Many Mansions?

Multiple Religious Belonging
and Christian Identity

FAITH MEETS FAITH

An Orbis Series in Interreligious Dialogue
Paul F. Knitter & William R. Burrows, General Editors
Editorial Advisors
John Berthrong
Diana Eck
Karl-Josef Kuschel
Lamin Sanneh
George E. Tinker
Felix Wilfred

In the contemporary world, the many religions and spiritualities stand in need of greater communication and cooperation. More than ever before, they must speak to, learn from, and work with each other in order to maintain their vital identities and to contribute to fashioning a better world.

The FAITH MEETS FAITH Series seeks to promote interreligious dialogue by providing an open forum for exchange among followers of different religious paths. While the Series wants to encourage creative and bold responses to questions arising from contemporary appreciations of religious plurality, it also recognizes the multiplicity of basic perspectives concerning the methods and content of interreligious dialogue.

Although rooted in a Christian theological perspective, the Series does not limit itself to endorsing any single school of thought or approach. By making available to both the scholarly community and the general public works that represent a variety of religious and methodological viewpoints, FAITH MEETS FAITH seeks to foster an encounter among followers of the religions of the world on matters of common concern.

FAITH MEETS FAITH SERIES

Many Mansions?

Multiple Religious Belonging and Christian Identity

Edited by
Catherine Cornille

ORBIS BOOKS

Maryknoll, New York 10545

Founded in 1970, Orbis Books endeavors to publish works that enlighten the mind, nourish the spirit, and challenge the conscience. The publishing arm of the Maryknoll Fathers and Brothers, Orbis seeks to explore the global dimensions of the Christian faith and mission, to invite dialogue with diverse cultures and religious traditions, and to serve the cause of reconciliation and peace. The books published reflect the opinions of their authors and are not meant to represent the official position of the Maryknoll Society. To obtain more information about Maryknoll and Orbis Books, please visit our website at www.maryknoll.org. To purchase our books on the Internet, visit www.maryknollmall.org

Manufactured in the United States of America.
Manuscript editing and typesetting by Joan Weber Laflamme.
To obtain more information about Maryknoll and Orbis Books, please visit our website at www.maryknoll.org.

Library of Congress Cataloging-in-Publication Data

Many mansions? : multiple religious belonging and Christian identity /
edited by Catherine Cornille.
    p. cm. — (Faith meets faith)
Includes index.
  ISBN 1-57075-439-X (pbk.)
  1. Christianity and other religions. 2. Syncretism (Religion) I.
Cornille, C. (Catherine) II. Series.
  BR127 .M27 2002
  261.2—dc21

                2002004751

Contents

1

Introduction

The Dynamics of Multiple Belonging

CATHERINE CORNILLE

I

In a world of seemingly unlimited choice in matters of religious identity and affiliation, the idea of belonging exclusively to one religious tradition or of drawing from only one set of spiritual, symbolic, or ritual resources is no longer self-evident. Why restrict oneself to the historically and culturally determined symbols and rituals of one religious tradition amid the rich diversity of symbols and rituals presenting themselves to the religious imagination? Why search for answers to the fundamental questions of life in only one religion when so many alternative proposals by time-honored traditions are readily available? Such questions point to the arrival of historical and cultural shifts at the level of religious identity. The erosion of religious territories formerly affixed by geography or politics seems now also to have come to affect the individual consciousness. A heightened and widespread awareness of religious pluralism has presently left the religious person with the choice not only of *which* religion, but also of *how many* religions she or he might belong to. More and more individuals confess to being partly Jewish and partly Buddhist, or partly Christian and partly Hindu, or fully Christian and fully Buddhist.

This sense or conviction of belonging to more than one religious tradition is thus clearly growing, at least in the West. It may be argued that in this, religion in Europe, America, and Australia is just coming to terms with a practice or a form of religiosity that has been prevalent for ages in most of the rest of the world, and especially in the East. The idea of belonging to only one religion has been more or less alien to most of the religious history of China and Japan, and in India and Nepal individuals visit shrines and temples and pray for blessings regardless of which religion a particular saint or temple might belong to. In the wider history of religion, multiple religious belonging may have been the rule rather than the exception, at least on a popular

1

level. In his essay, Jan Van Bragt problematizes the generally accepted assumption of the multiple belonging of the Japanese people by pointing out that Buddhism and Shinto were not always regarded as distinct traditions in the history of Japanese religions, and that the Japanese do not so much belong to different religions at the same time as they turn toward one or another as required by particular circumstances. It is nevertheless the case that religious exclusiveness runs against the grain of Japanese religiosity, which understands truth and goodness more in subjective and functional terms rather than in objective and absolute categories. From a purely historical point of view, one may wonder whether Western religiosity is not merely becoming more "Oriental" in nature.

Whereas the phenomenon of multiple religious belonging may thus seem relatively innocuous from a historical perspective and unproblematic on a modern existential level, it presents a number of serious philosophical, theological, and, of course, doctrinal questions and challenges. The contributions to this volume approach these challenges mainly from a Christian point of view. However, in order to avert the assumption that Christianity would be the only religion having trouble in accepting divided loyalties in its members, I wish to point out briefly that a total commitment and unitary belonging are ideals for most religions of the world.

II

It is undoubtedly the case that the idea of belonging to more than one religion at the same time presents itself as a serious problem predominantly for monotheistic religions. However, the difference with other, non-monotheistic religions may be a matter of degree, rather than nature. While monotheistic traditions tend to claim absolute and exclusive truth in all domains of existence, other religions may focus this claim, by nature or by necessity, on specific areas of ritual life and/or teaching. Some religions focus on healing practices, while others may have come to limit themselves to rituals relating to death and the afterlife. In these cases, simultaneous belonging to other, complementary religions may not present a problem. But it is doubtful that the healing religion will readily accept the participation of its members in radically different healing practices, or that the religion placing emphasis on funerals will applaud the simultaneous execution of alternative mortuary rites. Within their own area of religious expertise, most religions remain exclusive and jealous of other religious traditions, demanding single-minded commitment from their members. This brings us immediately to a rough-and-ready axiom: the more encompassing a religion's claim to efficacy and truth, the more problematic the possibility of multiple religious belonging. Conversely, it thus seems that the idea of belonging to more than one religion can be tolerated only when and where a religion has accepted the complementarity of religions, a point which is argued theologically in the contribution of Jacques Dupuis.

While the recognition of possibility of belonging to more than one tradition may thus arise from a position of humility, it may also result from a posture of superiority. Rituals and beliefs of other religions may be regarded as harmless, if not superfluous, from the perspective of the higher truth and efficacy that is offered in that particular religion. Such is often the case in new religions, which claim to be the fulfillment of some or all previously existing religions. But it is also a dynamic by which some of the more tolerant religions accept the existence of and the simultaneous belonging to another religion.

In the end, most religious traditions expect a total and unique commitment, if not from their followers at large, at least from their specialists or spiritual elite. Whereas the Chinese might have experienced a sense of simultaneous belonging to Confucianism, Taoism, and Buddhism, scholars or monks of each of these traditions were expected to demonstrate unswerving and single-minded commitment to their own tradition. This may be seen to flow from the very nature of religion, which might be understood—ideally—as the total commitment of will, feelings, and intellect to the ultimate reality. While the ultimate reality may itself transcend all historical forms and religious boundaries, it is nevertheless only through and ultimately to a particular person, symbolic system, and ritual tradition that this total commitment or surrender can take place. The selective and simultaneous belonging to various religions implies a discriminating and self-sufficient subject that is precisely what needs to be left behind in the pursuit of the highest levels of spiritual and religious attainment.

It is against the background of this ideal-typical understanding of religious belonging that the specific difficulties felt by the monotheistic religions, perhaps Christianity more than others, emerges in proper relief. The present state of the Christian tradition is characterized by a tension between all-encompassing claims to absolute truth and uniqueness on the one hand, and on the other hand an ever-more-independent or autonomous group of believers, at least in the West. It is the modern shift from a conception of truth and meaning framed in cosmology to one rooted in subjectivity that yields the radical sense of individual freedom and autonomy evident everywhere in Western culture today. As this autonomy extends its claims and entrenches itself, it enters into ever greater tension with the classical senses of religious belonging and identity. One need not think much further to notice a correlation between a strong form of modern freedom and autonomy and the self-understanding implied by those who approach multiple religious belonging. Individuals who no longer feel compelled to accept every single aspect of the tradition without question come to adopt a more piecemeal approach to doctrine, symbols, and practices governed by personal judgment and taste. From here, it is only a small step to the exploration and selective appropriation of elements of belief and practice of other religions.

III

There are various degrees and ways of understanding the phenomenon of multiple religious belonging. It may be associated with the form of religiosity generally called New Age, in which the individual chooses beliefs and practices from various religious traditions based on his or her own taste and judgment. While this may be understood as multiple religious belonging in the broadest sense of the term, it would be more appropriate to speak here of a complete absence of religious belonging. New Age is characterized by a rejection of the absolute truth claims of all institutionalized forms of religion. Insofar as this implies the rejection of the self-understanding of these religions, New Age believers cannot properly be said to belong to any of these religious traditions.

Religious belonging implies more than a subjective sense of sympathy or endorsement of a selective number of beliefs and practices. It involves the recognition of one's religious identity by the tradition itself and the disposition to submit to the conditions for membership as delineated by that tradition. Raimundo Panikkar discusses the need for both a subjective and an objective pole in any form of religious belonging with great subtlety.

If multiple religious belonging then implies a full commitment to at least one religion, there are still a number of ways in which one may extend that sense of belonging to include other religious traditions. The context in which this has come to pass within the Christian tradition is most often that of sincere dialogue with other religions and the inculturation of the Christian faith in non-Western cultures. In most cases, the encounter with other religions is framed by one's primary religious identity. Only those beliefs and practices of the other tradition are endorsed that are not in contradiction with the Christian faith, and the meaning of symbols and rituals that may be adopted is usually altered to fit the Christian ritual and doctrinal tradition.

There is, however, a more radical form of interreligious dialogue in which one may really come to identify fully with the other religious tradition. The attempt at understanding the other from within may in some cases lead to an unwitting conversion to the standpoint of the other, an endorsement of the worldview and practices of a different religious tradition. In this case, one no longer only understands the other from the perspective of Christianity, but also comes to understand the Christian tradition from the perspective of the other. Here we come close to speaking of multiple religious belonging, if indeed such a category is logically consistent. John Dunne speaks in this context of "passing over" as a deliberate and growthful experience. However, the experience of profound identification with one religion without losing one's attachment and commitment to another seems to be more often than not deeply confusing and spiritually unsettling. There is often no "coming back" from a deep identification with another religious tradition. Figures such as Henri Le Saux/Abhishiktananda, to whom several articles in this volume refer, come to find themselves in between traditions, unwilling to renounce the tradition of origin and unable to deny the truth discovered in the other tradition. It is here that we may speak of multiple religious belonging in the full and most dramatic sense of the term.

IV

While none of the contributors to this volume endorse or advocate the possibility of multiple religious belonging in the strong sense of the term, most attempt to rethink Christian identity and belonging in ways that would not exclude a certain degree of identification with a different religious tradition. Multiple religious belonging, understood in a broad sense of the term, is generally regarded as a positive challenge to Christian theology rather than a threat. John Cobb, for example, considers it an indispensable vehicle for interreligious reconciliation and transformation. Since the sins and injustices committed against other peoples and religions can only be understood from within those traditions, it takes individuals versed in both religions to bring about the insights and awareness necessary to promote peace and mutually inspiring interaction. However, Cobb insists that multiple religious belonging should be regarded as a means rather than an end in itself. The ideal is not to remain divided between two static religions, but to transform one religious tradition through inspiration from the other. This is a point sometimes evident in other contributions to this volume and speaks for the continued reflection on the ethical, but also the soteriological dimensions of the issues at hand.

There are a number of different ways in which the tensions and challenges inherent to multiple religious belonging might be addressed and resolved from within a Christian theological framework (or, for that matter, from within any particular religious tradition).

The first and probably most common way of understanding and legitimating the phenomenon of multiple religious belonging consists of focusing on the ultimate religious experience that lies at the base of all traditions. While belonging to different religious traditions may not be reconcilable on a theoretical or doctrinal level, it becomes more of a possibility if all religious traditions are regarded as different expressions of the same ultimate reality and experience. The belief in multiple religious belonging is indeed generally predicated on the belief in the unity of all religious experiences. The theoretical discussion on the unity or multiplicity of religious experiences has reached an impasse, with constructivists insisting on the dependency of religious experiences on the traditions from which they emerged, and the essentialists arguing for the possibility of a pure and universal religious experience. Without taking sides in this discussion, it might be pointed out that it is perhaps no coincidence that the individuals who appear most often as examples of multiple religious belonging belong to the spiritual branches of the traditions and that the intermonastic dialogue has offered much of the food for thought on this question.

A second way of understanding or resolving multiple religious belonging is by remaining faithful to the symbolic framework of one tradition while adopting the hermeneutical framework of another. This is what has taken place in advanced forms of inculturation, when the Christian faith has been reformulated in philosophical categories belonging to non-Western traditions. In the interaction between Christianity and the traditions of Asia, it is most often the tradition of Advaita Vedanta of Hinduism or the Mahayana tradition of Buddhism that has been appropriated in order to reinterpret traditional Christian theology. Joseph O'Leary, for example, argues that the reinterpretation of Christianity in Mahayana terms is not only possible but absolutely necessary in order for the church to face the challenges of the contemporary critique of traditional metaphysics. He presents his arguments in a critical discussion of the Vatican document *Dominus Iesus*. While the endeavor at cross-cultural hermeneutics is usually framed in the context of the secondary and auxiliary nature of philosophical renderings of an original faith experience, it generally derives from a strong identification with Christianity on the one hand, and a particular branch of Hinduism or Buddhism on the other. A different way of using categories of one religious tradition in order to reinterpret elements of another tradition may be found in Francis Clooney's exercise in intertextual reading. He demonstrates how both the Tamil tradition of Hinduism and the Jesuit Christian spirituality speak of the creative function of the human imagination in the encounter with God, who may meet us in "whichever form pleases us."

A third and final way in which theology may come to terms with the possibility of multiple religious belonging is by acknowledging the complementarity of religions. While Christianity is based on the belief in Jesus Christ as the full and final revelation of God, there are various ways in which the existence of other religions may be recognized, not merely over against, but alongside Christianity. This requires a strong awareness of the eschatological nature of Christian faith, as well as the belief that other religions play a distinct and revelatory role in God's plan of salvation. While Christians may or must believe they have a privileged understanding of the will of God in Jesus Christ, other religions may exercise a critical and constructive function in the process of discovery of the fullness of truth and the pleroma of Christ at the end of time. Jacques Dupuis speaks in his article of a mutual asymmetrical complementarity among religions as the theological grounds for multiple religious belonging. Whereas Christians may not be able to recognize the complete equality between religions, they certainly can acknowledge the authentic and distinct nature of truth operative in other religions, as well as the possibilities of growth through the internalization of religious experiences in more than one religion. The idea of multiple religious belonging is here used in the sense of *intrareligious* dialogue, a term originally coined by Raimundo Panikkar and used by several authors contributing to this collection. Belief in the complementarity of religions lies also at the basis of much of the attempt at dialogue and collaboration between Buddhism and Christianity in Sri Lanka. In "Double Belonging: Illusion or Liberating Path?" Elisabeth Harris discusses the history of the encounter between Buddhism and Christianity in Sri Lanka as well as the contributions of theologians such as Aloysius Pieris, who is known to have made concrete the idea of complementarity in terms of the relationship between *agape* and *gnosis*. A somewhat different notion of complementarity may be found in Claude Geffré's essay, in which he discusses the relationship not so much between Christianity as a religion and other religions, but between all religions and the spirit of the gospel. Geffré suggests that just as there are Christian ways of loving, working, and rejoicing, there might be Christian ways of being Hindu or Buddhist.

All of these reflections on the complementarity and the originality of Christian faith return us to the question of the concrete content of Christian belonging or the specificity of Christian identity. In "Belonging or Identity? Christian Faith in a Multireligious World" Werner Jeanrond tackles this question in a critical hermeneutical way. He points out that Christian identity is not a static and fixed reality but a fluid and dynamic process that defines itself in reaction to concrete challenges that present themselves in changing circumstances. After a lifetime of lived experience of multiple religious belonging, Raimon Panikkar emphasizes that religious identity and belonging are not only matters of subjective confession, but also of the recognition of this confession by the group. In the end, however, the group is constituted by individuals who are continuously engaged in the process of redefining their own identity and retracing the boundaries of belonging. In this very process, multiple religious belonging may present itself not only as a problem, but also as an opportunity for Christian faith to expand the horizons of its own self-understanding and to grow in faithfulness to the truth, which lies beyond the boundaries of any fixed identity and exclusive sense of belonging.

2

Multiple Religious Belonging of the Japanese People

JAN VAN BRAGT

JAPANESE RELIGIOSITY AS A MODE OF MULTIPLE RELIGIOUS BELONGING

It is very well possible—although I have no means of checking it—that the term *multiple religious belonging* has been used by scholars in religion for the very first time in connection with the Japanese traditional religious scene. Recently, the same term has come to be used to characterize a rather novel phenomenon or trend in the religious world of the West, namely, the case of the so-called hyphenated Christians (or Jews): people who do not want to choose between a Christian and a Buddhist identity but feel entitled to call themselves Christian-Buddhist or Buddhist-Christian (or any other combination of religious nomenclatures).

This confronts us immediately with the question whether this concept applies equally and in the same sense in both of these cases, and, since this looks very improbable, whether there is sufficient analogy between the two cases to justify the inclusion of a paper on the Japanese case in a collection of papers evidently intended to study the present Western case. As always, of course, the proof of the pudding will be in the eating. Nothing prevents us, however, from starting out with the hope that the Japanese case may throw a little sidelight on the present Western phenomenon, even if only by contrast.

One way of entering into our discussion might be to ask this question: Why is it that multiple religious belonging has apparently looked natural to the Japanese people for many centuries, while it looks very problematic, if not downright impossible, to most Westerners? Phrased in this way, the answer can only be, I submit—if I may anticipate my conclusion—because Japanese and Westerners understand the term, and each of its elements, in a thoroughly different way. In other words, viewed from its meaning in the Western context, the term *multiple religious belonging*, when applied to the Japanese situation, comes very near being a complete misnomer. It is clear enough, however, that, if I want this rather bold statement to be understood by non-Japanologists, I must first of all provide a general sketch of the Japanese religious situation.

The reader may know that Japan's population stands at about 126 million. According to the Japanese government, the number of Shinto adherents is about 100 million, and the number of Buddhists is estimated at about 95 million. This total far surpasses the population, not yet counting the followers of the many new religions, the Christians, the nonbelievers, and so on. Confronted with these statistics, Western observers must conclude that, unbelievable as it may seem, the Japanese consider themselves both Shintoists and Buddhists; they do not see any contradiction or inconvenience in belonging to two or more religions at the same time. Our question becomes whether, or how far, this conclusion is justified.

But, in order to tackle this question, we must first know something more about the Japanese religious world. In order to help my Japanese students grasp the specificity of the Japanese religious situation they are living in, I have often confronted them with the following three characteristics:

1. In contradistinction with most other countries, whose national ethos has been informed by one single dominant religion, the Japanese people have been living, for approximately fifteen hundred years, with many religions. Besides Confucianism (which in Japan played the role of a religion only in some exceptional cases), there were the native religion, which developed into the present Shinto, and the many Buddhist sects whose doctrines differ greatly from one another. Around the time of the Meiji Restoration (1868), this multiplicity was further augmented by the rise of many new religions of a very syncretistic character and the second entry of Christianity. In such a multi-religious context, the particular religions came to be perceived not as absolute but as relative, and religion itself tended to be experienced not as a matter of objective truth and obligation but as a subjective matter, something one could have recourse to if one felt the need for it.

2. The Japanese religious scene is further characterized by an unusually strong survival of the original native religiosity, often called primitive or tribal religion, which is strongly centered on the basic natural values of "Blut und Boden": *blood,* that is, the ancestors, the family *(ie)*; and soil, that is, the home ground *(furusato, uji),* ranging from the native village to the home country, Japan. In nearly all other cases, this native religion disappeared or went underground when one of the world religions took roots. In Japan, however, it managed to preserve not only its hold over the people but also its outward and inward identity even after a very long, strongly inculturated, and most of the time culturally and politically dominant presence of Buddhism.

It is thus often said that, even today, the Japanese perceive or locate "the sacred" primarily in the ancestors of the family and in the soil of Japan ("the land of the gods," where one's bones must be buried). It is only toward these two realities that the Japanese feel a real sense of religious obligation. One has characterized this persistence of the old, the original, notwithstanding the acceptance of new, and in a sense higher, cultural values by saying that the original became the matrix wherein the new was taken up and molded. Thus, one could say that in the blood-and-soil framework of original Shinto, Buddhism has been taken up and put in charge, as it were, of the veneration of the family ancestors (not the ancestors of the country).

Moreover, in this kind of religiosity, it is the social group rather than the individual that is the subject of religion (that which "belongs" to a religion). It could then be said that every Japanese is affiliated with Shinto as a member of the local community and is associated with Buddhism as a member of his or her family. A Japanese "belongs" to the Shinto religion by the fact of birth in Japan, "the land of the gods," very like a Jew belongs to the Judaic religion by the fact of belonging to the Jewish race. Indeed, for the majority of the Japanese, the fact of being Shintoist does not detach itself from the fact of being Japanese, to the extent that, when asked to name the religions they know, they will mention Buddhism and Christianity, and maybe Islam, Judaism, and others, but not Shintoism. On the other hand, the belonging of the great majority of the Japanese to Buddhism resides in the fact of their family having its tombs or the tablets of the ancestors in a Buddhist temple.

3. In Japanese history a certain "division of labor (or responsibilities)" has been worked out between the religions, in which religions take care of the sacred and of the blessings of the people, while Confucianism, which was not regarded as a religion, is put in charge of morality and the principles of social life. This constitutes, in fact, a strong case of secularization *avant la lettre*. It makes that, in Japan, one hears on all sides that religion is beyond ethics and social concerns. It also makes that religions in Japan very rarely confronted one another on ethical or social issues.

After this all too brief sketch of the particularities of the Japanese religious scene, we must ask our question again: How far is one justified in saying that the Japanese feel no qualms about belonging to two or more religions at the same time? In view of our general discussion, we could tentatively add a further question: Does the present trend toward multiple religious belonging indicate that the Western sense of religion is evolving in the direction of the traditional Japanese view?

JAPANESE RELIGION: MULTIPLE OR UNIFIED?

There appears to be some truth in the above-mentioned Western evaluation of Japanese religiosity. However, if we do not want to evoke in the Western mind a very wrong picture of the religiosity of the Japanese people, we must carefully circumscribe that judgment. Indeed, there seems to exist in Japanese religiosity a certain indeterminacy and multiplicity. It has been said, for instance, that the Japanese have an open-ended religiosity; that is, their subjective need to worship and to seek protection appears not to be very particular about the object at which it is directed. It is a moot question whether there is any difference in their inner religious attitude when they pray to the gods at a Shinto shrine and when they worship the buddhas in a Buddhist temple.[1] What has been said above about the particularities of Japanese religion may make this partly understandable.

When religions are not considered as matters of objective truth, their differences in doctrine lose much of their weight and their boundaries tend to blur: they appear less distinct and mutually opposed. It has often been pointed out that, for the Japanese, religion is, in the first place, a question of ritual and practices, and only very secondarily a question of doctrine (and organization). And when belonging to a religion does not impose any personal obligation, nor involve ethical and social consequences, multiple belonging is, of course, much less problematic.[2]

We may have to come back to these issues later, but at this point we may indicate that both concepts used in the phrase *belonging to a religion* have a thoroughly different meaning for a Japanese and for a Westerner. A Japanese does not spontaneously think of a religion as "a particular system of belief in a bounded community."[3] And a personal sense of belonging is not really an ingredient of the religiosity of most Japanese. One survey, published in 1979, asked people about their membership in organizations. With regard to religious organizations, only 13.6 percent said they were members.[4] From other indications it is clear that the number of people who "have faith" is much higher, of course. One may be inclined to interpret that lack of a sense of belonging in the following way. "Belonging to" implies "finding one's identity in," and it could be said that, for most Japanese, there is no perceived need for any identity besides being Japanese and having an identifiable place in Japanese society.

Let me quote two texts that may evoke something of the "flavor" of these differences:

> The Chinese did not perceive these [the "three doctrines" of China: Confucianism, Buddhism, and Taoism], through Western spectacles, as alternative religions, but as something more analogous to three interpenetrating fields of force within the continuous religious life of China.[5]

> The Japanese do not live in a system that demands full-blooded belief-oriented and exclusive commitment that precludes any other. Rather, their orientations are situational and complementary.[6]

The word "situational" in the second quotation may alert us to the fact that the third element in the Western judgment about the Japanese belonging to different religions *at the same time* is misleading. There is enough reason to say that Japanese religiosity tends to be syncretic, but the image of an amorphous mixture this might evoke is not the whole truth. The other half of the picture is that the Japanese love to keep some distinction among things of different origin, to assign them different roles or compartments in their lives, and to use one or the other according to the situation. To quote only one example: in Japanese restaurants Japanese and Western menus are kept rather scrupulously apart. The boundaries are clearly marked. For Japanese dishes chopsticks are provided, and for Western dishes fork and knife. The same rice is called *gohan* (the Japanese name) in the first case, and *raisu* in the latter.

This applies also, at least on a secondary level, to the distinction between the native religion, Shinto, and the imported religion, Buddhism. Each is assigned a different compartment, and circumstances decide which one comes into play. Putting it very crudely, it is said that Shinto is the religion for the living, and Buddhism is the religion for the dead. The Japanese feel themselves to be Shintoists in the cycle of the four seasons, at the times of planting and harvesting of the rice, at the New Year, at the festival of the tutelary deity of the village, and when a child is born. They feel themselves to be Buddhists at the times of funerals and services for the dead. Ian Reader, the author of the quotation above, speaks of a "latent sense of belonging, which would materialize when the situation and circumstances demanded and required it";[7] he uses the phrase, "the Japanese people [are not, but] 'become' Buddhists in certain circumstances."[8]

In this context, it is said that the Japanese are less concerned than Westerners about consistency in their lives and have an uncanny ability to compartmentalize their lives according to circumstances. The same man who, during the day, is a modern no-nonsense executive in a blue suit, indistinguishable from his Western counterparts, turns into a traditional Japanese gentleman writing calligraphic poetry in kimono at night. The Japanese, as a people, have compartmentalized (and, thus, separated) their lives during the war from their lives after surrender so hermetically that present demands for apologies for crimes committed during the war are felt as unreasonable or outlandish. And the girl who was a devout Christian as long as she lived in the ambience of a Christian boarding school may on graduation quite naturally leave Christianity behind together with the school.

All in all, we may recognize, I believe, that the Japanese show a special ability to belong to two or more religions—at least in the sense that several factors, which make it difficult for Westerners to do so, are less conspicuously present in the Japanese cultural context. But before venturing to posit any real conclusions, we must have a second look—this time a historical one—at the central case of the Japanese multiple religious belonging, that of their alleged simultaneous belonging to Shinto and Buddhism.

There is, of course, only multiplicity of belonging when the religions in question are recognized as distinct from one another. This, however, appears not to have been univocally the case with Shinto and Buddhism in Japanese history. Indeed, since the pioneering work of the Japanese historian Kuroda Toshio,[9] it has become widely recognized among scholars of Japanese religion that, in most of Japanese history, Shinto and Japanese Buddhism did not function (were not recognized) as two independent religions. Instead, they were so thoroughly amalgamated as to form a single religious worldview, wherein the beliefs and practices typically associated with Shinto were submerged and constituted particular facets and aspects. It was only after the forceful implementation of the 1868 Meiji decree of *shinbutsu bunri*, separation of Shinto and Buddhism,[10] that the two came to appear outwardly as two separate entities, each with its own sanctuaries, objects of worship, and rituals. It could be said that, before that event, Shinto and Japanese Buddhism have lived in such an intimate symbiosis that they appeared to the Japanese people not as two distinct religions but rather as one composite but organic unity, in which the two components maintained a separate identity only on a secondary level. There was no reason, then, for a Japanese engaged in that more inclusive religious entity to experience this as a double belonging.

The confines of this article do not permit me to convey a concrete picture of this Shinto-Buddhist syncretization or "fusion of gods and buddhas" *(shinbutsu shugo)*, but I must at least try to give an idea of the depth of the integration of the *kami* into the Buddhist framework or, conversely, the thoroughness of the Buddhist inculturation into the world of Shinto. A summarizing text by Kuroda Toshio may set us on the way:

Among the doctrinal explanations of the kami were the following: (1) the kami realize that they themselves are trapped in this world of samsara and transmigration and they also seek liberation through the Buddhist teachings; (2) the kami are benevolent deities who protect Buddhism; (3) the kami are transformations of the Buddhas manifested in Japan to save all sentient beings *(honji suijaku)*; and (4) the kami are the pure spirits of the Buddha *(hongaku)*.[11]

One can detect, of course, a chronological evolution in these diverse conceptions of the native gods. The idea of the kami as protectors of Buddhist institutions found early expression in the incorporation of a shrine to the god of the locality in Buddhist temple compounds (a custom observed up to the present day). By the end of the eighth century (second half of the Nara period) oracles are heard wherein gods lament the pains of their existence as gods and express the desire to entrust themselves to the "three treasures" of Buddhism (Buddha, Dharma, and Sangha) in order to find enlightenment and liberation. This inclusion of the gods among the suffering sentient beings, however, must have been experienced as an undue degradation, for soon, in the Heian period, we see them presented as enlightened beings, avatars, or local manifestations of buddhas and bodhisattvas for the benefit of the Japanese people. The native gods, then, one by one, while keeping their own name, acquire the name of the buddha or bodhisattva whose avatar they are alleged to be. Instead of being abased, the native gods now gain in status by this "buddhification." They are now enshrined in *jinguji* (a combination shrine and temple) and worshiped with ceremonies "which could not be distinguished specifically as Shinto or Buddhist,"[12] but which very often comprised the recitation of Buddhist sutras. Still, that this symbiosis never became a seamless one was proven in the later Edo period, when the gods revolted against their, after all, subordinate position, and came to be considered by some theoreticians as themselves "the real thing" *(honji)*, of which the buddhas and bodhisattvas were the avatars *(suijaku)*.

The spirit of this Shinto-Buddhist conglomerate was maybe best caught in a legend that a scholar residing in Dazaifu (Kyushu) around 1100 c.e. heard from the mouth of a priest of the local Hachiman shrine and noted down for posterity:

> The Buddhist monk Dogyo from Silla [one of the three Korean kingdoms from which Buddhism was originally transmitted to Japan] forced his way into Japan, tied up the gods, and pushed them into a bottle. Then, however, the god of the Atsuta shrine [situated in Nagoya and traditional repository of the sacred sword] endeavored to escape by changing himself into the sacred sword of Kusanagi, originally bestowed by the god Kusanoo. But the monk Dogyo wrapped the sword together with the other gods in his Buddhist surplice and tried to shut it up in the shrine of Usa Hachiman. The sword, however, rose into the sky and the monk could not stop it. When the monk had proceeded along the Sanyo highway as far as Bingo [Hiroshima], he was trampled to death by the god Usa Hachiman. Thereupon the other gods escaped one by one from the bottle and regained their former shape. All this is due to the protection of Amida Buddha, the real essence [*honji*] of the god Hachiman.[13]

We are entitled to conclude, I believe, that for most Japanese in history the allegiance to the Buddhist-Shinto conglomerate—and, thus, in a sense, to both Buddhism and Shinto—did not have to be accompanied by a sense of multiple belonging. The composite religious system in which they were born and which served equally the legitimation of the political system and the social integration of the nation did not present them with a real choice entailing the rejection of an alternative. If choice there was, it was rather in the sense of the possibility of different *specializations* on the basis of the acceptance of the system as a whole. The individual was free to choose one of the various Buddhist schools as a path to personal liberation, for example, by becoming a Tendai monk, but this step did not mean for the individual concerned a rejection of the syncretistic system. The situation of these individuals reminds me somehow of that of a Catholic choosing the Franciscan spirituality without any thought of rejecting thereby the rest of Catholic religiosity.

Winston Davis, an eminent scholar of Japanese religion, has made the following statement:

> Thus, unlike the Abrahamic traditions in which social integration rested on belief in one God, one faith, and one religious practice, the political and social integration of Japan has traditionally been based on a *multiplicity* of gods and faiths.[14]

True and significant as this statement may be, we must nevertheless remark that, precisely as integrating factor, this multiplicity constituted a unified system. A further quotation from the same author may now guide us to one more aspect of the Japanese religious scene that could be relevant for our question:

> Whereas in the west it was heresy (or pluralism, as it is called today) which seemed to threaten the unity of Christendom, in Japan it was monopraxis (emphasis on a single religious practice) that posed the greatest spiritual menace to the traditional integration of society.[15]

THE CHALLENGES OF RELIGIOUS EXCLUSIVISM IN JAPAN

In general, our present problem can be formulated as follows: Can we not detect in Japanese history a kind of counter-current to that all-embracing and multidirectional (indeed, "polytheistic") religious system that was avowedly dominant? In other words, can we agree with Futaba Kenko's "overall view of Japanese Buddhist history as a struggle between a particularist state-centered Japanese religiosity, legitimized by worship of the kami, and a universalist egalitarian vision of the Buddha-Dharma, reaching back to Sakyamuni himself?"[16]

In connection with this "struggle" or tension, two of the Buddhist schools that originated in the Kamakura era as distinct religious movements are often mentioned: the school of Nichiren (1222-82) and the *Shinshu* or True Pure Land school of Shinran (1173-1262). Indeed, in their origin both of these schools rejected the multiplicity of religious objects and practices found in the dominant religious system. Nichiren insisted on the sole worship of the perennial Buddha Sakyamuni, as embodied in the *Lotus Sutra,* and on the sole practice of the *daimoku,* the recitation of the title of the *Lotus Sutra,* "Namu myoho renge kyo." With fierce prophetic zeal, he condemned all the practices of the other Buddhist sects as leading the individual to hell and the country to perdition, and considered the persecutions by the religio-political establishment, which this inevitably brought upon himself, as a sure sign of election by Sakyamuni Buddha. Shinran, in the wake of his master Honen (1133-1212), elected the savior Buddha Amida as the exclusive object of worship and reliance, and advocated the *nembutsu,* the recitation of Amida's Name *(Namu Amida Butsu)* as the only practice conducive to salvation in Amida's Pure Land.

In these two Kamakura figures we can sense something akin to the "monotheistic pathos" that in the West keeps most Christians and Jews from multiple belonging. We find this spirit beautifully expressed by Bonnie Thurston:

> I admit to being one of those persons who holds to the traditional Christian insistence on a clearly demarcated religious identity. . . . Jesus Christ does make exclusive claims on my life, loyalties, and allegiances. . . . My understanding of my tradition does not allow me to be Christian *and* Buddhist.[17]

In the case of Nichiren and Shinran, their conviction might then be formulated in the following way: My Buddhist tradition, as I understand it, does not allow me to be Buddhist and at the same time an adherent of the dominant religio-political system. Among the points of incompatibility to which they were sensitive were the subservience of Buddhism to the state and the admixture of the native gods with the true object of worship, the Buddha.

On the first point, Nichiren appears to have taken the clearer standpoint by his insistence on the superiority of the "Buddha Law" over the "king's law":

> Nichiren asserted the authority of the *Lotus Sutra* in a way that significantly reworked both Tendai and other early Buddhist models of nation protection, making the state responsible for protecting the [Buddha] Dharma, and not the other way around.[18]

But Shinran too roundly criticized the emperor for harming the Buddhist Dharma by sending his master Honen into exile.

On the second point, Shinran probably was the clearer of the two. While the "patriotic" Nichiren always wanted Japan to be the center of the world and, therefore, could ill afford to give up the idea of Japan as "the land of the gods," Shinran clearly felt that the great importance given to the native gods detracted from the exclusive reliance due to Amida Buddha. Although he recognized the gods as protectors of the Amida believers, he prescribed their "non-worship." "If one has taken refuge in the Buddha, one must not further take refuge in various gods."[19] Still, of Nichiren also it has been written that "in his later thought, Nichiren came thoroughly to reject the *honji suijaku* notions that bolstered the authority of establishment Buddhism, and deemed the kami significant only insofar as they protect 'the world of the *Lotus Sutra.'*"[20]

All in all, it looks as if Nichiren and Shinran, in their single-minded adherence to one object of faith and to one single practice, offered a kind of religiosity that was genuinely different from, and even subversive of, the religiosity that undergirded the religio-political system of Japan. They can be said to have presented a genuine alternative and thus the possibility of a real choice (involving rejection). The question is how far their ideas were operative and socially influential in Japan's history.

There are sufficient signs of a tension with the general Japanese religiosity within these two movements in history and even today. However, it must be said, I believe, that these movements did not realize their revolutionary potential because later generations, under heavy social pressure, sufficiently curbed the provocative elements of their message in the direction of the socially accepted religiosity to be able to survive in peace in their social environment. Let me document this briefly in the case of *Shinshu* and its attitude to the native gods. Alfred Bloom summarizes the evolution as follows:

> Shinran and the Pure Land teaching to which he subscribed clearly rejected "mixed" practices. . . . [However,] historically there have been theories that enabled followers of Shin Buddhism to relate positively to the religious environment.[21]

Shinran's early descendants and successors as leaders of the *(honganji)* movement, Kakunyo and Zonkaku, already had started this process of accommodation:

> Zonkaku's attitude toward the Shinto *kami* was clearly at variance with Shinran's. Zonkaku perpetuated the prevailing concepts of Shinto-Buddhist syncretism of the period, construing the *kami* to be manifestations *(suijaku)* of Buddhas and Bodhisattvas. . . . Shinran never presented the *kami* in such a syncretistic fashion. The most he would say is that the *kami* act as guardians and protectors to those who have faith in the *nembutsu*.[22]

And it is Rennyo (1414-99,) rightly called the second founder of Shinshu, who is mostly credited with having made this accommodating attitude into the official policy of the Pure Land school. For example, in his catechetical letters to his followers he wrote:

> All the kami manifestations . . . will protect nembutsu practicers. Consequently, even if we do not worship the kami in particular, since all are encompassed when we rely solely on one Buddha, Amida, we give credence [to them], even if we do not rely on them in particular.[23]

We can speak, therefore, of an evolution from an exclusive centering on Amida to an inclusive attitude of "accommodation through a qualified acceptance of the other buddhas and the kami."[24]

MODERNITY AND MULTIPLE RELIGIOUS BELONGING

Until now we have directed our attention to Japanese religiosity as it was lived in the past. Would there be any real change in the present? In general it can be said, I believe, that in Japan modernity has stripped religion of much of its influence on social life and of its earnestness for the individual. But, while in the West the Enlightenment and anticlerical atheism, for instance, can be singled out as important factors in this evolution, no such upheavals can be pinned down in Japan. Indeed, the main dividing line in Japan—at least so far as our discussion goes—may rather be the above-mentioned decree of separation of Buddhism and Shinto and the fact that from that time on (the beginning of the Meiji era) Shinto has been used as a central element in nationalist ideology. Significant is also that, around the same time but apparently without causal nexus, a multitude of "new religions" started and Christianity appeared again on the Japanese scene.

Thus, not only was a real choice between Shinto and Buddhism possible (probably for the first time), but at the same time a much richer "supermarket of religions" was offered to the Japanese people. In the consciousness of the average Japanese, however, the traditional symbiosis of Shinto and Buddhism has survived all official policies to the contrary. With regard to most of the new religions, on the other hand, the Japanese people have been able to show their capacity for multiple religious belonging. Indeed, most of the new religions, while tending to offer a religion "for all seasons," do not demand of their believers the rejection of their traditional religiosity or affiliation to any other religion.

On the other hand, however, there is a small minority of people who want to reject the traditional religio-political system; they believe that it enslaves the individual. So there are now on the Japanese scene religions that demand exclusive belonging with rejection of the traditional syncretism. Among them is, of course, Christianity, but there are also some of the new religions that base their doctrine and praxis on Nichiren's teachings. In some cases, as with a considerable number of Protestant Christians, the rejection of the political ideology, centered on a divine emperor, plays an important role herein.

By way of illustration of the more general Japanese feeling, I want to insert here a brief note on the religious attitude of the scholars of the so-called Kyoto School of Philosophy, which has become known to some extent also in the West. What characterizes these philosophers (Nishida Kitaro [1870-1945], Tanabe Hajime [1885-1960], and Nishitani Keiji [1900-1990]) is their intention to philosophize out of their Eastern background and thus not simply to participate in philosophy as a Western enterprise. As such, they are anchored in Japan's national religiosity (inclusive of its socio-political context) but with a strong preference for the Buddhist intellectual tradition.

What strikes us then is their open attitude toward Christianity, their willingness even to embrace Christianity together with Buddhism (in our present language, their acceptance of hyphenation), and their, as it were, spontaneous search for the unity of the two. The following text by Watsuji Tetsuro is very revealing on this point:

> We cannot but recognize a number of religions as true. All of them are forever divine in that they have the same roots; in other words, reveal the Absolute. But

precisely because we recognize all these faiths equally, we cannot belong to any of them. We are on a new quest for God.[25]

It certainly looks as if we have to look for the roots of this openness (or "looseness," as one of them calls it) in the character of the traditional religiosity of Japan, as we have sketched it above. However, the big obstacle on their irenic path was, of course, the intransigent attitude of the Christianity of the time, its insistence on the necessity of exclusive belonging to only one true religion. Commenting on Tanabe's saying that he considered himself to be a *werdener Christ* (a Christian in the making) who is not able to become a *gewordener Christ* (an actual Christian), Nishitani once said the following:

> I have the impression that I understand Tanabe's problem very well. I myself am in a similar situation. . . . I cannot become anything more than a *werdener Christ*, in the same sense as Tanabe. For I cannot bring myself to consider Buddhism a false doctrine. . . . From the standpoint of Buddhism I can do this [be a Christian in the making]. . . . Christians are inclined to speak ill of such Buddhist "looseness," but I do not feel that way.[26]

Rather than analyzing the reasons for that attitude further, I must content myself with pointing out a—to me—still inexplicable expression of it. I refer here to the totally natural way in which these "actual Buddhists" make use of the idea of "God" and unhesitatingly place it at the center of their philosophy of religion. So, for instance, Nishida squarely declares: "Religion is about God. God is fundamental to religion in any form."[27] How can Buddhists—especially Buddhists who consciously build their worldview on the Buddhist idea of Emptiness—experience this as *fraglos* (without problems)?

Finally, we must come back to our initial question: Does the investigation of the modalities of Japanese religiosity throw any light on the contemporary (Western) problem of multiple religious belonging? I want to suggest here that a comparison with the Japanese situation can help us to gain a clearer consciousness of the presuppositions on the basis of which multiple belonging appears to us as a problem.

From the above analysis of the Japanese religious world it appears, I believe, that multiple religious belonging—although not as blatantly present as often said (in the Shinto-Buddhist case)—was on the whole not perceived as a problem. In the West, on the contrary, multiple belonging is perceived as fundamentally at odds with the traditional understanding of religion. It appears as a deviating state of affairs over against a presupposed normative pattern: exclusive belonging to a single religion, conceived as a particular system of beliefs in a bounded community. From a Japanese standpoint, it could be argued that the emergence of multiple belonging in the Western world indicates that, for all these reasons—and some others such as the disappearance of social pressure exerted by closed societies, the feeling that exclusive identity is divisive and impoverishing, the appearance of an attractive alternative, and others—the Western conception of religion is losing its monotheistic rigidity and drawing nearer to the Japanese traditional sense of religion, in which the idea of exclusive affiliation to one religious group, if not completely absent, certainly does not constitute the norm. A strong saying by a famous interpreter of things Japanese may be the right *coda* to end my scribblings:

> At the basis of Japanese religious ideas lies a view different from one that sees religion as a matter of conscious decision or subjective choice. . . . Ours has been a worldview that considers exclusive affiliation to a particular sect an essentially irreligious posture.[28]

NOTES

[1] I might even add here "and when they participate in a Christian ritual." When I once, at their own request, invited a group of believers of one of Japan's new religions to attend Sunday Mass at my native village in Belgium, the parishioners were so struck by their devout attitude that they were convinced that these people were fervent Catholics.

[2] Judaism and Islam, with their strong grip on secular life, might be the best counterexamples here.

[3] W. C. Smith, *The Meaning and End of Religion* (San Francisco: Harper & Row, 1978), xi.

[4] David Reid, *New Wine: The Cultural Shaping of Japanese Christianity* (Fremont, Calif.: Asian Humanities Press, 1991), 20. One cannot but think that the majority of the people who called themselves members of a particular religion were Christians or members of a new religion.

[5] Ibid., xiii. W. C. Smith elsewhere has the interesting comparison: "Some Western scholars have tried to estimate how many Taoists there are in China. This is not quite so misconceived, perhaps, as asking how many pragmatists there are in America; but almost."

[6] Ian Reader, *Religion in Contemporary Japan* (London: MacMillan Press, 1991), 16.

[7] Ibid., 3.

[8] Ibid., 16.

[9] Kuroda's ideas were made known to a wider audience in the West by a special issue of the *Japanese Journal of Religious Studies* 23/3-4 (1996). However, a similar viewpoint had already been defended by Western scholars, among whom Allan Grapard may have been the most influential. See especially Allan G. Grapard, *The Protocol of the Gods: A Study of the Kasuga Cult in Japanese History* (Berkeley and Los Angeles: University of California Press, 1992).

[10] This drastic political maneuver has been called by Allan Grapard "Japan's ignored cultural revolution" (*History of Religion* 23/3 (1984), 240-65.

[11] Kuroda Toshio, "Shinto in the History of Japanese Religion," in *Religions of Japan in Practice*, ed. George Tanabe (Princeton, N.J.: Princeton University Press, 1999), 458.

[12] Ibid.

[13] Translated from Yoshii Akio, *Shinbutsu Shugo* [The fusion of gods and buddhas] (Tokyo: Iwanami shoten, 1996), 179. Note how the very Buddhist Amida Buddha takes the side of the Japanese syncretistic religious complex (and thus of the native gods) against the (pure, monastic) Buddhism originally transmitted from Korea.

[14] Winston Davis, *Japanese Religion and Society* (Albany, N.Y.: State University of New York Press, 1992), 33.

[15] Ibid.

[16] Minor and Ann Rogers, *Rennyo* (Berkeley, Calif.: Asian Humanities Press, 1991), 29.

[17] Bonnie Thurston, "Joint Practice," *Buddhist-Christian Studies* 14 (1994), 177-78, 180.

[18] Ruben L. F. Habito and Jacqueline I. Stone, "Revisiting Nichiren," *Japanese Journal of Religious Studies* 26/3-4 (1999), 228.

[19] Shinan, in the *Keshindo* volume of his main work, the *Kyogyoshinsho* (no. 82).

[20] Jacqueline Stone, "Placing Nichiren in the 'Big Picture,'" *Japanese Journal of Religious Studies* 26/3-4 (1999), 391.

[21] Alfred Bloom, "A (Shin) Buddhist perspective on Dual Worship," *Buddhist-Christian Studies* 14 (1994), 164. On Shinran himself, Minor and Ann Rogers write: "In our view, Shinran's view presents a radical departure from Japan's tradition of religious syncretism" (in Rogers, *Rennyo*, 90 n. 50).

[22] James C. Dobbins, *Jodo Shinshu—Shin Buddhism in Medieval Japan* (Bloomington and Indianapolis, Ind.: Indiana University Press, 1989), 176.

[23] Rennyo, *Letters*, II-3 (quoted from Rogers, *Rennyo*, 176).

[24] Ibid., 89.

[25] Watsuji Tetsuro, *Shamon Dogen* [Dogen, The Monk], in *Gendai bukkyo meicho zenshu* [Collected masterpieces of contemporary Buddhism], ed. Nakamura Hajime et al. (Tokyo: Kokubunkan, 1965), 12.

[26] Nishitani Keiji, in *Sengo Nippon seishinshi* [Spiritual history of post-war Japan], ed. Kuyama Yasushi (Nishinomiya: Kirisutokyo Gakuto Kyodaidan, 1961), 194.

[27] Quoted from Nishida Kitaro, *Last Writings: Nothingness and the Religious Worldview*, trans. David Dilworth (Honolulu: University of Hawaii Press, 1987), 48.

[28] Yamaori Tetsuo, quoted from Okuyama Michiaki, "Approaches East and West to the History of Religions: Four Japanese Thinkers," *Japanese Journal of Religious Studies* 27/1-2 (2000). Available online.

3

Multiple Religious Belonging and Reconciliation

JOHN B. COBB JR.

I

Through most of history, most people's religious orientation has been determined for them by the communities into which they were born. Indeed "religion" was largely whatever bound the people of a community together in celebration, patterns of behavior, systems of belief, or worship. Most people have no more chosen their religion than their ethnicity or nationality.

From time to time this pattern was broken for some. During the time of the Roman Empire, various cults arose that invited people to join them. Joining was then voluntary. Usually one continued to participate in much of the religious ethos and cultus of the community from which one came, so the break was not sharp. But there were exceptions.

Among Jews, participation because of birth was normal and normative. But this pattern was qualified in two ways. First, Judaism was attractive to Gentiles, and a considerable number of them became Jews or at least adopted many Jewish beliefs and customs. Second, competing sects developed within Judaism, so that Jews were offered the chance to join and thus to shape their personal religious life by choice.

Christianity proved to be the most important of these sects. Also it became the most important of the cults inviting membership from the larger community. Its growth changed the religious landscape of the Roman Empire, so that for several centuries the inhabitants of the empire found themselves in the position of deciding whether to be Christians or continue in the traditional religious patterns. Furthermore, becoming a Christian constituted a sharp break from remaining a part of the traditional religious culture. This break was dramatically heightened during periods of persecution.

The choice continued for some time even after the establishment of Christianity but gradually ended. Now the more typical pattern was widely reinstated. One was born into Christianity, just as one had previously been born into the various ethnic cults. For the vast majority of people in Christendom, there remained many decisions about how serious to be about one's faith and just how to embody it, but there was no question of one's identity as a Christian. Of course, in areas of Christian expansion, the situation of choice repeated itself.

The situation was only a little different for Jews within Christendom. To be born of Jewish parents was to be a Jew, but from time to time they were under pressure to convert to Christianity. The vast majority paid the high price required of those who refused to do so, but that meant that there was an element of choice in remaining Jews.

In North Africa, the Middle East, and later the Balkans, the rise of Islam introduced choice about religion. Those who were Christian by birth as well as others could decide to become Muslim or to pay some price to remain what they were. Here, too, after a period of transition the more typical situation renewed itself in which the vast majority were throughout life whatever they were born to be.

The Reformation brought about a situation somewhat like that of the Jews in an earlier period. Several forms of Christianity bid for allegiance. Membership in one or another was a matter of choice. The choice often involved important consequences. In some parts of Europe, after a short period, choice largely disappeared for most people. But in other parts, such as Great Britain, it remained. The plurality of options was still more marked in America. Even here, over time, the importance of the choice among forms of Christianity declined. Today one may change from Baptist to Methodist to Presbyterian to Episcopalian without massive consequences. One may retain one's membership in one denomination while participating more actively in another. Or one may be a member of a congregation that is affiliated with more than one denomination. Multiple belonging among Protestant denominations does not usually involve formal membership in multiple congregations simultaneously, but, short of that, it is a well-established pattern.

Meanwhile, however, the voluntary character of religious self-identification has increased greatly. In the American colonies there were many who did not count themselves as participants in any form of Christianity or other religious institution. Despite the effectiveness of a series of revivals, this has been true throughout our history. In many parts of the country Protestantism was culturally established, so that those who declined to participate exercised the element of choice more clearly than those who agreed. But membership was also a matter of choice.

II

I have accented this voluntaristic element in religious belonging as background for the question of whether there can be multiple belonging. Without it, the question does not arise. With it, it arises in at least three ways. First, there are those who are by birth a part of a religious community and wish to remain so, who then encounter another form of religion they find attractive. Can they remain what they are and also participate in the new community? The answer, in our society, is that in many cases they can. A lifelong Methodist who decides to join a Zen meditation group is unlikely to be disowned by her Methodist congregation. But the answer is also that in other cases they cannot. A member of a fundamentalist Protestant congregation would be strongly discouraged from joining a Buddhist temple.

Between these two extremes are many intermediate cases. The Methodist woman would also find problems in being a full participant in a Pure Land Japanese Buddhist temple. If she has married a member of that temple and wants to support him without giving up her membership in the Methodist congregation, she may well receive some support from both congregations in dividing her energies. But there will be internal stress as well. The Buddhist temple is likely to be the bearer of Japanese culture as well as distinctive Buddhist practice, just as the Methodist congregation embodies mainstream American culture. Even if one could harmonize or synthesize the central beliefs of Wesleyan Christianity and Pure Land Buddhism, the cultural associations would limit the fullness of identification in both.

Second are those who are converts from one tradition to another, or descendants of such converts, who come to appreciate what they have lost through this conversion. An important and poignant instance is found among Native American Christians. As they come to realize how conversion to Christianity was bound up with oppression of their people and how it has alienated Native Americans from their culture and heritage, they seek to renew their ties to this heritage. Because there is also much in Christianity that has shaped them and that they cherish, they seek to recover their participation in Native American traditions without renouncing their Christian faith.

Analogous instances in Asia can often be resolved by the fuller indigenization of the Christian faith. But the differences between Native American and Christian ways of being are too deep for that. The former are oriented to land and space, the latter to transcendence of nature and to history. For now, double belonging seems to be the best solution.

Third, there are those who view all the religious traditions from without. They recognize values in several of them but see no reason to identify fully with any one. They can, of course, privately agree with some on one point and others on another without belonging to any. But they may want also to become part of living communities that practice these faiths. The question then becomes whether they can participate in more than one such community.

To minimize the cultural issues raised above, we can imagine that both religious communities are made up chiefly of Americans. Instead of joining a Japanese Buddhist temple, for example, one might join a group of American disciples of a Tibetan Buddhist teacher. This could be paired with a liberal Episcopal church. Would this work?

I assume that both groups would accept such a person as a member. To be a serious member of both groups would be demanding, but that is not the question here. Those interested in multiple belonging are generally willing to pay that price. Hence the answer is that this is possible. Indeed, it actually happens!

III

The real question for a Christian theologian is whether such arrangements are desirable. This is more difficult to answer and for that reason a topic well worth serious reflection. I will consider first the problems with or objections to multiple belonging from a Christian point of view. Then I will consider arguments in its favor.

Christianity is a way of ordering the whole of life and society. For the serious Christian, being a Christian provides one's primary identity. One may also be an American, a lawyer, a father, and a Rotarian, but one is not truly a Christian unless that identity is controlling. The real Christian decides what it means to be an American as a Christian, not the other way around. Hence, belonging to a Christian community is normatively a way of expressing one's primary identity. One may be a member of many other groups and organizations, but they must all be subordinated to this identity. If the other group understands itself in such a way that this subordinate role is possible, there need be no problem, but the term "multiple belonging" seems open to participation in more than one group claiming this primacy. That is highly problematic from a Christian point of view.

The issue, then, is whether other religious traditions make the same ultimate claim as Christianity. The answer is that they do not always do so. A group of Zen Buddhist practitioners may make such a claim, but they do not necessarily do so. They may offer a meditational discipline that has distinctive values and can contribute to the well-being of people in many communities. For this reason I suggested that the Methodist woman could join such a group and profit from it without raising questions about her Christian identity. Many Catholics practice Zen in this way.

On the other hand, there are Zen Buddhists for whom the authentic practice of Zen is a part of a whole way of being, understanding, and living. This is very impressive to Christians, and very appealing. But it is not at all clear that one could belong to the Zen Buddhist tradition in that full sense while retaining one's primary Christian identity. It seems to require that one's primary identity be Buddhist in such a way that one's participation in a Christian community must be subordinated to it.

A similar situation obtains with respect to transcendental meditation. This presents itself typically as a system that benefits people of all faiths and no faith. Indeed, it can be shown to do so. Christians are certainly at liberty to participate in groups of meditators who use the transcendental method. But the more deeply one moves into this meditation, the more distinctively Hindu elements appear; also, the more consuming is the demand for fullness of commitment and involvement. Belonging to a transcendental meditation group in this deeper sense almost inevitably subordinates one's Christian identity to something else.

The problem of multiple belonging among the Abrahamic faiths is even more difficult. Their monotheistic character encourages all of them to call for the primary commitment of their members. A Christian might decide to practice Subud, a meditational system arising in Islam. But to become a Muslim is to become part of a community whose practices shape the whole of life in a way that is different from Christianity. Even though one may continue to reverence Jesus as a Muslim, Jesus can no longer be the center of history. Christian identity is replaced, not supplemented, by Muslim identity.

IV

Despite all these problems, there are good reasons, from a Christian point of view, for experimenting with multiple belonging. Although the Christian ideal is that Christian faith order the whole of life, centuries of secularization have in fact relegated it for most adherents to particular areas of life. The recognition that there are other great religious paths has further relativized the meaning of faith for many of the most sensitive and perceptive Christians. It is unrealistic to oppose multiple belonging in the name of an ideal or norm that is largely inoperative. If there is to be a recovery of an effective religious vision, it is unlikely to come from any one religious community alone. It will have to grow out of the new situation of radical religious pluralism in which we now find ourselves.

Furthermore, we must recognize that today many of the most religiously sensitive and perceptive people find it impossible to identify themselves fully with any one of the competing traditions. To ask them to do so is to call for a surrender of their integrity that is alien to all these traditions. The choice is between distancing themselves from all communities of faith, creating a new one, or multiple belonging.

For these religiously sensitive and perceptive people to function only as individuals, cut off from community, is surely undesirable for them and for the future of religious life. They need community, and they are badly needed by existing communities. Some may find in Bahai the inclusive community they need, since Bahai understands itself as a drawing together of what is best in all the traditions. But for others, Bahai has become one more community with its specific values and limitations.

One possibility is for people of this sort to band together and create a new syncretistic religion. Perhaps something of this sort will happen, and perhaps it will point the way into the future. But it is doubtful that either these individuals or the wider culture is ready for this. For one thing, there is no agreement as to just what elements from what traditions should be integrated into a new religion. For another, any specific integration now coming into being would be destined to be one more tradition alongside the others, subject, in time, to similar limitations.

This leads us back to experiments in multiple belonging. Those of us deeply rooted in one tradition or another will not be attracted to this. But we can be grateful that there are those who are. As they participate seriously in more than one community of faith, they will come to understand the contributions and limitations of these communities in ways that will otherwise remain invisible. They will also discover ways in which these communities can support one another and supplement one another. They can interpret us to one another. They may discover new forms of self-identity appropriate to a pluralistic age.

We should view this as genuine experimentation. That means that we cannot chart the results in advance. It also means that the major result may prove to be failure. We may learn that exclusive particularity is so important to each religious community that to transcend it is to lose the values of that community. But the fact that an experiment may fail does not mean that we should discourage those willing to try. On the contrary, it indicates the importance of our collective support.

V

Although I support the experiment in multiple belonging for the reasons indicated above, I do not see it in itself as the primary pointer to the desirable future. I see it, instead, as a contribution to those who work inside individual traditions to move them forward. It is this development of particular traditions to which I am committed, primarily, in my case, Christianity.

As a Christian I agree with those who find strengths and weaknesses in all traditions, including my own. The point at which I part company with those who seek multiple belonging is that I do not find it problematic to belong to a community with strengths and weaknesses. I would find that problematic only if that community refused to acknowledge its failings. In principle, and to a considerable extent in fact, Christianity is open to repentance, and it is this openness that provides hope for its continuing contribution to the salvation of the world.

The terminology of weaknesses and failings is far too moderate in the case of Christianity. Our history is one replete with persecution of Jews and heretics. We have sanctioned and sanctified conquest and slavery. We have undergirded patriarchy in extreme and horrific forms. We have ignored the consequences of our actions for the well-being of the natural world, thus threatening the human future on this planet. We have used political and economic power to force our beliefs on others.

Of course, I believe that we have also done much good in the world. If our role had been only villainous, there would be little point in identifying with this tradition! The point here, however, is not to brag about positive achievements but rather to emphasize that at the heart of our tradition are deep reasons for self-criticism and self-transformation. In such self-criticism and transformation we see Christ at work in our midst. It is only a penitent and transformed Christianity that can work effectively for the salvation of the world.

The penitence and openness we need today has much to do with how we relate to other religious traditions. We have much to repent of in this respect. Most of all we must repent, and are repenting, of the anti-Judaism that has cursed us so long and so deeply. We must transform both our teaching and our practice to embrace our elder brothers and sisters in the Abrahamic faith. We must learn from them about who and what we have been and also about ways in which we can incorporate elements of their wisdom into our lives.

Our crimes against Muslims have also been monumental. In the Crusades we rallied Christendom against "the infidel," even though Muslims worshiped our God and reverenced Jesus. In more recent times we have colonized Muslim lands, and to this day we tend to vilify Islam in ways unthinkable in relation to other religious communities. We have much of which to repent and much fresh thinking to do. We should listen to Muslim critiques not only of our practice but also of our teaching, and we should undertake to change what is validly offensive. If we had not presented Jesus as a god, the Trinity as a polytheistic doctrine, and grace as a substitute for righteousness, Mohammed might have become a Christian prophet! We have much to learn from the purity and clarity of Muslim monotheism.

The encounter with Indian traditions challenges us to repentance in a quite different way. There is the history of European imperialism in India and in some Buddhist nations. We must confess the role of Christianity in sanctioning this imperialism and in using imperial power to implement its proselytizing projects. But we must also reflect on the negative character of the dominant ways we have described God in all the Abrahamic traditions as this is perceived by Hindus and especially by Buddhists. Our rethinking of what we mean by God in light of the wisdom of India is a major task for the Christian community. It must be associated with rethinking of the nature of reality and of thought in general. Only a Christianity that has been transformed by the wisdom of India can make its full contribution to the salvation of the world.

Most difficult of all may prove the transformation demanded of us by what we learn from our fresh encounter with Native Americans and other primal peoples. Especially because we have been newly sensitized to our crimes against nature by the ecological crisis, we are drawn to the truth and value of their orientation to the land. We recognize that ancient Israel felt a somewhat similar attachment, but we have long prided ourselves on transcending such parochial understanding. We do not associate the divine with particular locations, and we pride ourselves on what our historical orientation has enabled us to accomplish. The whole emphasis of this essay on repentance and transformation belongs to that historical emphasis. How can we then learn from primal peoples the importance of appreciation for the Earth as our nurturing mother and particular localities as our home?

Difficult as this is, it is a task we cannot evade. Today we cannot avoid the recognition that the dominantly historical orientation of Christianity has been part of the problem. Not only has it led us to an aggressiveness toward others that has blocked their hearing of the gospel and often done immeasurable harm, but it has also blinded us to the needs of the natural world. Merely calling for attention to these needs and proposing changed practices for historical purposes will not effect the deep changes needed. For the sake of the salvation of the world to which we are committed, we must transform ourselves far more deeply.

VI

How does double belonging relate to this process? Repentance must be the act of one who identifies fully with the guilty party. One cannot repent another's sins. To whatever extent one identifies fully as a Christian, one can confess the sins of Christians against Jews and Muslims, even when, as an individual, one has not participated importantly in those sins. Repentance (*metanoia* in Greek) begins with confession but is chiefly a matter of changing direction. Leadership in changing direction can also come only from one who is fully identified with the community that needs to change.

Can the multiple belonger contribute to that process? He or she can certainly help Christians understand the crimes they have committed and the importance of confession and change. This is an important contribution. But one who belongs also to the community of those who have been sinned against can probably not lead in the confession and change. That leadership must be in the hands of those whose belonging is not thus divided.

The limitation may go deeper. Many multiple belongers, especially of the third type considered above, are likely to be such because of their desire to identify with what is positive in each tradition without identifying with the negative. A certain distance from the actual tradition and history seems inevitable. As one who does not identify with the Christian tradition in its entirety, the multiple belonger cannot really participate in the confession and repentance at all. At a time when repentance is so central to the Christian calling, this is a severe limitation. There is danger that the multiple belonger does not really belong at all.

The case of Native American Christians considered above illustrates this problem. There is no question that Christians collectively have sinned grievously against Native American peoples. There is also no question but that Native American Christians can be leaders in helping us to understand the depth of our crimes. But when they call us to repent, they seem to do so as Native Americans rather than as the Christians who need to repent.

This limitation would be very serious, even decisive for normative judgment, if it were not the case that many single belongers also fail to accept corporate responsibility for the past sins of the church. In our individualistic society they, like multiple belongers, want to belong to the church without full identification with it in its crimes as well as its virtues. Despite this, we welcome them into our congregations. A multiple belonger brings to the church all that these single belongers do, and something else besides—an insider's understanding and appreciation of another community. To recognize that in some crucial respects they cannot lead is in no way to disparage the positive contribution they can make.

Nevertheless, I have no doubt made it clear that I do not see multiple belonging as the primary way into the future. The primary way is the transformation of the particular religious traditions, at least in the Christian case, through their new encounter with other traditions. As Christians learned much from Greek philosophy and from modern science, so they can learn much from a new appreciation of Judaism, Islam, Hinduism, Buddhism, Native American traditions, and other religious traditions. This is not a matter just of information about them, important as that is, but of a wisdom and practice that Christians need to appropriate into the mainstream of their own faith. To this end, Christians can gratefully benefit from the distinctive knowledge and experience of multiple belongers.

VII

I am a Christian theologian, so I have written from this perspective and directed my attention to the role of those who are Christian as well as something else. In conclusion I will offer my impressions as to whether other religious communities can benefit in similar ways. The communities differ from one another profoundly, so that what makes sense for some is far less relevant to others.

It is my impression that repentance and transformation, as I have described them, are far more central to Christianity than to most other traditions. This may be in part because we have more of which to repent, but it is also because of the distinctive nature of our tradition. We are oriented to the historical future of the world. Jesus pointed us to the reign of God, the situation in which God's will is done on earth as it is in heaven. We know that we have always been and continue to be drastically incomplete and inadequate instruments of God's work to this end. Hence, learning what we can from others is central to our shared mission.

Of course, there are other emphases in the Christian tradition. There are many who want to claim for existing Christian knowledge a completeness that it does not have. They point back to what happened once for all in the Christ event rather than to the future toward which Jesus directed us. They want to absolutize the Bible or church pronouncements in a way that blocks appreciation for any ideas that come from other sources. They are even inclined to deny that Christianity as a whole, or at least their branch of Christianity, has committed crimes against humanity and nature. But in inner-Christian terms, these refusals to acknowledge our guilt and incompleteness are themselves sins of which we need to repent.

Other religious communities are often less oriented to a changed future and to the historical process of moving toward it and more oriented to a practice or pattern provided in the past or to an ahistorical fulfillment. Their orientations toward other religions are, therefore, not informed by the same needs and considerations.

Nevertheless, other religious communities for other reasons are open to learning from one another and from Christians. To them, too, multiple belongers can contribute. Perhaps most of these multiple belongers will in the end become single belongers enriched by their experience in other faith communities. But perhaps not. Perhaps for the foreseeable future this stance will grow. Perhaps it will provide a valuable option for the many religiously sensitive and concerned people who find it arbitrary and limiting to give total loyalty to any one community in the context of religious pluralism. In either case they have their role to play, and we can rejoice in the quality of those who choose this difficult path.

4

Toward a Buddhist Interpretation of Christian Truth˙

JOSEPH S. O'LEARY

My models of "double belonging" are the late Winston and Jocelyn King. They meditated together every morning, he as a Buddhist Christian, she as a Christian Buddhist. Here was a marriage of traditions that left all theological cavilling far behind, demonstrating that there is no fundamental contradiction between the gospel and the Buddha's path. One might try to maintain that each spouse had a primary and total commitment to one tradition and only an auxiliary commitment to the other one. Yet in the lived symbiosis of traditions it may be doubted whether such questions of priority were of any great moment. Jocelyn liked to quote Hakuin's slogan: "Great faith, great doubt, great effort." Great faith is practiced both in the initial total commitment to one's own tradition and in the subsequent generous embrace of the other tradition. Great doubt arises in the mutual testing and purification of the traditions. Great effort is called forth by the horizon of spiritual searching and questioning that the meeting of traditions opens up.

VATICAN WARNINGS

The immense mutual enrichment that religious pluralism brings was noted with joy by Pope John Paul II during his recent visit to Israel. A contrasting note is struck in the recent declaration of the Congregation for the Doctrine of the Faith, *Dominus Iesus*: "The Church's constant missionary proclamation is endangered today by relativistic theories which seek to justify religious pluralism, not only *de facto* but also *de iure*" (par. 4). This document has the merit of pointing to real dangers of the interreligious encounter. Theologians should ponder its warnings about

the difficulty in understanding and accepting the presence of definitive and eschatological events in history; the metaphysical emptying of the historical incarnation of the Eternal Logos, reduced to a mere appearing of God in history;

29

the eclecticism of those who, in theological research, uncritically absorb ideas from a variety of philosophical and theological contexts without regard for consistency, systematic connection, or compatibility with Christian truth; finally, the tendency to read and to interpret Sacred Scripture outside the Tradition and Magisterium of the Church (ibid).

Religious relativism is popular today, partly because of the repulsion and fear excited by its polar opposite, fundamentalism. There is also a strong pressure on theologians to abandon the high claims made for Christ not only at Nicea and Chalcedon but in the New Testament.

However, dangers are sometimes unavoidable, even salutary. The encounter of Christianity and Buddhism of its very nature puts a question mark against definitive eschatological events, demands a less substantialist ontology of the Incarnation, sets up a play of ideas that cannot be reduced to systematic connections, and uncovers meanings in scripture that are thinly represented in traditional church teaching. Theologians dealing with these pressures will usually try to maintain the definitive character of what God has done in Christ, including a view of the Incarnation that can claim fidelity to the truth of Nicea and Chalcedon. But their striving for orthodoxy will inevitably seem insufficient to those who refuse to take Buddhist questions and insights seriously. As to "uncritical" syncretism, one is tempted to ask to what degree it is in the eye of the beholder. The alternative to it, in any case, is not a purism that would refuse to use any non-Christian or non-Western concepts, but rather a discerning "syncretism" of the kind practiced by the Fathers when they took on board the riches of Greek philosophical theology. The Vatican document offers little positive advice on how to proceed here, and in the context of the discouragement of study of Asian religions in Asian seminaries one suspects that it is fomenting panic about relativism in a rather obstructionist way.

Vatican documents of this kind, ever since *Pascendi* (1907), tend to erect theological questions or problems—problems usually posed by the realities of the cultural context or by the results of historical research—into fixed "presuppositions" forming a system of errors to be overthrown. These errors are then dismissed by citation of the Creeds or of other Vatican documents, citation that can be highly selective (witness the fate of Paul VI's left-leaning texts *Populorum Progressio, Octagesima Adveniens*, and *Evangelium Nuntiandi* in contrast with the use of his *Creed of the People of God* as a litmus test of orthodoxy). The hermeneutics implied in this procedure is one of circular transparency between modern questions and ancient texts. There is no recognition that the ancient texts, unless sensitively interpreted for the modern context, have an abrupt and rather scandalous character, due not to the truth they contain but to the inadequacy of its archaic expression. The same unresolved question of the need for translation of ancient creeds into modern categories underlies the skirmishes between the Vatican and hermeneutically alert theologians such as Rahner and Schillebeeckx. Of course, it is very frustrating and discouraging for theologians to have to explain the elements of hermeneutics to uncomprehending church authorities again and again, especially when their patient clarifications are rewarded with contumely. Doctrinaire impatience with hermeneutics also plays into the hands of those who would dissolve the Christian tradition, for instance by labeling two millennia of Christian thought as anti-Semitic, anti-woman, or "metaphysical."

The encounter with Buddhist thought enhances the hermeneutical task of theology by opening up the possibility that Christian truth today can be more luminously presented in a discourse influenced by Buddhist analytical methods and ontological insights than in the old frameworks formed in dialogue with Greek ontology. In order to dissolve the theoretical objections to a Christian-Buddhist symbiosis, without trivializing them, one needs to trace the points of contention to their historical roots. This is a vast and unending hermeneutical task. In our non-Eurocentric culture it is unconvincing to dismiss the ontological analyses of Buddhism as simply erroneous while conferring on those of Thomas Aquinas a perennial validity. A thoroughgoing philosophical dialogue between the traditions of Western and Eastern metaphysics is called for, with a constant attempt on both sides to rejoin the phenomena themselves, the *Sachen selbst*, from which no philosophical or theological discourse can stray with impunity. Buddhists, like Christians, have always sought to understand the nature of reality itself, both in metaphysical analysis and in meditative contemplation of the "suchness" of things. When they share their quests, they are unlikely to find a systematic connection between the two ontological traditions; nor is it likely that one tradition will simply refute the other. Currently, Buddhist philosophy seems to reinforce the deconstruction of substance-ontology that has been going on in the West since Kant and Hegel, with some help from quantum physics. Yet Buddhism can also provide a deep underpinning to the modern philosophies of subjectivity, language, and phenomena, revealing ultimacy at the heart of the realms they open up and preserving them from nihilistic forms of reduction. Buddhist ontology could also perhaps restore insights of classical metaphysics, but we do not yet have serious Buddhist readings of Plato, Aristotle, or Aquinas. Conversely, Western philosophical analysis may be necessary to give Buddhism an articulate modern voice, for the great debates of the Madhyamika or T'ien-t'ai schools, so fascinating to scholars, seem tangential to contemporary questions unless this hybridization is allowed. The exchange between Buddhism and Western philosophy is far more vibrant, at least intellectually, than the Buddhist-Christian dialogue, and it is flourishing unchecked by any supervising agency such as the Vatican. "Double belonging" in the realm of philosophy has its tensions, to be sure, but they are of a purely intellectual order. In the realm of religion we seem happy to confine ourselves to a dialogue of contemplation or praxis, which eschews the clash of ideas and the opening up of questions. The all-importance claimed for spirituality or for politically correct causes produces a discourse in which Christianity and Buddhism taste exactly the same, a bland spiritual chewing gum.

The first questions raised in Buddhist-Christian encounter may seem like tired chestnuts, not worth fretting about. The question of God, for example, is already so blurred and confused after centuries of discussion in the West that one can scarcely summon hope that Buddhism could renew it. With its stress on universal impermanence, Buddhism is uneasy with the idea of an eternal God, or rather it is positively hostile to the idea. Even when Buddhists teach that Buddhahood is a constantly abiding reality, identical with the very suchness of things, this Buddhahood, as Dogen stresses, is not a substance but the event of becoming Buddha, an event constantly renewed. Thus if "impermanence itself is Buddha-nature" and thus "constantly abiding" (a difficult paradox), conversely, Buddhahood itself is impermanent in its fabric. Buddhism begins by dismantling the Brahmanist idea of a securely substantial God, whereas Christianity is firmly rooted in Jewish monotheism and even reinforces it by Platonic structures of transcendence wherein God is located as supreme eternal being. Here we seem confronted with an irresoluble contradiction that makes "double belonging" impossible.

But this may be tackled as a challenging koan, pointing to a subtler conception of the meaning of monotheistic language. The doctrines of non-self and emptiness do not annihilate human personhood but free it for a more authentic existence. Similarly, an empty God, who is non-self, is closer to the dynamic Johannine and Pauline conception of God as an event of Spirit, light, agape, than to the God of classical metaphysical theology. Even within metaphysical theology, when God is spoken of as "being itself" or as "beyond being," we are asked to think of God as an empty space attained when we put speech aside *(apophasis)* and suspend our desire to grasp conceptually *(akatalepsis)*. When God is spoken of in this way, Buddhists may sense an affinity with their own positive conceptions of ultimacy, the notion of *dharmakaya*, for example. In Buddhism and Vedanta, apophatic thinking serves to bring us into the presence of ultimacy here and now, an immanent ultimate, rather than to transcend the present world in a Platonic ascent to a world beyond. But in Christianity, for instance in Meister Eckhart and even in Plotinus, *apophasis* can be a means of awakening to present reality, finding oneself where one already is. Buddhism encourages the overcoming of Platonic dualism through a more thoroughly phenomenological and contemplative method of thinking. Just as Buddhist conceptions of Buddhahood or the *dharmakaya* are supposed to be quarried from the experience of realizing Buddhahood in meditation, a new concept of God could be discerned by sifting our inherited God-language through a thinking that hews to the phenomena. (The peculiar clumsiness of process theology derives from its lack of a secure grounding in the phenomenology of how God is encountered; the same may be said of the bloated trinitarian speculation so popular of late.) Eternity can be translated into phenomenological terms as the discovery that God is "always to hand"—*pantote* in the sense of "the poor you have *pantote* with you" (Jn 12:8). To be sure, the inherent quality of that which is encountered undoes the application of temporal categories; love, grace, spirit are not subject to temporal categories, just as Buddhahood in its nirvanic ultimacy and emptiness cannot be tracked by them, though each of these noumenal realities is always being realized in a lived here and now. Perhaps the nearest analogue to Buddhahood in Christianity is the Holy Spirit. When we call the Spirit an "eternal being," we feel we are missing the phenomenon of the Spirit, ever active in the here and now.

CHRISTOLOGY

As even the title of *Dominus Iesus* indicates, the most persistent objections to Christian acceptance of Buddhist thought stem from Christology. The accents of Buddhist ontology can have a refreshing impact here. The language of substance, nature, and hypostasis as applied to Jesus has tended to shield the humanity of Jesus from contingency and impermanence (Buddhist *anitya*) in a docetistic fashion. Buddhism allows a more thorough appreciation of the kenotic character of Christ's humanity, its full participation in the dependently co-arising texture of samsaric existence. Even apart from Buddhism, theologians are constrained to envision the definitive eschatological role of Jesus Christ in light of the radically contingent texture of human evolution and history. The singular meaning emergent in the life, death, and ongoing life of Jesus needs to be credibly placed within the general perspectives of history as we currently discern them and particularly within the history of religions. The metaphysics of the Incarnation need not be an inexplicable amalgamation of two substances, human and divine. A step back to the perspectives of Origen or the quasi-adoptionist language of the New Testament (Acts 2:36; Rom 1:3-4; and so on) can suggest that the divine Word is manifested, becomes historical, in a unique and full way in and across the entire history of Jesus in his connections with Israel and the entire human community. Never to be forgotten is the fact that Logos is God and that Jesus is a man. The "hypostatic union" of the Logos and the man as one and the same Lord Jesus Christ has always been seen as an unfathomable mystery. Yet if we approach it "from below," along the pathways of the history in which the figure of Jesus emerges as the divine Word spoken into the heart of that history, and of all human history, then the dogma acquires a certain phenomenological profile; the mystery comes into focus without ceasing to be mystery. The contingent, dependently arising events of the Christian "history of salvation" (embracing Israel, the fleshly Jesus in his various interconnections with others, and the history of the church) reveal ultimate reality in a distinctive way, summed up in the phrase "the Word became flesh" (Jn 1:14). Phenomenologically, the claim that Jesus is savior and divine is grounded in the way that in the story of Jesus divine ultimacy and human historical struggle click together in a cogent and potent way, unknown elsewhere.

A metaphysics of emptiness can greatly enhance these efforts to rethink Christology in a phenomenologically accessible style. To see Jesus as a man empty of own-being, and therefore manifesting in his dependently co-arising existence the ultimate reality of divine emptiness, is a vision that chimes well with many aspects of the gospel. John P. Keenan shows this in his remarkable commentary *The Gospel of Mark*.[1] Even Johannine Christology could be re-envisioned in these terms; it is in his abandonment of vain claims to substantial self-nature that Jesus becomes the true Word of the empty God and can enter the dimension of glory and become the source of Spirit for all who accept him and live the same "empty" life.

But it may very legitimately be feared that Buddhist analysis will ultimately have a corrosive effect on the language of Christology. Converting it from a language of being into a language of emptiness carries the great risk of losing its integral content. The temptation that lies nearest, and to which *Dominus Iesus* is particularly attentive, is that of a "Nestorian" separation of the eternal Logos and the man Jesus. The doctrine of the Atonement raises a further series of problems. René Girard offers pointers to rethinking atonement as a human process, the dismantling of human mimetic rivalry and its murderous outcome through the prophetic nonviolence of Jesus, given universal presence in the symbol of the cross. (Girard's humane sensitivity as a literary critic contrasts with the unwieldy contraptions of theologians who speculate on the "creative suffering of God" and other far-fetched unbiblical notions.) Jesus draws on himself the violence generated by human greed and ambition, eloquently countering it in his death with an expression of forgiveness, compassion, humility, and love: "Father, forgive them; for they know not what they do" (Lk 23:34). Jesus has a bodhisattva's insight into the bondage of his enemies to delusive passions and delusive objects of passions, rooted in a delusive idea of self, and he exerts educative compassion on their condition, to release them from suffering. Wherever the cross is made known, the same compassionate education is continued. The truth revealed in the event of the cross is as old as creation—the truth of divine loving-kindness constantly pressing on God's creatures despite their closed hearts. "God was in Christ, reconciling the world to himself" (2 Cor 5:19), not by magic but through the eloquent expression of forgiveness and compassion in all the gestures of Jesus culminating in his death. Wherever the cross is remembered, God's work of healing, through the Spirit, is something phenomenologically accessible. To human arrogance it is a stumbling block or mere folly, but when its meaning is discerned this exhibition of failure and weakness is understood to be "the power of God and the wisdom of God" (1 Cor 1:24). It may be objected that the cross has been an emblem of violence and tyranny in crusades and colonization. That means that the cross has not been understood. Today we understand it better, because we see more clearly how damaging is the disease to which the cross brings the cure. The three poisons of greed, hatred, and delusion are writ large in contemporary history and are studied in depth by psychoanalysts and socio-biologists. Alongside the wisdom of the Buddha, the power of the cross is increasingly being recognized as the supreme antidote. (Buddhist gentleness suggests to us the question whether the harshness of biblical language—especially in the gospel denunciations of Pharisees and "the Jews"—has been an appropriate method of conveying the wisdom of the cross.)

Against substantializing and magical theories of the Atonement, we do well to set in high relief the salvific impact of the cross as registered in human experience. That impact reaches far, to the very depths of humankind's biological and psychological makeup, and it can correct even what is all too human in the letter of scripture and the activities of the church in history. Redemption, too often conceived as a magical "behind the scenes" process, is worked out in history as the deconstructive impact of the figure of the cross, dissolving the barriers set by human arrogance and fixation against the liberating space of divine ultimacy. God's reconciliation of humankind with Godself takes phenomenological profile as the power of the cross—epitomizing an entire trajectory of awareness and enactment—to put humans back in touch with gracious ultimacy. What is experienced as dramatic divine intervention can also be grasped as the human process of opening to the ever-available ultimacy, an opening supremely expressed and enabled in the life and death of Jesus. A phenomenology of breakthroughs of ultimacy need not overlook the conventional processes that are the vehicle and the basis of such breakthroughs. Indeed, it is only by deepening our awareness of the sheer conventionality or contingency of religious languages, in a kenotic spirit, that we can preserve their functionality as vehicles of ultimacy.

Focusing on these phenomena, we realize that grace is not an abstruse, invisible substance. It is the core of reality itself, constantly operative, awaiting our realization of its power and presence. One might compare this presence of grace with the notion

of "original enlightenment," central in Japanese Buddhism and now powerfully reha-
bilitated in Jacqueline Stone's recent work.[2] For Buddhism, at least in the optimistic
form that prevailed in medieval Japan, the status of Buddhahood is open in principle
to any human being; indeed, we already have the Buddha-nature and need only wake
up to the fact; why, even grasses and trees can be Buddha, or rather already have the
Buddha-nature just as they are! The reason for this is that Buddhahood is identical
with the suchness of things; to become a Buddha is to be what one is and to be it to
the full. This is attained not by the intercession of a Buddha but by each individual
discovering and following the path to Buddhahood, or simply awakening to Buddhahood. Such a system of salvation seems a blank denial of Christian claims about sinful
humanity's radical need of a redeemer. But let us remember that Christian thinkers
have always rejoiced in the radical goodness of being, none more so than that prince
of soteriological pessimists, Saint Augustine. All that exists is good to the core, and
evil is a mere deficiency in being. Ultimate gracious reality is revealed in all beings and
is at work in all beings. When we say that salvation is found only in Christ or only in
the church, the meaning of "salvation" here must be a highly specific one. Perhaps the
completeness of historical eschatological salvation is what is meant, the idea that Christ
brings to fulfillment and leads to its ultimate destiny the universal creative-salvific
process that is always going on in all religions and in all life. Paul VI had a beautiful
flight of eloquence in his Christmas sermon for 1975: "I see all the religions of the
world converge around the crib of Bethlehem, and as I say this my voice trembles, not
with incertitude, but with joy—*la mia voce trema, non d'incertezza, ma di gioia.*" This
was the vision of Vatican II, albeit imperfectly expressed in its documents, a vision
rooted in a Teilhardian sense of the dynamic of life.

THE UNIVERSAL MEDIATION OF THE INCARNATE WORD

The claim that all grace is mediated by the incarnate Christ and his church, so
strongly stressed in *Dominus Iesus*, could be interpreted more gently if one first stressed
this universal constant presence of grace at the core of reality. Christ and the church
are definitive historical ciphers of grace, its eschatological incarnation, but they make
sense only against this broader background. In theologies like that of Karl Rahner this
background is expressed in abstract metaphysical terms, but we can discern it in its
concrete richness if we interrogate the witness of the great religions, all of which speak
of the miracle of grace. In the Fourth Gospel Jesus tells his disciples that they still have
a lot to learn and that the Spirit will lead them into all truth (Jn 16:12-13). One of the
places where that truth should be sought is in the religious witness of humanity. In-
trinsically, Christ as the Word Incarnate is the fullness of truth, but to discover this
divine fullness in the concrete words and signs in which it is deposited is an infinite
labor in which all humanity participates. Christ is always ahead of us, waiting to be
fully known.

Jacques Dupuis's book *Toward a Christian Theology of Religious Pluralism,*[3] under
investigation by the Congregation for the Doctrine of the Faith in the two years preceding the publication of *Dominus Iesus*, is perhaps the target of the following remark:

The theory of the limited, incomplete, or imperfect character of the revelation of Jesus Christ, which would be complementary to that found in other religions, is contrary to the church's faith. Such a position would claim to be based on the notion that the truth about God cannot be grasped and manifested in its globality and completeness by any historical religion, neither by Christianity nor by Jesus Christ (*Dominus Iesus*, no. 6).

The phrase "the theory" seems to lump together many different possible positions, to consign them all to the dustbin of heresy.

The document states, "Theological faith (the acceptance of the truth revealed by the One and Triune God) is often identified with belief in other religions, which is religious experience still in search of the absolute truth and still lacking assent to God who reveals himself" (no. 7). Here again an important nuance risks hardening into a black-and-white opposition. All religions have faith in the sense of generosity of vision and existential trust that goes beyond the warrant of narrow empiricism and implies a relation to gracious ultimacy. On the other hand, there is the specific recognition of God at work amid God's people Israel (Jewish faith) or in Jesus (Christian faith), which corresponds to that extra something, that definitive eschatological fullness of salvation, that scripture proclaims. But the quest-structure of human experience pervades all religions. According to Augustine, God "can be found while he is being sought" *(inveniri posse dum quaeritur);* God is "sought in order to be found more sweetly, and found in order to be sought more eagerly" (*Nam et quaeritur ut inveniatur dulcius, et invenitur ut quaeratur avidius* [*De Trinitate* XV 2]). All religions have their mighty finds and their ongoing quests. The incompleteness of their understanding does not mean that they have not found what they seek; and the fact that Christians securely possess the fullness of divine truth does not mean that they are not seeking still for what they have found. The attempt to view this universal process of human religious seeking and finding as the medium and mode of even biblical revelation, and conversely to find a divine revelatory activity at work in the non-biblical trajectories of religious experience and questioning, seems to me an irreversible path of theological reflection, imposed on us by the facts of religious pluralism themselves. To see only its dangers and not its promise seems fainthearted and ungenerous. To insist that "the sacred books of other religions, which in actual fact direct and nourish the existence of their followers, receive from the mystery of Christ the elements of goodness and grace which they contain" (no. 8) may be logical, in that the eternal Word (God) is the source of all goodness and grace (and truth, unmentioned here), and this Word is most fully and definitively incarnate in the Christ-event and the Christ-process. But this logical claim has had deleterious effects on Christian understanding of Judaism in the two millennia during which the Hebrew scriptures have been read as testimonies to Christ that the Jewish people, due to their blindness, were unable to read correctly. Applied with equal bluntness to the sacred texts of Hinduism or Buddhism, it would amount to the claim that only Christians, full of the Holy Spirit, are capable of understanding the true import of, say, the teachings of the Buddha. The stubborn realities of history and of pluralism are in tension with bluntly expressed theological claims here, and this tension cannot be resolved in a wholesome way by simply shutting out awareness of the other, as happened in Christian exegesis of the Hebrew scriptures in the centuries between Jerome and Calvin.

"The theory which would attribute, after the incarnation as well, a salvific activity to the Logos as such in his divinity, exercised 'in addition to' or 'beyond' the humanity of Christ, is not compatible with the Catholic faith" (no. 10). Nor is there any "economy of the Holy Spirit with a more universal breadth than that of the Incarnate Word, crucified and risen" (no. 12). According to theologians such as Karl Barth, even the creation of the world is mediated by the humanity of Christ, and the idea of Christ's descent into hell implies that Abraham, Isaac, and Jacob were saved not simply by their faith in God but by their prophetic faith in the humanity of Christ. An inflated Christocentrism, even Christomonism, had a debilitating effect on much of Barth's and Von Balthasar's thought. Hasty insistence on stamping Christ and the church on every phenomenon of creation and history leads to a counter-intuitive vision of reality and leaves no breathing space for the diversity of humanity and the transcendence of the divine. That is why missioners are mistrusted; they are too quick to stamp Christ on local cultures or to stamp out these cultures to make room for Christ. In Asia the church is perhaps beginning to define itself as "defender of faiths" as well as propagator of the faith. Interreligious dialogue is not to be used as an instrument of mission, but rather it is out of dialogue that authentic mission may emerge.

At an abstruse, transcendental level the claim that adherents of non-Christian religions mysteriously participate in Christ's paschal mystery, and not merely in the universal light of the Logos, may belong to the logic of Christian faith, even though it must be admitted that the "logos spermatikos" doctrine by which Fathers such as Justin Martyr were able to discern traces of the divine Word in Greek philosophy and religion often sounds as if the *logos asarkos* (the non-incarnate Logos) is being spoken of. In the actual practice of interreligious thought, however, it may often be indiscreet and positively distorting to introduce the humanity of Christ as an explicit theme. Britten's chamber opera, *The Rape of Lucretia*, has a narrator who comments on the ancient Roman story from a Christian point of view; the effect is an unconvincing clash of styles. The beauty of Mozart's music is mediated by the humanity of Christ and not just by the disincarnate divine Logos; but such a claim offers only the most nebulous guidance for a theology of music, and could license the most insensitive intrusion of gospel themes on the fabric of the musical work. There is a lot of Zen in the gospel and there is a lot of the gospel in Zen, but this communion of the two traditions is not brought to light by dogmatic fiat. Christians may find it more convincing and more tactful to say, along with Vatican II, that "the Spirit" is moving in all hearts, and if pressed they will of course affirm that this Spirit is none other than that breathed forth in the fullness of its power by the dying and risen Jesus. The paschal mystery is universal because it touches the essence of human living and dying; this universality is not imposed from without, by preaching Christ, but discovered from within, in every human destiny, as a horizon of hope, given a certain definitiveness in the cross. Modesty is de rigueur in making such claims, since we are dealing with realities of faith, not of final vision. An eschatological proviso, a *docta ignorantia*, must qualify all our affirmations. We grasp only dimly and from within a human historical perspective what the Spirit is saying to the religions and to us through the religions.

We may measure what we grasp against what we have grasped of our own scriptural revelation, and the result may be that our grasp of our own tradition deepens and changes. Thus the normative and complete character of God's salvation in Christ does not exclude a lot of give and take in practice, given the radical limitations of our understanding of God and even of Christ. That stress on limitations need not signify a modernist neo-Kantian agnosticism; what the Vatican document understresses is the degree to which this emphasis can draw on sources deep within Christian tradition itself.

Theological claims need not blind us to empirical reality. The claim that Christ and the church are universal needs to be qualified by a recognition of the historical and culture-bound limitations of Christian discourse as it has actually existed. Only at the end of time will the universality of Christ be an actually realized phenomenon. For now it is a projected perspective of faith, a regulative idea guiding the dialogue between Christian tradition and other traditions. In that dialogue Christianity is in quest of its own universality. The fullness of truth dwells in Christ, but as particular historical movements the churches do not exhaust the totality of truth; there is always more of Christ to be discovered. Many new things are to be learned from Judaism, Islam, Buddhism, Hinduism, things not precontained even implicitly in the treasury of Christian truth that the church effectively possesses, though they are precontained in the fullness of the Incarnate Word. Christian truth is not in any case primarily a set of theories but the living memory of an event, the death and glorification of Christ. Our interpretations of this event, including the labor of dogma that produced the Nicene Creed and Chalcedon, remain very imperfect. Western philosophy has been found to be of great value in the ongoing task of interpretation, and Buddhism should prove of greater value still. Christianity, viewed in its history, is best seen as a dynamic and open project that is far from being able to grasp its own significance completely; still less can it grasp completely the significance of other religions, judging them from a superior vantage point. The normativeness of the Christian project is an open-ended and fluid thing, as is the normativeness of the project of Western reason or of the Western quest for human rights. This normativeness is enriched if it can ally itself with kindred projects in other traditions.

The categories of classical dogma have a role in orienting Christian faith toward its object, if they are skillfully deployed. But the fundamental thought of religious people does not move on the conceptual plane. When we rethink our images of God in light of a Buddhist insight into emptiness, for example, the dogmatic prohibitions of atheism, pantheism, and so on, provide only a safety net rather than powerful, positive direction. Dogmatic criteria are less central than the criteria inscribed in the gospel itself: the primacy of love, the superiority of the life-giving Spirit to the letter that kills, the abundance of grace and of divine mercy, justification by faith in Christ, the primacy and assured triumph of the eschatological kingdom. These are mysterious criteria, demanding ongoing contemplative perception, and cannot be summarized in cut-and-dried categories. Even within the Bible these criteria functioned in a subversive way, as signs of contradiction. They remain troubling to the church whenever it becomes excessively bureaucratic. One of the wonders of Vatican II was that these criteria again came unmistakably to the fore.

BACK TO THE PHENOMENA THEMSELVES

If we identify the Christian essentials as love, Spirit, grace, we must be careful not to reify the saving event these terms indicate. We must not freeze our understanding of these terms, making them fetishes. When we meet an alternative discourse of ultimate spiritual life, such as the Buddhist discourse of Wisdom and Compassion, our mono-Christian terminology may be felt to be insufficient, parochial. The universality of love, Spirit, grace is perhaps already lost if we remain within the furrow of biblical language and refuse to confer an equal dignity and centrality on the Buddhist terms. The great religious founders were amazingly free people and showed little concern with packaging their doctrine in an exclusive set of orthodox categories. The realm of religious truth is fundamentally that realm of pneumatic freedom, only very secondarily a realm of doctrinal propositions. Consider this description:

> There is an important connection between the image of the Zen master as unhesitating and unflinching and the central Buddhist realization of the emptiness or groundlessness of all things. The Zen master is the one who no longer seeks solid ground, who realizes that all things and situations are supported, not by firm ground and solid self-nature, but rather by shifting and contingent relations. Having passed through this experience of the void at the heart of everything, the master no longer fears change and relativity. The Zen master is undaunted by the negativity in every situation and every conversation. He no longer needs to hold his ground in dialogue, and therefore does not falter when all grounds give way. What he says is not his own anyway; he has no preordained intentions with respect to what ought to occur in the encounter. Indeed, on Buddhist terms, he has no self—his role in the dialogue is to reflect in a selfless way whatever is manifest or can become manifest in the moment.[4]

This description could apply very well to Jesus, especially as he appears in the sayings tradition and in Mark. The awakened person is in tune with the movement of life itself. The kingdom of God, the main theme of Jesus' preaching, is beyond the register of control and calculability. Perhaps his prophetic statements about its future coming were never intended to be taken literally but rather functioned to awaken people to the divine at work in their midst. The future triumph of the divine is assured, but the assurance rests on "whatever is manifest or can become manifest in the moment," and it is here that the teaching of Jesus becomes precise and penetrating, whereas the references to past and future depend on the conventional symbolic framework of the time. Church teaching, too, should center on awakening people to the presence of God here and now, relying less on the secure grounds presented by the past or by promises about the future. The burden of worrying about these grounds weighs down the Christian present and creates a musty, shabby idea of religious truth as consisting chiefly in claims about what happened or will happen at other times and places. The history of salvation is a necessary backdrop to Christian preaching, but it is less substantial than is supposed, as can be seen from the fact that our understanding of it has changed so much over the centuries. The significance of the past and the promise of the future are always things to be quarried anew from the experience of the present. The tendency of Christian thought to see the present only in light of a mythicized past and future, instead of the other way round, stifles spiritual creativity. Projecting our perspectives on past and future from the Zen groundlessness and emptiness of the present, we can reground past-oriented faith and future-oriented hope in the present movement of the Spirit, a movement that itself has no firm ground but blows where it will in shifting and contingent relations and encounters.

Reductions of dogma to what is phenomenologically accessible have been afoot in theology since Schleiermacher. They defuse the basic tensions between Christianity and Buddhism. Other tensions are more a matter of accent and atmosphere, for instance, the stereotypical opposition of Buddhism as an impersonal, rational, equanimous religion or philosophy and Christianity as personal, emotional, and based on faith in authority. Different personality types flourish on different types of religion. Buddhism does a better job than everyday Christianity in catering to those whose religious sensibility is impersonal and rational; Christianity is richer in resources for those of more existential and affective temper. But Christianity is no more lacking in fearless rational analysis than Buddhism is in passion and compassion. Rather than think of Buddhist equanimity as a cool, self-protective attitude, we should see it as guaranteeing the authenticity of compassion; a busy nurse cannot direct effective compassion to a succession of patients unless he or she is deeply grounded in equanimity. The wealth of equanimity, as a spiritual attitude of wisdom and freedom, is so great that it can found and fund compassion. Conversely, Buddhists tempted to stereotype Christian piety as emotional should consider that sentimentality can be a skillful means for some people and that a radical purification of emotion is available within Christianity in such masters as John of the Cross. Generally, any totalizing criticism of a great religious tradition will fall flat. Cardinal Ratzinger's comment that "Buddhism is a form of spiritual auto-eroticism" is a case in point, at least if read as a remark about the entire tradition rather than about some irritating local Zen enthusiasts. British Buddhologist Paul Williams claims that this remark was instrumental in his conversion to Catholicism, and that as a Buddhist he was unable to get outside his own mind. But the attractions of mind-only idealism are not unknown in the Christian West, and each tradition has its antidotes to the extremes of solipsism or other forms of mind-based nihilism, just as it has its antidotes to substantialist reification.

All religions have to do with salvation and healing. A religion that is no longer effective in healing the ills at the root of human existence risks being numbered among those ills itself. For Buddhism, religions are skillful means, expedients adapted to the concrete situations of suffering beings. That does not mean they are merely lies or fictions; each in its own symbolic language functions as a mode of the Buddha's presence. In Japanese esthetics, even the poetic naming of a tree or the spring rain can be such a presencing of Buddhahood. Christianity has not had this sense of itself as a pragmatic construction and has not been very generous in admitting a providential healing function in all other religions as well. It has sought to center its identity on the rock-like security of doctrinal truth, often at the expense of healing efficacity. Perhaps we have been too anxious to pin down the truth, imitating the methods of philosophy and seeking foolproof guarantees. We have been more anxious for proof that there is a

God than for an understanding of what is meant by the word *God*. Energy invested in shoring up doctrinal certitude carries a charge of violence, violence against our own questioning minds, which can overflow into violence against others who revive the repressed questions.

"Unlike the modern European focus on epistemological concerns—the concern to attain accurate representation through avoiding error—Buddhists envision a systematic distortion that pervades all human understanding."[5] Buddhism avoids the trap of anxious attachment to views, content to let the experience of following the Buddhist path speak for itself. Buddhist tolerance of and respect for a variety of religious paths seems flabby to Christians, consonant neither with the biblical insistence on one saving truth nor with Greek rationality. But there is a twofold wisdom in the Buddhist approach. On the one hand, there is a clear insight into the relative character of any linguistic formulation of truth. Formulations belong to the register of conventional, not ultimate, truth, and they are characterized by an inbuilt inadequacy. On the other hand, Buddhists are optimistic about the power of truth to make itself felt in any language, always adapting itself to the capacities of the hearers. Applying this to Christianity, we may say that it is in its very brokenness that Christian language speaks with provisional adequacy of Christ crucified and of God. God is revealing Godself and acting for salvation in all languages, religious or secular, and even in the mute trees and stones. The Christian will hear the divine Logos in all things and in all religions, and even the Logos Incarnate, as in Joseph Plunket's poem, "I See His Blood upon the Rose." The language of Bible and church is a key for interpreting the other languages. In Buddhism a similar economy prevails: a canonical text such as the *Lotus Sutra* provides the perspective wherein all others are read. But whereas the *Lotus Sutra* marks itself as merely a provisional means of perception, the Christian Bible seems to have been absolutized in a way that makes it an obstacle to generous perception of grace and truth outside its pages. We need to find the places in the Bible itself where it marks its own status as an instrument of perception, to be used imaginatively.

The task of interreligious theology is "to explore if and in what way the historical figures and positive elements of these religions may fall within the divine plan of salvation" (*Dominus Iesus,* no. 14). One way in which Buddhism may fall within the divine plan is as a pharmacopoeia of antidotes for the sickness of religion. Christianity, like Buddhism, is a self-critical religion; the Bible has been seen as containing the remedies for every kind of religious pathology, including many enacted within the Bible itself. But the self-critical prowess of Christianity, even as renewed by the Protestant Reformation and sharpened by the challenges of the Enlightenment and modern atheism, today needs to be supplemented by the gentler arts of Buddhism. Buddhism tempers the elements of fixation, irrationality, emotivity, and violence in Christian thinking and presents a peaceful, reasonable, wholesome mode of being present religiously to the contemporary world. Buddhist-Christian encounter and symbiosis do not concern primarily the confrontation of two sets of doctrines. We misread Buddhism when we assimilate it to historical Christianity and think of it as centered on institutions and doctrines. The Buddhist Christian is not a speculative synthesizer, but one who draws on the rich and various resources of Buddhist tradition when and where they are found to be useful and illuminating. In an age when religious fundamentalism and sectarian strife are more virulent than ever, the healing critique of Buddhism has perhaps a more central role to play than the classical dogmas of Christianity, at least at the forefront of history, whatever the ultimate shape of "the divine plan of salvation."

What needs to be lived and thought is this concrete symbiosis. The pontifications of theologians about inclusivism, exclusivism, pluralism, and relativism are part of that in-house ecclesiastical wrangling that is the mark of a theology disengaged from a living context. I would add that the dogmatism of liberal theologians who discard the notion of truth or who dismiss tradition instead of overcoming it could equally be a symptom of disconnection. The encounter of Buddhism and Christianity is an encounter of truths embodied in historical trajectories. The self-critical labor forever going on within each of the traditions is enhanced when they embrace in mutual appreciation and critique. Traditions may appear as conventional, contingent, culture-bound, human constructs; yet they provide a necessary defense of and medium of transmission for the breakthroughs of truth in primary enactments of spiritual vision. A tradition is a finger pointing at the moon, fragile, provisional, changing as the moon moves across the sky. Yet without that fragile indicator few would see the moon, and there would be no sharing of the vision. The errors and distortions of tradition can be overcome only by a respectful hermeneutical retrieval of tradition, drawing on its salutary core to overcome these darker aspects. Theologies that escape from the historical concreteness of tradition and the critical labors it demands of us, and theologies that substitute a benign relativism for the scholarly and spiritual weight of interreligious encounter, may create an atmosphere in which new questions are opened up, but more often their vacuous rhetoric is an obstruction to the advance of theological insight.

The symbiosis of religions may take the form of a mutual aid wherein the weak points of one religion are healed and corrected by another. To say that Buddhism has no right to play that healing and correcting role toward Christianity is like saying that the Samaritan had no right to bind the wounds of the man left for dead on the Jericho road. In real life the religions need one another, whatever their utter self-sufficiency on the plane of abstruse theological claims. The religions, as human historical trajectories, are inevitably marked by incompleteness and tragic failures. The tensions between them are not to be suppressed by dogmatic self-affirmation but to be interpreted as the tension of "truth" itself, making itself felt within the finitude and brokenness of the human language striving to express it. Just as a married couple give each other a sense of perspective and prevent each other from falling into megalomanic, egocentric delusion, so Buddhism and Christianity in their irreducible otherness are good for each other, helping to keep each other open-minded and sane. It used to be said that a good Catholic needs to be a Protestant, while a good Protestant needs to be a Catholic; today, we might add, a sane Christian needs to be a Buddhist.

NOTES

[1] John Keenan, *The Gospel of Mark: A Mahayana Reading* (Maryknoll, N.Y.: Orbis Books, 1995).

[2] Jacqueline Stone, *Original Enlightenment and the Transformation of Medieval Japanese Buddhism* (Honolulu: University of Hawaii Press, 1999).

[3] Jacques Dupuis, *Toward a Christian Theology of Religious Pluralism* (Maryknoll, N.Y.: Orbis Books, 1997).

[4] Dale S. Wright, *Philosophical Meditations on Zen Buddhism* (Cambridge: Cambridge University Press, 1998), 100-101.

[5] Ibid., 137.

5

God for Us

Multiple Religious Identities as a Human and Divine Prospect

FRANCIS X. CLOONEY, S.J.

A straightforward way to approach the issue of multiple religious identities, of course, would be to begin with a review of the resources within one's own tradition—those that already shape one's identity—in order to see what is permissible and sanctioned according to the tradition. I, for instance, might look to the Catholic and Jesuit traditions to consider clues regarding how to relate to other religions. Or one might postulate universal religious experience and then stress its implications for the possibility of multiple religious identities. But in this essay I begin elsewhere, in what I have been learning more intentionally through years of the study of Hinduism. I shall turn secondly to consider my own tradition in light of this excursion into a Hindu tradition.

A VERSE, A CLUE

In 1984-85, my first year as a professor at Boston College, I taught a course on saints of the Hindu religious traditions. For a section of the course I translated a 1940s Tamil-language and popular life of Antal, the ninth-century south Indian saint who composed two poetic works in Tamil, *Tiruppavai* and *Nacciyar Tirumoli*.[1] This account by K. R. Govindaraja Muthaliyar is really an elevated hagiography that reconstructs Antal's life with clues extrapolated from her poetry. Govindaraja recounts her birth so as to suggest that she is a goddess, but his account of her childhood and growing up treats her like a young person distinguished by her intense love of her God—Lord Narayana—and God's favoring her. In one key incident, little Antal becomes accustomed to wearing beforehand the fresh flowers intended solely for use in temple worship. When her father discovers this "tainting" of the purity of the flowers, he is horrified. But Narayana appears to him in a dream and assures him that the flowers are all the more pleasing because they have been worn by Antal. Finally, the Lord chooses her for his bride, and she is invited to the great temple at Srirangam for her wedding with the Lord who resides there.

The latter part of the account narrates this journey to Srirangam. On the road, the women accompanying her are skeptical that the Lord would approach a human in this way in their time and place, even selecting someone like Antal as his bride. In response, Antal says or sings this verse:

> Whichever form pleases his people, that is his form;
> Whichever name pleases his people, that is his name;
> Whichever way pleases his people who meditate without
>   ceasing, that is his way,
> That one who holds the discus.

As we love God, God adjusts and comes to us accordingly; if someone loves like a bride, God comes as a groom.

This charming account has been useful in courses aimed at illuminating Hindu devotional piety, and it provides an interesting counterweight to Antal's own poetry. But it is the verse that has most of all stayed with me, distilling and focusing my understanding of a Hindu way of thinking. Although the verse appears in a very specific devotional context, it is strikingly universal. I wondered about the mode of love of God it encourages, how general and how specific. The verse seemed to deserve closer attention, so I began to look deeper into its meaning. Much of this essay is about what I have found in that search, and what I have learned by thinking about it. As we shall see, it has provided me a way to respond to this volume's thematic question regarding multiple religious belonging. My hypothesis is that in contemplation we construct a path of religious belonging that suits our own spiritual imagining; we do this according to our traditions but also the possibilities available in our time and place. In all of this, God agrees to meet us there; if our contemplation happens to cross religious boundaries, God agrees to meet us there too. But let us see how I arrived at this hypothesis.

WHAT HINDUS THOUGHT ABOUT THE VERSE

When I searched out the source of Antal's lovely verse, I discovered right away that she had not composed it. Rather, it is verse 44 from a work known as the *Mutal Tiruvantati,*[2] attributed to Poykai Alvar, a Vaisnava saint *(alvar)* who lived a generation or two before Antal. Poykai Alvar was by tradition "found" by his parents nestled in the wall of a water tank. By tradition too, he and two other saints, P'y and Bhut, found their mission by chance. During a wild thunderstorm they one by one took refuge in a small shelter and found themselves mysteriously and increasingly squeezed together by a fourth and unseen presence. In fact, they were being overwhelmed by the growing presence of Lord Narayana, who had unexpectedly visited them and was crowding in upon them. Upon realizing this, they burst into song, each composing

100 verses, of which Poykai's verses are placed first and known simply as the *Mutal Tiruvantati.*

Poykai Alvar's general question has to do with how God has been accessible to humans, and how one learns to see God now. The verses of the *Mutal Tiruvantati* immediately preceding verse 44 set up its context. Poykai Alvar had been reflecting on the ways in which God is both great and merciful, and how the divine justice, though uncompromised, leaves room for a gentle compassion and a divine intention to find devotees wherever they may be. The Lord focuses intently on those who depend on him (25); he is the cause of the world, yet also compassionate to individuals in their individual needs (29); he has expressed his gracious intent in deeds performed in past divine *avataras* (34, 35, 36), but also in certain places, most important, the temple on Mount Tiruvenkatam, where he is easily accessible, though remaining transcendent and mysterious (37-43). After verse 44, Poykai Alvar continues to investigate the path toward union with the Lord, the simplicity of true meditation, the power of evoking the sacred name, and so on.

Verse 44 thus serves as a kind of intermediate summation: the transcendent Lord, source of the universe, who has engaged in astounding deeds in ancient times and who dwells most graciously in the temple at Tiruvenkatam, is also present in every place, any time, wherever devotees may be. God remains creative and accommodating now. Because of this, God can be found now, in meditation, however devotees imagine him.

Since first impressions are not always correct, I was reluctant to read the verse out of context or to overextend it interreligiously merely according to my own wishes. My next step then was to ask how the Vaisnava tradition actually interpreted the verse and its claim about divine graciousness. I found two ancient commentaries directly on the *Mutal Tiruvantati*: a detailed commentary by Periyavaccanpillai in the thirteenth century, and a prose summation by Appillai in the fifteenth century.

LIVING THE VERSE

Periyavaccanpillai offers a straightforward exegesis of *Mutal Tiruvantati* 44 that also puts it in a larger textual context. Most important, he emphasizes the specific realizations of divine graciousness in form, name, and deed by linking each of the first three lines of the verse to an illustrative parallel. The first line, "Whichever form pleases his people, that is his form," is illustrated with an anecdote about an unusual and humble divine form. The great teacher Ramanuja was out walking near the Srirangam temple and saw some boys at play. In fact, they were playing priests, and for this had outlined a shrine of Lord Narayana in the dust. Ramanuja not only was not offended by this but indeed was certain that the Lord was present even in so trivial a form as that produced by playful boys. So he prostrated himself before the image sketched by the boys and even took its dust as *prasadam* (the food given to one who worships in a temple).

Periyavaccanpillai illustrates line 2, "Whichever name pleases his people, that is his name," with an anecdote recollecting the favorite name by which Nanciyar, an earlier teacher, evoked God. Lord Narayana appeared to a teacher named Visnucittar, and asked for alms, identifying himself as "the cowherd God." When Visnucittar asked him why he answered to that unusual name, he replied that this was the name that pleases Nanciyar, so it pleased him as well.

Line 3, "Whichever way pleases his people who meditate without ceasing, that is his way," prompts an anecdote about Rama's self-forgetfulness in the *Ramayana* (*Yuddha Kanda* 117). Although Prince Rama was really Lord Narayana come down on earth, and his kidnapped wife Sita was really his eternal consort Laksmi, Rama became absorbed in his earthly deeds and acted as if he were simply a human being. He even thought of dismissing his wife Sita, whom he had just rescued from captivity, on the grounds that perhaps she was defiled by her captor, Ravana. The gods spoke to Rama, lamenting that he seemed to have forgotten his real identity as supreme Lord of the universe, and likewise his wife's true divinity, and also that in his true nature he was not susceptible to the cruel doubts that divide other men from their wives. Rama responded by admitting that he had indeed been so immersed in his mission that he had forgotten his divine identity. Accordingly, he asked the gods to remind him of who he was, and Brahma, spokesman for the gods, did so. Periyavaccanpillai's point, of course, is that the Lord is like that: he becomes immersed in his salvific tasks even to the point of self-forgetfulness. Similarly, God always thinks more of "us" than God's own self.[3]

These anecdotes—Ramanuja's simple commitment to finding God in all things, the Lord taking for himself the name Nanciyar enjoys, Rama's self-forgetfulness in service—illustrate *Mutal Tiruvantati* 44 and give a rich contextual "feel" to the notion that the Lord actually accommodates his devotees. Accordingly, the reader is encouraged to recollect such anecdotes along with the verse and thus to be more confident in encountering God.[4]

THE VERSE AND ITS WIDER CONTEXT

In addition to direct commentary on the verse, Periyavaccanpillai explicates it by linking it to a verse from the much more well-known Sanskrit-language *Bhagavad Gita*:

> However someone takes refuge in me, in that way do I favor them, Partha! (*Bhagavad Gita* 4.11).

Thereafter this *Gita* verse serves as a kind of all-India Sanskrit double for the local Tamil insight of *Mutal Tiruvantati* 44.

The *Gita* verse has an appropriate theological tradition of its own. Ramanuja, the key teacher of the tradition to which Periyavaccanpillai belongs, had used *Gita* 4.11 as an occasion for summarizing the double purpose of divine descent, that is, the restoration of righteousness and the promotion of divine accessibility. According to Ramanuja, the divine descents are first of all freely chosen divine acts aimed at defeating evildoers and uplifting the good. But more important, in fact, these acts of divine entry into the world provide devotees with more immediate access to God, an access that is distinctive and good in itself, an opportunity that the Lord graciously provides for his people. *Mutal Tiruvantati* 44 is understood to be making the same point: God desires to accommodate his people, meeting them wherever they happen to be.

The message of *Gita* 4.11 and *Mutal Tiruvantati* 44, that the Lord is near and available, is also taken by Periyavaccanpillai as referring particularly to divine temple images. At *Mutal Tiruvantati* 44 he also cites *Visnudharmottara Purana* 103.16, a puranic text that makes explicit the value of constructing a temple image of gold:

> The lovely form of Visnu, his image, his pleasing face and
> glance—
> making this image in a way that pleases him, from gold or
> silver,
> he should then honor it, bow before it, love it, meditate on it.
> His flaws removed, he will then reach that form of Brahman.

The point of *Mutal Tiruvantati* 44 is thus made even more concrete: the Lord is willing to be present in whatever material form and shape his devotees construct for him, and the temple image—idol—expresses the same accessibility known in ancient times through the divine descents. We are thus reminded of Antal's approach to Lord Narayana at Srirangam, where, for all his enduring transcendent mystery, God can be found all the time, every day.

Appillai summarizes the meaning of the citation of *Visnudharmottara Purana* 103.16 in this way:

> Thus the Lord does not consider his own greatness, but holds as his own forms, names, deeds, etc., those which please people who take refuge in him. Thus Poykai Alvar reflects on and makes known the excellence of the nature of the image-form with which the Lord serves those who take refuge in him.

Later Srivaisnava theologians confirm what had clearly become a standard belief in the tradition: as devotees seek the Lord, so the Lord makes himself found by them. The fourteenth-century Vedanta Desika, for example, makes the same connection of *Mutal Tiruvantati* 44 with the same *Gita* text:

> The person surrendering should meditate on the Lord's making himself dependent on those who seek his protection in a manner that cannot be understood by the mind or described in words. As it says, "However someone takes refuge in me, in that way do I favor them" (*Bhagavad Gita* 4.11); the same is also stated in Tamil, "Whichever form pleases his people, that is his form" (*Mutal Tiruvantati* 44).[5]

AN ASIDE ON HOW TO SEE GOD
AND ON HOW GOD WILLS TO BE SEEN

To deepen our sense of the meditative process and theology of divine accessibility promoted by *Mutal Tiruvantati* 44, let us detour for a moment by taking a look at the interpretation of another alvar song, *Tiruvaymoli* 3.6, one from among the hundred by the poet Satakøpan. Here is a characteristic verse from among the eleven that compose the song:

> Never manifest, never decaying, yet he does both,
> unique in form, the bright-eyed Lord abides,
> so that one who receives both his grace and anger can enter
> >   beneath his feet;
> fragrance, manifestation, taste, sound, approachability:
> all of this is my bull of the heaven-dwellers—
> except for him I have belonged to no one else, not even for
> >   seven births.

This song is traditionally understood as a key locus for reflection on temple presence, and in this light it was commented on extensively by an earlier teacher, Nampillai, the teacher of Periyavaccanpillai.[6] In explaining *Tiruvaymoli* 3.6, Nampillai introduces *Mutal Tiruvantati* 44, along with *Gita* 4.11 and *Visnudharmottara Purana* 103.16. But he also extends the intertextual connection by introducing several other interesting references that enrich our understanding of the kind of contemplation this tradition had in mind in commenting on *Mutal Tiruvantati* 44 and *Bhagavad Gita* 4.11.

First, Nampillai cites a section of the fourth-century *Visnu Purana* (5.17), in which we hear of the visualization practice of Akrura, the minister of a king Kamsa, a fierce enemy of Krsna (who is Lord Visnu come down on earth). Akrura himself is a good man, deeply devoted to Krsna and intent on seeing Krsna, who has made himself accessible to humans. When Akrura finally met Krsna, he notes in rich detail the details of the person before him—Krsna's color, his physical features, how he walked, the clothing he wore, the flowers in his hair. The next day Akrura went down to the river to bathe and meditate, this time visualizing Krsna anew by recollecting what he had already seen and re-creating in his imagination those same vivid details of Krsna's appearance. After this powerful visualization, Akrura met Krsna once again and was able to confirm the reality of his contemplation: "I saw a marvel at the river, and now I see it before my eyes, in bodily form. For it is you that I encountered in the waters, Krsna. The entire world is filled with your marvelous presence." God is really present, in direct encounter and as one recollects God in meditation.[7]

Second, Nampillai connects *Tiruvaymoli* 3.6 with the practice of *uruvelippatu*, visualization. The Lord is accessible according to how intensely the devotee imagines the divine presence. In introducing the song he cites a scene from the *Ramayana*, *Sundara Kanda* 21.19, where Sita, kidnapped and captive, spoke to King Ravana, her captor. In warning Ravana to allow Rama to rescue her, she referred to Rama as if he were actually present, next to herself and Ravana. She was so preoccupied with Rama that he was vividly present in her imagination, wherever she herself might be. Likewise, Nampillai notes, Ravana himself became increasingly preoccupied with Rama, who was coming to fight him and take back his wife, so he too could not help but visualize Rama's presence everywhere around him. Sita's longing, Ravana's guilt—the intensity of emotion, the longing or fear—made Rama vividly present. This process could be imitated in the more reflective process of meditation.[8]

In introducing *Tiruvaymoli* 3.6, Nampillai also indicates the importance of the visualization that occurs regularly in the temple context by citing the *Srirangarajastavam,* a hymn composed by Ramanuja's disciple Parasara Bhattar in praise of divine accessibility:

> Let us stop counting your births
> which overflow with auspicious qualities
> and let us stop numbering all that is good about you, O
>   Lord of Srirangam!
> Your real delight is being worshiped in this world
> In temples, homes, and hermitages, bearing all things and
>   in a condition of complete dependence upon the
>   temple priests.
> Tenderhearted persons are stunned at this character of
>   yours! (2.74).

That is, the Lord is tenderhearted because he is present in temples, homes, and hermitages, enduring all things, and remains in a condition of complete dependence on temple priests. That this point is the same as made in *Mutal Tiruvantati* 44 is made clear by Nampillai's series of cross-references, as he connects for us *Mutal Tiruvantati* 44, *Bhagavad Gita* 4.11, *Tiruvaymoli* 3.6, and *Srirangarajastavam* 2.74. These linked texts support one another, and all confirm the basic theological point: the Lord is willing to make himself approachable in a form suitable to humans.

In the fifteenth century the great teacher Manavalamamunigal closes this particular circle by citing *Mutal Tiruvantati* 44 along with *Srirangarajastavam* 2.74, emphasizing the connection of both to temple worship:

> "Whichever form pleases his people, that is his form." That is, as [the Lord] takes that form for himself that the devotees imagine as his divine body, he makes himself present in any material the devotees choose, such as gold, silver, or stone. Here it is not like the specialties of manifestation, incarnations such as Rama, Krsna, and so on, where he made himself present with a fixed norm, with respect to places such as Ayodhya, Mathura, and so forth, regarding the time such as 11,000 years, 100 years, etc., regarding the fitness of the person, Dasaratha, Vasudeva, and so on. Here there is no norm regarding place, as it is said, "[Your real delight is being worshiped in this world] in temples, homes, and hermitages." Here there is no rule that limits time, place, form in some already established way. The Lord overlooks the shortcomings of devotees, since he is tolerant—as it says, "Bearing all things" (*Srirangarajastavam* 2.74).[9]

In modern times the same interconnections of text, image, and affect are reaffirmed, for instance in the modern Tamil editions and commentaries by Krishnasami Ayyangar, today's premiere Srivaisnava editor and commentator. After linking *Bhagavad Gita* 4.11 to *Mutal Tiruvantati* 44, and also to other texts we have seen, *Visnu Purana* 5.17.5 and *Tiruvaymoli* 3.6.9, he extends the intertextual connection by adding a citation from the Sanskrit-language *Jitante Stotra* 1.5, which notably reinforces the theme of divine accessibility:

> You have no form, no shape, no weapons, no abode,
> But nonetheless you shine forth in the form of the Person
>   for those who love you.

Ayyangar interprets this verse too as stressing the extreme nature of the Lord's accommodation: God has no form, shape, power, place; indeed, he is nothing, except insofar as he formulates himself in accommodation of his devotees:

> In the previous verse you were described as the means; this verse explains how you make yourself and what is proper to you suitable to those crossing over worldly existence *(samsara)*. The fact that devotees and their proper nature exist for the Lord is indeed due simply to what is proper to them; but that he should make himself and his proper nature exist for their sake is due rather to his tenderness, good character, etc. Therefore, this verse explains his tenderness, good character, etc., such that he is the object of refuge. For tenderness, good character, etc., are supporting aspects of the definition of him as the object of refuge who is both transcendent and accessible.[10]

When we return finally to K. R. Govindaraja Muthaliyar's telling of Antal's story in the 1940s and review his decision to use *Mutal Tiruvantati* 44 in illumination of Antal's hope, we can see clearly that by putting this verse in her mouth he aligns himself with the old tradition of citing it when there is a need to stress that the Lord's determination is to be accessible to his devotees according to their wishes—even as Antal might dream of marrying God. He also stresses the value of the accessibility of temple presence and accentuates the remarkable, counter-intuitive ease of this access. This "modern" reformulation poses the old value in the face of skeptics represented by the women: in the past God came very close to us, as a bridegroom, but "it does not seem right that now, in his temple form, the Lord would marry Antal." She replies with verse 44, and adds, "if he has appeared to people in the past, why should it be extraordinary now?"[11] The long tradition of reflection on the immediacy of God's presence, particularly in temples, is represented vividly when Antal is given the verse to quote.

Mutal Tiruvantati 44 itself is just one key to one traditional Hindu way of seeing God and God's accessibility, incorporating the piety of ancient teachers, practices of meditation and worship, and a powerful theology of divine accommodation. As I traced the verse in its various contexts, I was also learning to think and imagine along with the commentators and to see more vividly for myself some of the possibilities opened by the verse and its logic of human-divine accommodation; the promises made by Narayana to these Hindu writers come alive as promises I can at least imagine as made to me as well. While the tradition has not extended its reflection on *Mutal Tiruvantati* 44 in support of a theology of God's presence in other religions—it remains thoroughly focused on the Vaisnava tradition itself—I can well imagine how that extension might appropriately be made.

NOTICING ONE'S FIRST CITIZENSHIP:
REFLECTION ON IGNATIAN IN-SIGHT AND MY HOME CITIZENSHIP

But we really cannot talk about the acquisition of a new, more complex identity unless we are also clear about our first belonging and how it functions in shaping our consciousness, as a limit and as a resource. So let us turn to the topic of "first belonging," mine in particular. If I have made some progress in learning about Hindu spiritual theology by my study of *Mutal Tiruvantati* 44, the process would still fail to be satisfying were there no application to what I know of God and how I know it. How does one's first "religious belonging" shape what follows thereafter, one's new loyalties?

I myself work from a fairly clear and rather traditional religious identity. As mentioned earlier, I am a Roman Catholic priest and a member of the Society of Jesus, the Jesuits. This tradition of Catholic Christianity also places a priority on contemplation, the value of visualizing God—in Jesus Christ—and on a gradual approach to God's presence. Throughout the preceding reflection on *Mutal Tiruvantati* 44 I have already and naturally had in mind Ignatius Loyola's *Spiritual Exercises*, the basic text that guides Jesuit meditation and contemplation. Some comments on this Ignatian resource are in order.

Ignatian spirituality is of course deeply rooted in the gospel narratives, which recount the life, words, and works of Jesus of Nazareth. Even apart from the specific theologies of each gospel, there is affective power in the stories the evangelists tell about Jesus and the people he met, those who followed him and loved him, those who killed him. If one reads the gospels imaginatively, one begins to visualize his birth and childhood, his time in the desert where he was tempted, the outpouring of the Spirit and the beginning of his ministry. We see him teaching the people, healing the sick, raising the dead. We follow him as he walks up to Jerusalem to meet his destiny and fulfill his Father's will. We mourn as we see him die on the cross, and we rejoice in his resurrection and recognize that we too are filled with his Spirit and sent forth to make him known in the world. Christ became like us in all things—that we might likewise become like him.

WHAT IGNATIUS HAD TO SAY

Drawing on a medieval contemplative tradition,[12] Ignatius makes particular use of this tradition of gospel contemplation by his concerted practice of applying the imagination to scenes from the life of Christ, composing such scenes so as to encourage the active engagement of the meditator. Indeed, Ignatius organizes much of his *Spiritual Exercises* in relation to these simple gospel mysteries, for it is here that God and humans meet. In Jesus we find a common ground, and in a marvelous sense God and humans become adequate to one another. Ignatius offers a series of contemplations that invite meditators to enter upon the scenes themselves, to find their place in the famous stories, and to engage in conversation with Jesus. They are to make a mental construction of the "place for contemplation" so as to be able to see the relevant spiritual and mental realities more clearly and to enter affectively upon the scene. Consequently, these meditators are asked to ponder each scene lovingly, composing the details of the place as vividly as seems profitable; for example, imagining Jerusalem or the shore of the Sea of Galilee, the room prepared for the Last Supper, the tomb in which Jesus was laid. In describing a meditation early in the "second week" of the *Exercises*, Ignatius sets the pattern:

> First Prelude. This is the history of the mystery. Here it will be that our Lady, about nine months with child, and, as may be piously believed, seated on an ass, set out from Nazareth. She was accompanied by Joseph and a maid, who was leading an ox. They are going to Bethlehem to pay the tribute that Caesar imposed on those lands.
>
> Second Prelude. This is a mental representation of the place. It will consist here in seeing in imagination the way from Nazareth to Bethlehem. Consider its length, its breadth; whether level, or through valleys and over hills. Observe also the place or cave where Christ is born; whether big or little; whether high or low; and how it is arranged.[13]

Once the scene is set, one enters it as a participant:

> First Point. This will consist in seeing the persons, namely, our Lady, St. Joseph, the maid, and the Child Jesus after His birth. I will make myself a poor little unworthy slave, and as though present, look upon them, contemplate them, and serve them in their needs with all possible homage and reverence. Then I will reflect on myself that I may reap some fruit.
>
> Second Point. This is to consider, observe, and contemplate what the persons are saying, and then to reflect on myself and draw some fruit from it.
>
> Third Point. This will be to see and consider what they are doing, for example, making the journey and laboring that our Lord might be born in extreme poverty, and that after many labors, after hunger, thirst, heat, and cold, after insults and outrages, He might die on the cross, and all this for me. Then I will reflect and draw some spiritual fruit from what I have seen.[14]

As the meditator imagines Christ in these locations, Christ becomes present to the person, as if there, now. Although the forms are understood as rooted in historical fact, Ignatius presumes that God is willing to accommodate the images generated by the person who contemplates that history now. The great energy behind imaginative practice in the *Exercises* is rooted in Ignatius's expectation that there can be an immediate relationship between God and the person who meditates, by way of the vehicle of the meditator's honest use of the imagination. As Ignatius explains in his introductory notes, contemplation gives the meditator a "taste" of God:

Second Annotation: The reason for this is that when one in meditating takes the solid foundation of facts, and goes over it and reflects on it for himself, he may find something that makes them a little clearer or better understood. This may arise either from his own reasoning, or from the grace of God enlightening his mind. Now this produces greater spiritual relish and fruit than if one in giving the Exercises had explained and developed the meaning at great length. For it is not much knowledge that fills and satisfies the soul, but the intimate understanding and relish of the truth.[15]

This imagining is not a mere connection with ancient events but also the event of direct contact with God:

15th Annotation: But while one is engaged in the Spiritual Exercises, it is more suitable and much better that the Creator and Lord in person communicate Himself to the devout soul in quest of the divine will, that He inflame it with His love and praise, and dispose it for the way in which it could better serve God in the future. Therefore, the director of the Exercises, as a balance at equilibrium, without leaning to one side or the other, should permit the Creator to deal directly with the creature, and the creature directly with his Creator and Lord.[16]

God engages the individual in a deeply personal way, preventing even traditional images of God and ordinary mediating authority structures from standing in the way of an active and effective use of the imagination.

SOME CONTEMPORARY VIEWS OF THE INTENSIFICATION AND EMPTYING OF THE IMAGINATION IN THE *EXERCISES*

Roland Barthes's *Sade Fourier Loyola* is one of the freshest studies of Ignatius's meditation techniques. It focuses in part on his strategies for the purification and intensification of the active imagination. Barthes is intrigued by Ignatius's project, seeing it as a controlled manufacture of certain feelings and emotions in the meditator, a clearing out of old images and an intensely defined admission of the new. Barthes notes that "anyone reading the *Exercises* cannot help but be struck by the mass of desire which agitates it," and

the immediate force of this desire is to be read in the very materiality of the objects whose representation Ignatius calls for: places in their precise, complete dimensions, characters in their costumes, their attitudes, their actions, their actual words. The most abstract things (which Ignatius calls "invisibles") must find some material movement where they can picture themselves and form a *tableau vivant*: if the Trinity is to be envisioned, it will be in the form of three Persons in the act of watching men descending into hell; how, the basis, the force of the materiality, the immediate total of desire, is of course the human body; a body incessantly mobilized into image by the play of imitation which establishes a literal analogy between the corporeality of the exercitant and that of Christ, whose existence, almost physiological, is to be discovered through personal anamnesis. The body in Ignatius is never conceptual: it is always *this* body: if I transport myself to a vale of tears, I must imagine, see *this* flesh, *these* members among the bodies of the creatures.[17]

Yet in the midst of this concreteness, as Barthes rightly notes, exterior images are stripped away, in effect giving the interior person full control over the construction of images:

In the isolated and darkened room in which one meditates, everything is prepared for the fantastic meeting of desire, formed by the material body, and of the "scene" drawn from allegories of desolation and the gospel mysteries. For this theater is entirely created in order that the exercitant may therein represent himself: his body is what is to occupy it.[18]

The role of the meditator is focused on Jesus throughout:

The very development of the retreat, throughout the final three Weeks, follows the story of Christ: he is born with Him, travels with Him, eats with Him, undergoes the Passion with Him. The exercitant is continually required to imitate twice, to imitate what he imagines: to think of Christ "as though one saw Him eating with His disciples, His way of drinking, of looking, of speaking; and try to imitate Him."[19]

Key to Barthes's understanding of Ignatius's method is this project of combining acts of imagination with the emptying of the imagination. Established images are noted and observed, and then stripped away so that the meditator can create more immediately his or her own image of the scene chosen for meditation; personal engagement in the contemplative process is given maximal opportunity. By extension, I suggest, the religiously plural and interreligious environment too provides genuinely religious opportunities for the disciplined meditator who both uses and empties the imagination.

In a recent essay on Ignatius's understanding of seeing in the *Exercises*, Richard Blake, S.J., notes Barthes's insights and further sharpens our understanding of the dynamic of emptying in the *Exercises*:

The one making the contemplation deliberately empties the mind of past images, like a favorite painting, statue, or pictures derived from the words of Scripture, from poetry, or ascetical writing; thus the retreatant begins with a blank canvas, and the process of filling it provides the opportunity for "the Father in heaven [to meet] His children and [speak] with them," much as God does with the words of Scripture. In other words, creating the images from nothing without adapting prior material can, under the guidance of grace, become an experience of divine inspiration. . . . The personal, private image created under God's inspiration clearly holds a greater value than the image recollected and reconstructed from external sources.[20]

Blake goes on to observe that this imaginative process is virtually "limitless, and thus not bound by historical or archaeological reality." Rather, everything is accommodated to one's own desire, as one imagines God in one's own way, and finds God anew in strikingly novel places:

> For example, rather than trying to picture the clothes and utensils Jesus used, the look on his face (as suggested from prior experience of a painting, perhaps), and the sound of his voice (speaking the American English of a fine actor or radio announcer), it may be just as "accurate" for the purposes of contemplation to see Christ in the face of a loved one, in the wasted body of an AIDS patient or in the African or Asian features of those we join in ministry. Perhaps, too, the school or parish or prison may provide a more suggestive setting for meeting the Lord than Galilee as presented in the pages of the *National Geographic* or as reproduced in biblical movies.[21]

The *Exercises'* concluding "Contemplation to Attain Love" moves out from the specificity of the Christocentric focus to a wider and deeper imagining of Christ everywhere in one's world:

> Ignatius encourages a series of reflections on images of concrete, visual realities, but in characteristically schematic fashion. As in so many instances, he provides stark outlines, like drawings in a coloring book. He expects the exercitants to color in the details form their own favorite collection of oils, water colors, or Crayolas.[22]

The meditative process is concrete and imaginative. God operates in accord with the very acts of imagining undertaken by the persons who meditate. There is a delicate and important balance between the insistence that preestablished or traditional, even scriptural images, decisively limit and focus meditation, and the insistence that we can imagine God—in all the ways one can imagine—and know, in humble awareness, that God will find us there.

MULTIPLE RELIGIOUS BELONGING, HUMAN BUT ALSO DIVINE

In the first part of this essay I outlined in detail—more detail perhaps than readers of this volume may have expected—a traditional interpretation and intertextualization of a Tamil verse about God's accessibility and reflected on the kind of religious consciousness that is cultivated among both learned and simple readers. In the second part I returned to my own spiritual tradition, paralleling *Mutal Tiruvantati* 44 with a few suggestive (and hardly original or complete) comments on the imaginative religious practice of Ignatius Loyola, the founder of the Jesuit Order to which I belong first of all.

In Ignatius's understanding of meditation, as in *Mutal Tiruvantati* and the texts related to it, there is an emphasis on the constructive aspect of meditation and the possibilities for real encounter with God through specific experiments in human imagining. Two different meditative traditions remain different, yet both teach us to see how God wishes to be recognized in recognizable terms. Accordingly, each can be reviewed in light of the other, as old and new visions of God are refracted in the proximity of the two. I do not wish to claim that the two traditions have the same view of human religious imagining or identical theologies of divine accommodation, but I do assert that the similarities are real and striking, that in our time the dynamic of their visions of divine accommodation enmeshes the traditions with one another, and that today this shared dynamic enables us to understand multiple religious belonging at a deeper and richer level. I conclude with several reflections on these new possibilities.

First, while one could focus on shared religious experience, the common features of human nature, or the imperative of the biblical tradition toward universalism, my choice has been to stress rather that multiple religious belonging is in important ways as accessible and ordinary as any process of attentive reading. Reading across boundaries is not entirely different from religious reading within particular religious traditions. With some focused effort a Christian reader can pick up and read a Hindu text such as *Mutal Tiruvantati* 44, trace the use of it within the Hindu tradition, reread it in light of some remembered Christian parallels, and then reread some Christian sources in that new light. In some cases, at least, this complication and expansion of the reading process changes us religiously. We do read; we do learn from what we read; we do ponder our reading; this does affect how we read other texts; and all of this does have a yet deeper effect on how we imagine our encounter with God. If a Christian reads a Hindu verse and ponders it according to traditions of Hindu learning, this eventually has an effect—salutary, I suggest—on how he or she thinks and reads, contemplates and encounters Jesus of Nazareth, who even today wishes to encounter us.

This religious reading offers a renewed contemplative practice that complexifies and deepens how we imagine and see God. We are what we read, and if we read in complex ways we become persons with complex religious identities. Reading Poykai Alvar and reading Ignatius end up as mutually complicated acts of reading; the texts become intertexts—which can now be cited in both commentarial traditions. At least, thus far, *Mutal Tiruvanati* 44 has now been cited by a Jesuit who reflects on the meaning of Ignatius's heritage. Ignatian spirituality disposes one to understand Poykai Alvar's point; even if one is deeply devoted to Lord Narayana's accommodating approach to devotees like Poykai Alvar and Antal, this need not be a barrier, intellectual or spiritual, to learning from Ignatius's imaginative practices. If in the end we bring to our spiritual understanding and practice images that belong to more than one tradition, we ourselves begin to belong to those multiple traditions in new and complex ways. In a sense we are "intertexted" in our spiritual practice. Even the most cautious believer need not find anything in this process of learning that has to be dangerous or objectionable. There is no good reason to avoid cultivating an awareness of God's active accommodation to human effort as appreciated in both traditions.

At a secondary level we are also given a new consciousness of what God and we are doing when we use our imaginations in Christian contemplative prayer. Grace comes first, but we remain agents in the construction of our own religious self-identity and our understanding of God and, according to the contemplative practices endorsed by Poykai Alvar and Ignatius, God graciously meets us where we manage to be. If we ponder what we know and what we learn from *Mutal Tiruvantati* 44 and the *Spiritual Exercises*, we then see our original belonging differently, understand God's initiatives and responses more broadly, and so have at least an initially richer and more complex starting point for reflection on where and how God can be found in the future. Apart from any specific theoretical commitment, one begins to *imagine* differently.

In both the Vaisnava and Christian traditions—and of course more broadly too—God remains sovereign over the possibilities of encounter. Since God can come in *any* form, then *any* form will suffice if humans imagine sincerely and God responds. A purification process may be involved, of course, but this will not rule out in advance images that occur to us inside and outside our original tradition. This is a kind of vacancy, an expectation for which the way has been cleared, which in practice is simply a recognition that there are no obstructions—sin, ill will, and ignorance aside—that must necessarily prevent us from contemplations that cross religious divides. Instead of merely being confronted with myriad competing images of God—and there are many, in both traditions and in other traditions—an attentive emptying that leaves room for true encounter with God also leaves the traditions unobstructed by one another in the minds of meditators who draw on both traditions. In this context, multiple religious identities receive a deeply spiritual foundation.

One might consider the texts together, to absorb more deeply the basic insight:

But while one is engaged in the Spiritual Exercises, it is more suitable and much better that the Creator and Lord in person communicate Himself to the devout soul in quest of the divine will, that He inflame it with His love and praise, and dispose it for the way in which it could better serve God in the future.	Whichever form pleases his people, that is his form; Whichever name pleases his people, that is his name; Whichever way pleases his people who meditate without ceasing, that is his way, That one who holds the discus.

How we meet God depends in part on how generously open—imaginative, vacant—we stand in expectation of this God who promises to adjust to us, accommodating us as we are.

In conclusion, it is important to emphasize that this complexification of religious identity is not just a human production. Rather, as in every instance where we grow spiritually because we continue to share a living relationship with God, this too is a response to God in interaction with a God who responds to us. It is a matter of acknowledging a truth that has to do with God's way of accommodating us and meeting us. In the past Srivaisnavas have meditated on the graciousness of Narayana's accommodation to the variety of ways people imagine, name, and tell stories of God; those of us who are Christians have found the gospel stories of Jesus, imagined and extended differently in different times and places, to be graced points of encounter with the living Christ. Today it seems to be the case that God is approached in acts of contemplation that are in part the fruit of new images generated by meditators who expect that God will still come near and be accessible—even when they are praying along with Poykai Alvar and Ignatius at the same time. The traditions remain different in important features, and at some level may seem contradictory, but these differences do not cancel out a common spiritual expectation: God is everywhere, one finds God everywhere and in everything. We seek in new ways, and God responds accordingly, agreeing to meet humans who find God differently because they imagine and remember in more than one religious tradition. It seems now to be the case that the form, name, deed, and condescension of God can all become consciously interreligious on God's part too—not simply because humans are responding to pluralism differently, so as to project different images of the divine, but because those who meditate are complicating and rearranging the names, and forms, and deeds according to which they are pleased to wait upon God. Accordingly, and as ever, God meets them in these new ways.

On a theoretical level we can therefore propose that it is not necessary to assert that God is immobile and unable or unwilling to respond to the new situation of multiple religious belongings. If a considerable number of good, sincere, genuinely God-seeking (and God-finding, being-found-by-God) human beings learn, think, reflect, and see across religious boundaries, and bring a new multiplicity to their prayer and reflection, then it seems proper to assume that God can graciously accommodate us and meet us in the complexity of this new spirituality, theology, community.[23]

On a practical level, we can say that humans who truly seek God have honestly created new religious situations in which God bears more complex names, forms, histories. It is not unimaginable then that God, who is not confined by what we are accustomed to and who does not hesitate to reach out to those who meditate, would graciously agree to encounter us in this new situation in new ways. Multiple religious belongings may at an early stage seem merely or uncomfortably multiple, until we—who are Christian, who are Hindu—notice that even when our imaginations have become religiously more complicated and diverse, it is still the same God who is seeking us out, accommodating us where we are. Govindaraja was on to something perhaps more universal than he realized when, in order to respond to skeptical bystanders who complain that nothing new can happen in our time and place, he put Poykai Alvar's words into Antal's mouth:

> Whichever form pleases his people, that is his form;
> Whichever name pleases his people, that is his name;
> Whichever way pleases his people who meditate without
>   ceasing, that is his way,
> That one who holds the discus.

Even in our time and place, God still graciously enjoys the possibility of finding us where we are pleased to look for God.

NOTES

[1] K. R. Govindaraja Muthaliyar, "Antal," in *Alvarkal Varalaru*, Part 1 (Madurai: The South India Saiva Siddhanta Works Publishing Society, 1975 [1948]), 142-68.

² That is, the "First Set of Verses in the Antati Style"; *antati* indicates a style in which the last word of each verse is the first word of the next.

³ See *Ramayana, Yuddha Kanda* 117.8-11.

⁴ At line 4 the question is why the Lord is called "the one with the discus." Are there reasons—other than meter or the need for filler of some sort—for mentioning this particular detail of popular iconography? Periyavaccanpillai notes that the "discus"—the war discus, a standard item in the assemblage of the divine instruments—stands for all that assemblage, and thus for all the regal and divine splendor and power. But the point is that this splendid Lord graciously takes simple and humble forms for the sake of his people: "The one who was the creator of all and controller of all has become one who is created and controlled."

⁵ *Srimadrahasyatrayasara*, chapter 15; page 155 in the translation (Kumbakonam, n.d.) by M. R. Rajagopala Ayyangar. U. T. Viraghavacharya, a modern commentator on Desika, notes that these verses show us how the Lord goes well beyond the act of divine descents, accommodating himself to whatever his devotees conjure in their minds.

⁶ Indeed, we can presume that his connection of these texts at *Tiruvaymoli* 3.6 provides the background for Periyavaccanpillai's similar collocation of verses.

⁷ *Visnu Purana* V.17-19; adapted slightly from the translation of H. Wilson (Delhi: Nag Publishers, 1980).

⁸ On Srivaisnava visualization practice, see Francis X. Clooney, S.J., "*uruvelippatu*: Notes on a Tamil Practice of Visualization and Its Larger Significance," *Commemorative Volume*, 8th World Tamil Conference (Tanjore, 1995), 83-88 (English).

⁹ Adapted from the translation by Anand Amaladass, S.J., in *Tattvatrayavyakhyanam* (Chennai: TR Publications for Satya Nilayam Publications, 1995), 208.

¹⁰ *Mutal Tiruvantati of Poykai Alvar with Commentary of Periyavaccan Pillai and a Modern Commentary by the Editor* (Trichi: Sri Navas Press, 1986), 204-9.

¹¹ Govindaraja, "Antal," 160-61.

¹² Most notably, the contemplative use of the gospels in the *Life of Christ* of Ludolph of Saxony, a massive tome that Ignatius encountered during his famous bedridden recuperation and gradual conversion of life (see Paul Shore, "The *Vita Christi* of Ludolph of Saxony and Its Influence on the *Spiritual Exercises* of Ignatius of Loyola," *Studies in the Spirituality of Jesuits* 30/1 [January 1998]).

¹³ Louis J. Puhl, S.J., *The Spiritual Exercises of St. Ignatius: A New Translation* (Westminster, Md.: The Newman Press, 1957), 52 (nos. 111-12).

¹⁴ Ibid., 52-53 (nos. 114-16).

¹⁵ Ibid., 1-2 (no. 2).

¹⁶ Ibid., 6 (no. 15).

¹⁷ Roland Barthes, *Sade Fourier Loyola*, trans. Richard Miller (Berkeley and Los Angeles: University of California Press, 1976), 62.

¹⁸ Ibid., 63.

¹⁹ Ibid.

²⁰ Richard A. Blake, S.J., "Listen with Your Eyes: Interpreting Images in the *Spiritual Exercises*," *Studies in the Spirituality of Jesuits* 31/2 (March 2000), 13-14.

²¹ Ibid., 14.

²² Ibid., 17.

²³ On the fact that multiple religious belonging is not merely a private phenomenon but rather also formative of new communities, see my essay "Extending the Canon: Some Implications of a Hindu Argument about Scripture," *Harvard Theological Review* 85:2 (1992), 197-215.

6

Christianity and Religions

Complementarity and Convergence

JACQUES DUPUIS, S.J.

The question of a complementarity and convergence between Christianity and the other religions of the world arises in the context of a theology of religions that while holding clearly to the essential and constitutive elements of the Christian faith, attributes to the other religious traditions a positive value in the order of salvation for their members and a positive significance in the plan of God for the whole of humankind. I have developed such a theology in a recent book, of which it may be useful to recall from the outset some fundamental positions.[1] I have insisted that the history of salvation does not start with the story of Abraham, to extend only to the Judeo-Christian tradition, but with the beginning of the world, from creation, and embraces the entire history of humankind. I have also affirmed that throughout that history God has manifested himself personally to the peoples of the world through the Word and the Spirit, and that the religious traditions of the world preserve the memory of such divine interventions in the history of the nations. I have further stressed the fact that such historical manifestations of God are always composed of both words addressed by God to people and of divine saving actions on their behalf. Thus, the foundational sacred books of the nations may preserve words addressed by God to them as "seeds of the Word" who has been operative among them, while their ritual and "sacramental" practices and their moral code may keep enshrined in them "seeds of holiness"; in the words of the decree *Ad Gentes*, "elements of truth and of grace" (no. 9).

I have thus held that the history of salvation extends to the entire process of God's personal dealings and involvement with the whole of humankind. The historical event

---

This chapter was completed before the publication of *Dominus Iesus* by the Congregation for the Doctrine of the Faith on 5 September 2000 and the *Notification* of the same Congregation on 24 January 2001 concerning Dupuis's book *Toward a Christian Theology of Religious Pluralism* (published by Orbis Books in 1997).

of Jesus Christ stands at the center of this process, of which it constitutes the culminating point; it represents the climax of God's personal engagement with humankind and, as such, is the key for understanding the entire process of divine-human relations. The various religious traditions of the world are in turn various manners in which God has through history been dealing with the nations and are, even today, "ways" along which God's truth and grace reach out to them. I have thus been able to conclude that the reality of religious plurality, of which we have in recent years acquired a deeper awareness, must not be viewed as a mere fact of life to be reckoned with but as a divine grace to be thankful for and an opportunity to be seized—a gift and a task. Religious pluralism, not only de facto but in principle, is based on God's initiative in searching for people throughout history in order to share with them, "in many and various ways" (Heb 1:1), God's own divine life, even before human beings could ever search for him, "in the hope that they might feel after him and find him" (cf. Acts 17:27).

Such a theology of religious pluralism leads to the concept of a true complementarity and convergence between Christianity and the religious traditions of the world, which in turn is not unrelated to the question of the possibility of a simultaneous "double belonging" of singular individual persons to two distinct religious traditions. The burden of this essay does not primarily consist in showing the various ways in which belonging to two religious traditions may present itself or the different degrees in which joint personal commitment to each of the two traditions concerned may be conceived; much less does it intend to pass an a priori, positive or negative, judgment as to the concrete possibility or theological justification of a deliberate personal belonging to two traditions. Double religious belonging is a delicate field, in which theology ought to abstain from a priori pronouncements, arrived at by way of deduction from accepted principles and traditional positions. Here, more perhaps than in any other field in the theology of religions, any considered opinion must take into account seriously and primarily the lived experience of those sincere and trustworthy persons who have attempted and claim to have succeeded to an extent—not without pain and sustained tension—to combine in their own life of faith and religious practice their Christian faith and their life commitment to the person of Jesus with another faith experience and religious pursuit. Such cases are not unknown today; they are even on the increase. Behind those to whom we may be able to bear witness today stand some spiritual masters of great stature who continue even today to inspire others by their extraordinary achievements and spiritual heights. To them are due the most profound attempts ever made to inculturate the life of Christian faith and to practice interreligious dialogue at its deepest level of shared religious experience. We will have the opportunity later to refer to some of these pioneers. Meanwhile, let it be noted that theology needs to be inductive before claiming to deduce dogmatic statements from preestablished principles.

The aim of this contribution consists in showing in what sense it seems legitimate to speak of a complementarity and convergence between Christianity and the other religious traditions, in such a way as would provide some theological foundation and justification for the claim made by some trustworthy Christians of a "double simultaneous belonging," to their Christian faith of origin, on the one hand, and to another religious experience they have encountered in their own life of faith, on the other. I will first address the demands of openness to the other that a sincere practice of dialogue with another religious faith already makes on those who earnestly enter into that practice. The second part of the paper will discuss the complementarity and convergence that may be affirmed between Christianity and the other religious traditions and that may serve as a possible theological foundation for the further step of a double personal belonging. The road from the practice of *intrareligious* dialogue in the context of *interreligious* dialogue to a personal engagement with and commitment to two distinct religious faiths is anything but obvious. Indeed, it is long and arduous, full of obstacles and hardships, even possible pitfalls. However, it should not for that matter be closed a priori as being either humanly unpractical or divinely forbidden. Concrete reality witnesses to the contrary. In the last part of the essay I will make a discreet attempt to show the way open for a double belonging on the foundation of the personal experience and witness of great pioneers who have dared to take that narrow path.

THE CALL TO INTRARELIGIOUS DIALOGUE

While the sincerity and the honesty of interreligious dialogue with members of other religious traditions presupposes that one enters into it with the integrity of one's personal faith, it also requires openness to the faith of the other in its difference. Each partner in the dialogue must enter into the experience of the other in an effort to grasp that experience from within. In order to do this, he or she must rise above the level of the concepts in which this experience is imperfectly expressed to attain, insofar as possible, through and beyond the concepts, to the experience itself. It is this effort of "com-prehension" and interior "sym-pathy"—or "em-pathy"—that Raimon Panikkar has termed "intrareligious" dialogue, an indispensable condition for interreligious dialogue.[2] This has been described as a spiritual technique consisting of "passing over and returning." "Passing over" means encountering both the other and the religious experience that the other bears within, together with his or her *Weltanschauung*. Frank Whaling has described the procedure as follows:

> To know the religion of another is more than being cognizant of the facts of the other's religious tradition. It involves getting inside the skin of the other, it involves walking in the other's shoes, it involves seeing the world in some sense as the other sees it, it involves asking the other's questions, it involves getting inside the other's sense of "being a Hindu, Muslim, Jew, Buddhist, or whatever."[3]

Under these premises it can already be asked what might be involved in sharing two different religious faiths. Is the concept of a "hyphenated Christian"—or, to put it more positively, of a double belonging—contradictory in itself to the extent that one could not be a Hindu-Christian, or a Buddhist-Christian, or the like? To assert this, as has been suggested above, would contradict the evidence, as such cases are neither rare nor unknown today. However, account must be taken of the various possible understandings of the concept, which it would in any case be a mistake to label hybrid. To be a Hindu-Christian, for example, might mean joining in oneself the Hindu culture and the Christian faith. Hinduism would then not be considered as a religious faith, strictly speaking, but as a philosophy and a culture, which, with the necessary adaptations, could serve as a vehicle for Christian faith. In this case the problem of the Hindu-Christian would be that of the inculturation of Christian faith and doctrine in Hindu culture. Here, obviously, the concept of a Hindu-Christian would offer no difficulty in principle. But does this explanation fully correspond to reality? Hinduism, while it is not primarily and uniformly doctrinal, nevertheless involves a genuine religious faith in the concrete lives of men and women. The distinction between religion and culture is difficult to maintain. Representing as it does the transcendent element in culture, religion is scarcely separable from culture. This, in fact, is true especially where the Oriental traditions are concerned. The question then remains whether one can simultaneously embrace Hindu faith and Christian faith. We shall have to return to this later, after showing which theological foundation might make double faith belonging possible. It needs, however, to be noted already that double belonging, understood at its deep level of a personal life commitment to two different objects of faith, is not without serious, apparently unsurmountable difficulties. To what extent is it possible to make each of the two objects of faith one's own and to combine both at once in one's own religious life? Even apart from any interior conflict that might arise in the individual, every religious faith constitutes an indivisible whole and calls for a total commitment of the person. It may easily seem a priori impossible that such an absolute engagement might be divided, as it were, between two objects. To be a Christian is not only to find in Jesus values to be promoted or even a meaning for one's life; it is to be given over to his person, to find in him one's way to God. Is it then possible to be, at one and the same time and on the same level, given over to Jesus and to another person, such as Gautama the Buddha, in order to trace our way to God? Or is it possible to live equally by the revelation which God has made of himself as universal Father in Jesus Christ and in the message of the gospel, and simultaneously by the mystical *advaita* experience of identity with Brahman as contained in the Hindu *Upanishads*? We must return to this later. Meanwhile, it can be stated as certain that, in order to be true, interreligious dialogue between persons of different faiths requires that both partners make a positive effort to enter into each other's religious experience and overall vision insofar as is possible. We are dealing here with the encounter, in one and the same person, of two ways of seeing and feeling, of thinking and being. This intrareligious dialogue is an indispensable preparation for any deep exchange between persons in interreligious dialogue. A long-time practitioner of dialogue in depth, Henri Le Saux, expressed this pointedly as follows:

> Each partner in dialogue must try to make his own, as far as possible, the intuition and experience of the other, to personalize it in his own depth, beyond his own ideas and even beyond those through which the other attempts to express and communicate them with the help of the signs available in his tradition. For a fruitful dialogue it is necessary that I reach, as it were, in the very depth of myself to the experience of my brother, freeing my own experience from all accretions, so that my brother can recognize in me his own experience of his own depth. The detachment and the freedom required by such dialogue is no

doubt enormous; yet at no lesser cost is real fellowship and communion possible between men. Interreligious dialogue is something too important to be taken lightly.[4]

If such are the demands made by the practice of interreligious dialogue in depth between two partners of different faith commitments, one may surmise what will be involved in one person's existential simultaneous commitment to two distinct faiths. Can such a double commitment be theologically grounded?

COMPLEMENTARITY AND CONVERGENCE: IN WHICH SENSE?

In light of the premises laid down from the outset, we may ask what kind of complementarity and convergence may be theologically conceivable between Christianity and the other religions of the world? Clear distinctions ought to be made here in order to dispel misunderstandings and objections coming from opposite directions. The complementarity intended here is not a mere simple complementarity, understood as a "one-way traffic." Such a one-way complementarity would mean that, while it is true that the other religions must find their "complement" in Christianity, these have nothing to contribute to Christianity. To hold such unilateral complementarity would amount to going back to the "fulfillment theory" in the theology of religions, according to which all other religions represent but different expressions, in the various cultures of the world, of the universal aspiration of human beings for union with the divine mystery. All would then be merely "natural" religions, destined to find the fulfillment of their aspirations in the only "supernatural" religion, which is Christianity. It is easy to see that this theory, largely abandoned today by theologians, makes true interreligious dialogue inconceivable. Christianity would have nothing to receive but only to give, nothing to learn but only to teach. There could be no dialogue between religions, but only a Christian monologue directed to others.

This one-way model of complementarity is clearly not what is intended as a foundation of dialogue, much less as a possible theological justification for a double belonging. The complementarity with which we are concerned is by necessity a reciprocal complementarity, or a mutual complementarity, such as would allow for "two-way traffic" in the process of dialogue and for a mutual enrichment of both partners involved as well as of their respective religious traditions. This, however, does not necessarily imply that both religions concerned are, theologically speaking, to be placed on one and the same level. There may remain differences in the evaluation of the value and significance of the respective religious traditions in accordance with the faith persuasion of the religious practitioners involved. However, the very idea of mutual complementarity presupposes that, differences in theological evaluation notwithstanding, both the traditions involved are considered as embodying some divine self-manifestation in words and deeds, and, to that extent, would both be approached with the respect due to God's word and to God's saving deeds in history.

From the viewpoint of Christian theology, a further qualification seems to be required. The complementarity under consideration is a mutual but asymmetrical complementarity. The reason is that Christian faith holds that the Christ-event represents the climax of God's personal dealings with humankind in history; the word which God speaks to humankind through Jesus Christ is, by virtue of his personal identity as the Son of God made man, the fullness of divine revelation. The historical event of his human life, and in particular the paschal mystery of his death and resurrection, are for Christians the culminating point of salvation history in which God's will to save is fully realized. While it may be true that there exists a mutual complementarity between Christianity and the other religions, it cannot be said that this mutual complementarity is a symmetrical one, identical in both directions. Whereas Christianity can truly be enriched through the process of dialogue with other divine self-manifestations in history, it nevertheless represents God's decisive engagement with humankind and is, in that sense, the "fullness" of divine revelation and salvation. In other words, the enrichment that Christianity can derive from the process of dialogue with other divine manifestations in history may not be conceived of in terms of a gap or a vacuum that would be left open in Christian revelation itself and could only be filled through the contribution made to Christian revelation by other divine revelations. If such were the case, Christian revelation by itself would fall short of its own fullness, and the fullness of divine revelation in Jesus Christ would tend to be denied. Christian theology then maintains that the complementarity of revelation and salvation between the Christ event and other divine manifestations to humankind is to be qualified as at once reciprocal and asymmetrical.

This being said, it is, however, important to add one more qualification to the complementarity at work between Christianity and the religions. The mutually asymmetric complementarity that obtains between them is of the *relational* order. This means that, notwithstanding the singular place and the unique significance proper to the mystery of Jesus Christ and to the Christ-event in the overall process of God's involvement with humankind in history, this unique event must be viewed as essentially *relational* to all other divine manifestations in history. The eternal God has conceived only one design for humankind; it is that unique plan of revelation-salvation that has been progressively unfolding throughout history and that continues to unfold even today. In this unique design and in its historical unfolding Jesus Christ is the center of gravity, the key to understanding, but this unique event is essentially correlated to the entire process. The Christ-event, in which revelation and salvation are achieved, did not take place in a vacuum with no previous divine interventions, but as the climax of what God had through the centuries been achieving among the peoples of the world. The stories of God with the nations and God's story with the world in Jesus are essentially mutually related. The former are inconceivable without the latter, and vice versa. This is where an effort needs to be made by the insightful theologian to enter, as far as possible, into the mind of God, to discover from within the intrinsic consistency of God's unique design for humankind.

Objections are made, however, to the language of complementarity suggested above between Christianity and religions, and this in different directions. These need to be rapidly considered and answered. In one direction, objection is raised against considering the elements of truth and grace contained in the other religious traditions as additional and autonomous benefits in relation to Christianity. The meaning of the expression should, however, be clear. The endowments found in those traditions cannot be reduced to mere stepping stones toward Christian revelation and religion, since divine truth and grace can be discovered in other religions which is not brought out with the same rigor and clarity in God's revelation and manifestation in Jesus Christ. This does not in any way contradict the transcendence of God's unique manifestation in Jesus or the essential relatedness, in God's unique plan of salvation, of such endowments of truth and grace to the historical event in which God's self-manifestation to humankind culminates. *Autonomy* is not here opposed to *relatedness*. As Claude Geffré put it recently, "Just as the church neither integrates nor replaces Israel, in the same way she neither integrates nor replaces the part of authentic religious truth of which another tradition can be the bearer."[5] And again, "The truth to which Christianity witnesses is neither exclusive nor inclusive of all other truth; it is related to all that is true in other religions."[6] Divine truth and grace in other religious traditions are not absorbed by Christian revelation and salvation. Christians can truly learn some divine truth and encounter some divine deeds in interreligious dialogue. All truth comes from God who *is* Truth and needs to be honored as such, whatever the channel through which it comes to us. More divine truth and grace are found operative in the entire history of God's dealings with humankind than are available simply in the Christian tradition.

On the opposite side, fear is expressed that talk about the complementarity between Christianity and the religions may fail to do full justice to these in their difference and specificity and thus obscure their intrinsic coherence as wholesome visions of reality. There may be a real danger of seeking too easily to assimilate the truth and the grace contained in other religions to the Christian reality and mystery, thus falling again into the trap of the fulfillment theory, instead of accounting for the mutually irreducible character of distinct, apparently irreconcilable, systems of thought and visions of life. The "embarrassment" that some experience with complementarity language, and the fear they express that less than full respect may thereby be manifested for the intrinsic otherness and original self-consistency of the other religious traditions, may be exemplified by the case of the relationship between Judaism and Christianity. Rather than standing in a relationship of mutual complementarity, Israel and Christianity are often found face to face in a certain reciprocal contestation, each considering itself as the one embodiment of a self-same promise. Christian theologians are becoming more keenly aware today that Israel will continue to stand on its own as the embodiment of the promise, without seeking a complementarity with Christianity, even if this complementarity were to be duly conceived as reciprocal. The case of the relationship between Judaism and Christianity, it is thought, is emblematic of the mutual oppositions and contradictions between the overall visions and approaches to reality characteristic of the different religious traditions in relation to Christianity, and of the irreconcilable nature of their respective inner coherence with the Christian message. Without denying these contradictions, it may still be noted that where Judaism and Christianity are concerned, Christianity is inconceivable without Israel, from which it originated, while Israel has been willed by God as the people from whom his Son would be born. Is there no mutual complementarity involved here, according to the divine plan? However different and mutually irreducible Israel and the church may be, they are nevertheless also mutually relational. Similarly and analogically, it may be noted that, all differences notwithstanding, the various religions represent many personal self-manifestations of God to peoples in history and many gifts of God to the nations. As such, they are all mutually complementary to and essentially relational with the Jesus Christ event, in which culminates the one and only plan devised by God for humankind.

But another difficulty may arise for the concept of a mutual complementarity between Christianity and the religions of the world, taking place in history. One may fear that to claim that a complementarity can already be realized in time amounts to unduly projecting back to the present time what can only be realized in the *eschaton*. We may well conceive that in the fullness of time all things will be "recapitulated" in Christ (*anakephalaiosis*, cf. Eph 1:10), according to the Christian promise. We may even think that such eschatological recapitulation will respect and preserve the irreducible character that God's self-manifestation through his Word and his Spirit has impressed upon the different traditions. But to speak of a recapitulation in history is to anticipate unduly what remains in store for the end-time, thus forgetting the "eschatological remainder." Such complementarity and convergence would seem to betray a theological optimism that is belied by concrete reality. To prevent collapsing the eschatological times into present history, it will be important to distinguish clearly between the initial and incomplete mutual convergence between Christianity and the other religions that can be realized in time from the full recapitulation in Christ of all things, religions included, which remains in store in the eschatological future. An incomplete mutual complementarity and convergence are possible, the complete realization of which, however, will only be unveiled in the *eschaton*. Examples of the possibility of a real, though incomplete, convergence, beyond the apparent contradictions and the irreducible differences, would be the possible symbiosis between the non-duality *(advaita)* of Hindu mystical experience and the mystery of interpersonal communion in the tri-personal God of the Christian tradition, or else—in the words of Aloysius Pieris—the "agapeic gnosis" of Christians and the "gnostic *agapē*" of Buddhists.[7]

Mutual complementarity, even partial and initial, makes a reciprocal convergence possible. It is the task of interreligious dialogue to turn the potential convergence inherent in the religious traditions into a concrete reality. We have exposed—without complacency—the demands interreligious dialogue makes upon the partners at the level of religious experience and theological discourse, if it is to be fruitful. More needs to be said. Reference must also be made to the mystery of communion in the Spirit existing between the partners of dialogue, which flows from their common sharing in the universal reality of the reign of God. This anticipated communion guarantees that actual convergence through dialogue is possible—with full respect to the differences between faith commitments.

Interfaith dialogue thus contributes to building up the reign of God in history. But, as we know, the reign of God in history remains directed toward its eschatological fullness at the end of time. It is permitted to think that convergence between the religious traditions will also attain its goal in the fullness of the reign of God. An eschatological recapitulation (Eph 1:10) in Christ of the religious traditions of the world will take place in the *eschaton*. As noted above, such recapitulation would preserve the irreducible character that the distinct self-manifestations of God in history have impressed upon the various traditions. This eschatological recapitulation will coincide with the last "perfection" of the Son of God as "source of eternal salvation" (Heb 5:9), whose influence remains, until this final achievement, subject to an "eschatological remainder." It seems possible, then, to speak, after Pierre Teilhard de Chardin, of a "marvelous convergence," which is to take place in the *eschaton*, of all things and all religious traditions in the reign of God and in the Christ-*omega*; of a "mysticism of unification" toward which Christianity and the religious traditions of the East tend together.[8] Such eschatological convergence does not in any way over-shadow the historical event of Jesus Christ: he is the end *(omega)* because he is the beginning *(alpha)*, the "central axis." It is in this eschatological sense that Teilhard looked toward a "convergence of religions" in the "universal Christ": "A general con-vergence of religions upon a universal Christ who fundamentally satisfies them all: that seems to me the only possible conversion of the world, and the only form in which a religion of the future can be conceived."[9] The eschatological fullness of the reign of God thus appears as the common final goal of Christianity and the other religions.

FROM COMPLEMENTARITY AND CONVERGENCE TO DOUBLE BELONGING

Can a double simultaneous belonging of individual persons to two religious tradi-tions be considered as a partial anticipation and initial realization in time of the full recapitulation in Christ of all religions, Christianity included, which in God's design is fulfilled at the end of times? The question is difficult and does not admit easy solutions. As has been hinted earlier, here perhaps more than anywhere else theology must start "from below," that is, from the lived experience of trustworthy witnesses, and must build inductively on such testimonies before it may claim to contribute, by way of deduction, "from above" (from established principles), some apodictic and dogmatic answers that would run the risk of being unduly restrictive. If little of rel-evance and interest can be anticipated in general from a theology of religions that would be built on abstract considerations without any personal experience of, and lasting exposure to, the concrete reality of other religious traditions as it is lived and experienced by members of those traditions, this holds all the more where a theologi-cal opinion is asked as to the practicability and spiritual worth of personal attempts at double belonging. In this matter, then, the "first theological act" must consist of re-flecting on the concrete experience of some of the pioneers who have relentlessly en-deavored to combine in their own life their Christian commitment and another faith experience. A striking example of such relentless search—who has, moreover, inspired many others desirous of taking the same path—is Henri Le Saux, Abhishiktananda by his Indian name.

There is no need to retrace his spiritual journey, even with rapid strokes. It is well known, and our knowledge of it has been enriched in recent years by many publica-tions of considerable worth. What may be useful is to see in his writings some clear indications as to how he himself understood and evaluated the experience he was living at the core of his being. This can best be done by referring, however rapidly, to some observations of his intimate journal and other occasional writings.[10] To put it in a nutshell, double belonging for Abhishiktananda consisted in combining in his own experience and life his Christian commitment with the advaitic experience of Hindu mysticism. How and to what extent, according to his own estimation, did he succeed in living both simultaneously? Did he experience the mutual lived encounter of both as mutual complementarity and convergence, or rather as a face-to-face incompatibility and reciprocal contestation? And if so, were the differences and contradictions eventually overcome in a reciprocal symbiosis of both faith commitments?

In order to evaluate what is at stake in such questions, it is necessary to attempt first a quick and necessarily incomplete description of what is meant in Hindu mysticism by the experience of *advaita*. *Advaita* experience may be described, it would seem, as an entry, or better an assumption, into the knowledge that the Absolute has of itself, and thus as a view of reality literally from the viewpoint of the Absolute. From the special viewpoint of this absolute awareness, all duality *(dvaita)* vanishes, since the Absolute alone is absolute, is One-without-a-second *(ekam advitiyam)*. From this viewpoint the universe, and history have no absolute meaning *(paramartha);* their existence pertains to the domain of the relative *(vyavahara)*, God's *lila* (God's play in creation). At the awakening of the experience of *advaita*, the ontological density of the finite seer itself vanishes. The awakening of absolute awareness leaves no room for a subjective awareness of self as a finite subject of cognition; there remains only the *aham-* ("I") awareness of the Absolute in the epiphenomenon of the body *(sariram): Aham brahmasmi.* The experience of *advaita* thus implies a radical disappearance of all that is not the Absolute. When the consciousness of the absolute *Aham* emerges in the seer, the latter is submerged in it. "Who knows and who is known?" asks the *Upanishad.* Henceforth it is no longer a finite "me" who—regarding God and regarded by God—contemplates and addresses a prayer to God. What abides is the awakening of the one who knows to the subjective consciousness of the Absolute itself. And it is not an objective knowledge of the Absolute by a finite me. In the process of illumination the human "me" gives way to the divine *Aham.* Such is the radical demand of *advaita.*

And such is the experience of the Absolute into which Abhishiktananda allowed himself to sink progressively but unremittingly. It became more and more absorbing, imposing upon him, over and above the outer renunciations of his hermit-like life, the supreme renunciation of himself, and over and above that, the still more radical renunciation of the divine "Thou" encountered in prayer. He observed in his diary that night invades the soul that can no longer address its God in prayer as an "I" addresses a "Thou." Over and above and beyond the interpersonal encounter with God, there is the "Other Shore," the "I am," where alone truth is entire. While Abhishiktananda did learn to combine in his concrete life the two planes on which he would henceforth have to move, it is sure that, on the level of mental synthesis, the eventual reconciliation of both did not cease to be problematic for him, almost to the end of his pilgrimage. It is no derogatory exaggeration to say that his whole life was marked by the quest for a synthesis—ever elusive, never accomplished save in what he called "the discovery of the Graal," that is, the heart failure that swept him away.

The questions posed to Abhishiktananda by the *advaita* experience must not be underrated. In general terms the question is that of the value of the traditional representations of God, the world, and the human being. Do the Christian tri-personal

God, the Christian concept of creation, and the Christian view of the human being in a personal dialogue with God stand up against *advaita?* Does history actually have the density that Christianity attributes to it? And what becomes of the Christ-event, considered as the total engagement of God in human history? Has not Christian dogma been unduly absolutized, whereas in reality, when all is said and done, it is only relative?

These questions became progressively more pressing as Abhishiktananda allowed himself to be more immersed in the *advaita* experience and sought to discover its mutual compatibility and complementarity with Christian faith. While during the first years of his journey some doubt remained in his mind regarding the validity of the *advaita* experience, certitude on this account grew over the years. Thus, he could write one day (May 11, 1971), not without enthusiasm, "The experience of the Upanishads is true, *I know it.*" [11] The fear, however, that the two experiences might be irreducible seized him progressively. He had in fact written at an early stage (November 27, 1956), "I cannot be at the same time Hindu and Christian, and I cannot either be simply Hindu or simply Christian."[12] The reading of the diary reveals alternatively either the exaltation of *advaita* or the fear that it might but be a mirage; at some times the nostalgia he experiences for the Christian mystery, at other times his radical questioning of the same. Serenity will dawn as Abhishiktananda resolves to live both experiences in an irreducible tension, beyond theoretical conciliations. He notes on December 5, 1970, "The best thing is, I think, to hold, even if in extreme tension, these two forms of a unique 'faith,' till dawn may arise."[13] And, writing to a friend on September 2, 1972, he explains:

> Less and less do I think that time has come to discover the concepts which will allow an exchange of experience between East and West. . . . I believe that the present task is simply to allow oneself to be invaded by the experience—by the two experiences, if you wish—and also, together with those who will share in this dislocating experience, to ensure the foundations of later intellectual dialogue.[14]

These few observations may suffice to show with what sincerity and what intensity Abhishiktananda lived the purifying, even crucifying, but also simplifying and unifying encounter in his inmost self of two faith experiences, the mutual complementarity and convergence of which eluded him unremittingly on the notional plane. One is then able to understand better the "anguish" that invaded him and held him in its sway over many years; one better appreciates his determination—which never failed—to "hold, even if in extreme tension, these two forms of a unique 'faith,' till dawn may arise." The dawn, the awakening, finally burst through, carrying everything in its unconquerable light. It was through the "discovery of the Graal," Easter, and the ultimate encounter.

The case of Abhishiktananda is, admittedly, a limit case. It can, however, guide us in proposing some theological reflections on the problem of a simultaneous belonging to two distinct religious traditions and of a simultaneous personal faith engagement vis-à-vis two distinct objects of religious faith. The terms of the problem ought to be clearly defined from the outset. We are not merely concerned with the problem of inculturation of the Christian faith in a different cultural and religious context in which one may find oneself involved. Nor is there primarily question of what baggage of one's previous cultural and religious tradition one may, and indeed should, carry with oneself on eventually becoming a Christian and joining the Christian community. The primary concern is with those committed Christians who, in the concrete circumstances in which they have found themselves, have come into contact with another tradition of religious faith to such an extent as to choose deliberately to combine, in their own personal life, two distinct objects of faith into the "two forms of a unique 'faith.'" The case of the religious baggage eventually carried over with one on becoming a Christian can, nevertheless, help us to discover the ground for the feasibility of double belonging in the opposite direction. For, to the extent that Hindus, on becoming Christian, may and should preserve not only their Indian and Hindu culture, but together with it, and unavoidably so, some elements of their previous religious faith, then also to that extent it seems permissible for Christians to adopt such elements of another religious faith that they have encountered in depth, as seem compatible with the Christian faith, or even complementary to it and convergent with it. That such elements in harmony with Christian faith exist and can be combined and integrated with it is a matter of fact. These, indeed, will serve to enrich the Christian faith if it is true that other faiths contain divine revelation and divine grace, "seeds of the Word" sown in them by the Word of God and "elements of grace" due to the active universal presence of the Spirit of God. The difficult question arises when two wholesale, self-contained, and self-consistent visions of reality claim the faith allegiance of a person, each with its intrinsic coherence and distinct outlook and perspective. Here is where a keen discernment is especially required.

The interaction between Christianity and the Asian religions, Hinduism and Buddhism in particular, has been conceived differently by various promoters of interreligious dialogue and practitioners of interfaith belonging. Aloysius Pieris sees the Christian tradition, on the one side, and the Buddhist tradition, on the other, as "two religious models which, far from being contradictory, are, in fact, each incomplete in itself and therefore complementary and mutually corrective." They represent "poles of a tension, not so much geographical as psychological. They are two instincts emerging dialectically from within the deepest zone of each individual, be he Christian or not. Our religious encounter with God and human beings would be incomplete without this interaction." Pieris calls these two complementary poles the *agapeic* (Christianity) and the *gnostic* (Buddhism).[15] A parallel suggests itself naturally between the two historical founders Jesus the Christ and Gautama the Buddha. The question being asked is that of a possible complementarity between the saving values that they represent and that are found enshrined in the traditions bearing their names. Pieris sees it as the complementarity between Buddhist gnosis and Christian agape. The mutual complementarity of the two traditions, in spite of their obvious differences, is based on the innate inadequacy of the basic "medium" proper to each, which leaves them open to completion. Pieris writes:

> In Buddhism the core-experience lends itself to be classed as gnosis or "liberative knowledge"; the corresponding Christian experience falls under the category of *agapè* or "redemptive love." Each is *salvific* in that each is *a self-transcending*

event that radically transforms the human person affected by that experience. At the same time, there is an undefinable contrast between them, which largely determines the major differences between the two religions, differences quite obvious even to the casual observer. And yet, it must be recognized that both gnosis and *agapè* are *necessary,* precisely because each in itself is *inadequate* as a medium, not only for experiencing but also for expressing our intimate moments with the Ultimate Source of liberation. They are, in other words, complementary idioms that need each other to mediate the self-transcending experience called "salvation." Any valid spirituality, Buddhist or Christian, as the history of each religion attests, does retain both poles of religious experience—namely the gnostic and the agapeic. The movement of the spirit progresses through the dialectic interplay of wisdom and love.[16]

The first major obstacle to a core-to-core dialogue between Buddhism and Christianity, Pieris observes, is

> the failure on the part of Buddhists and Christians to acknowledge the reciprocity of these two idioms; their refusal to admit that gnosis and *agapè* are both legitimate languages of the *human spirit* or (as far as the Christian partner of dialogue is concerned) that they are languages that the same *divine* Spirit speaks alternately in each one of us. . . . The core experience of Christianity is not *agapè* pure and simple, but *agapè* in dialogue with gnosis; conversely, the core experience of Buddhism is not mere gnosis, but a gnosis intrinsically in dialogue with *agapè*.[17]

John A. T. Robinson, on his part, speaks of two "eyes" of truth and reality: Western Christianity represents one eye, Hinduism the other; more generally, the West stands for the first, the East for the second. Robinson sees the polarity of the two "centers" as that between the male and the female principles. He too calls for a mutual complementarity between the two centers.[18] John B. Cobb, in turn, advocates a "mutual transformation," beyond dialogue, between Christianity and Buddhism. Such a mutual transformation will result from osmosis between the complementary approaches to reality, that is, between the worldviews characteristic of both traditions.[19]

Raimon Panikkar's focus is different. He insists that the various religious traditions differ and must keep their distinct identity. He rejects a facile "eclecticism" that would destroy the respective identities. Faith cannot be "bracketed" *(epochè)* to ease the dialogue. But, while the "cosmotheandric mystery," the object of faith, is common to all religious traditions, "beliefs" differ in each. Between these beliefs Panikkar advocates a cross-fertilization—which he terms syncretism—in view of a mutual enrichment.[20] Panikkar has returned to this topic more than once. More recently he has described what he regards as the profile of the horizon of interreligious dialogue for the future. Going now beyond the problematic of cross-fertilization, he calls for a further stage in which, transcending the static doctrinal identity of their respective traditions, the partners of dialogue will be able to contribute mutually to a deeper self-understanding.[21]

In this variety of opinions on the benefits that may be derived from the practice of interreligious dialogue, what can be concluded with regard to a personal engagement in intrareligious dialogue that stretches out to a search for double belonging to two distinct religious traditions? Some of the explanations mentioned above seem too neat to be able to account for the drama experienced by Abhishiktananda. To the comparison of the two eyes combining in one vision could easily be opposed that of a prism, whose different facets it is not possible to embrace at one glance. We must, however, remember that the first agent of religious dialogue—*intra-* as well as *inter-* —is the Spirit of God, who animates the persons. The Spirit is at work in both traditions, the Christian and the other; thus the dialogue—inter- or intra—cannot be a monologue, cannot be one way. The Christian tradition, the fullness of revelation in Jesus Christ notwithstanding, does not possess a monopoly on truth. Christians as others must allow themselves to be possessed by the truth. Those among them sincerely engaged in the hard asceticism of a double belonging may derive from it a double advantage. On the one hand, they may win an enrichment of their own faith. Through integrating in their own life of faith the "seeds of the Word" enshrined in another tradition, they may find their own life of faith deepened and enriched. They will discover at greater depth certain dimensions of the divine mystery that they had perceived less clearly and that have been communicated with less force by Christian tradition. At the same time they will gain a purification of their faith. The shock of the inner encounter will often raise questions, force them to revise gratuitous assumptions and to destroy deep-rooted prejudices or overthrow certain overly narrow conceptions or outlooks. It needs to be perceived clearly that the insights on the divine mystery contained in the various religious traditions, in spite of their differences and apparent contradictions, have in the last analysis the same origin, if they are genuine and authentic. History and interiority are two equally valid channels for a true experience of the divine; he who acts in history according to the Judeo-Christian tradition is he who is experienced in the "cave of the heart," according to the Hindu. The God of history is also the "ground of being." Experiencing God under both forms through engagement in a double faith may, if practiced in earnest, deepen one's perception of the divine mystery and one's commitment to it.

NOTES

[1] Jacques Dupuis, *Toward a Christian Theology of Religious Pluralism* (Maryknoll, N.Y.: Orbis Books, 1997).

[2] Raimon Panikkar, *The Intrareligious Dialogue*, 2d ed. (New York: Paulist Press, 1999).

[3] Frank Whaling, *Christian Theology and World Religions: A Global Approach* (London: Marshall Pickering, 1986), 130-31.

[4] Henri Le Saux (Abhishiktananda), "The Depth-Dimension of Religious Dialogue," *Vidyajyoti Journal of Theological Reflection* 45 (1981): 214.

[5] Claude Geffré, "Le pluralisme religieux comme question théologique," *La vie spirituelle* 4 (1998), 584.

[6] Claude Geffré, "La singularité du Christianisme à l'âge du pluralisme religieux," in *Penser la foi: Recherches en théologie aujourd'hui: Mélanges offerts à Joseph Moingt*, ed. Joseph Doré and Christoph Theobald (Paris: Cerf-Arras, 1993), 358.

[7] Aloysius Pieris, "The Buddha and the Christ: Mediators of Liberation," in *The Myth of Christian Uniqueness*, ed. John Hick and Paul F. Knitter (Maryknoll, N.Y.: Orbis Books, 1987), 162-77; idem, *An Asian Theology of Liberation* (Maryknoll, N.Y.: Orbis Books, 1988).

[8] Ursula King, *Towards a New Mysticism: Teilhard de Chardin and Eastern Religions* (New York: Seabury Press, 1980), 159-62.

[9] Pierre Teilhard de Chardin, *Christianity and Evolution* (New York: Harcourt Brace Jovanovich, 1971), 130.

[10] See Henri Le Saux (Swami Abhishiktananda), *Intériorité et révélation. Essais théologiques* (Paris: Editions Présence, 1982). English translation: Abhishiktananda, *Ascent to the Depth of the Heart: The Spiritual Diary (1948-73) of Swami Abhishiktananda (dom Henri Le Saux)* (Delhi: ISPCK, 1998).

[11] Quoted in ibid., 18.

[12] Ibid., 19.

[13] Ibid.

[14] Ibid., 20.

[15] Aloysius Pieris, "Western Christianity and Asian Buddhism: A Theological Reading of Historical Encounters," *Dialogue* new series 7/2 (1980), 64. See also idem, *Love Meets Wisdom: A Christian Experience of Buddhism* (Maryknoll, N.Y.: Orbis Books, 1988).

[16] Aloysius Pieris, "The Buddha and the Christ," 163; idem, *Love Meets Wisdom*, 111.

[17] Pieris, *Love Meets Wisdom*, 111, 119.

[18] John A. T. Robinson, *Truth Is Two-Eyed* (London: SCM Press, 1979).

[19] John B. Cobb, *Beyond Dialogue: Toward a Mutual Transformation of Christianity and Buddhism* (Philadelphia: Fortress Press, 1982).

[20] Panikkar, *The Intrareligious Dialogue.*

[21] Raimon Panikkar, "Foreword: The Ongoing Dialogue," in *Hindu-Christian Dialogue*, ed. Harold Coward (Maryknoll, N.Y.: Orbis Books, 1990), ix-xviii.

7

Double Belonging in Sri Lanka

Illusion or Liberating Path?

ELISABETH J. HARRIS

We know not that there is an individual near us, from the highest to the lowest, who would not receive us gladly, and allow of the people assembling about his house to hear the Word of God – not that they have renounced Buddhism, or the Worship of Devils; their eyes are not yet open to discern the sin and folly of their former vain superstitions and idolatry. But they have a sort of respect for religious ceremonies; and while they believe our religion to be a good one, they still regard their own as good also.

—Rev. Robert Mayor, Church Missionary Society missionary
Writing from Baddegama, Sri Lanka, in the early 1820s

Our religion is not exclusive. We consider it no sin to attend Christian worship. All that I have heard at your church was good. Probably I should go there often, but I could not do so in my present position without incurring reproach from my countrymen, that I was a Christian and not a Buddhist, and therefore unfit for my office.

—The Guardian of the Sacred Tooth Relic in Kandy, Sri Lanka
Speaking to Sir William Gregory, Governor of Sri Lanka, 1872-77

RELIGIOUS BELONGING IN NINETEENTH-CENTURY SRI LANKA

When missionaries from newly formed evangelical missionary societies in Britain reached Sri Lanka between 1812 and 1818, they were pleasantly surprised to find that Sri Lankans were not at all averse to listening to them.[1] Thomas Squance, Methodist missionary, could write with euphoria in 1815 that he was able to draw two thousand to hear him preach in an open field in Galle, on the south coast, and goes on to explain that when he preached in the bazaars people would lay aside their business "to listen with great attention."[2] Disillusionment and sheer bafflement, however, set in when they realized that willingness to listen among the people, even apparent readiness to agree, did not mean that Buddhism would be rejected and Christianity embraced. Missionary records at this time overflow with the complaint that Sri Lankan Buddhists seemed unable to grasp that Buddhism and Christianity were mutually exclusive, that they were different and that the differences were incompatible. Rev. Robert Spence Hardy, Methodist missionary, writing *Jubilee Memorials* for the year 1865, claimed that lay Sri Lankans in the early decades of the century saw no "culpable inconsistency"[3] in professing themselves both Christian and Buddhist; he admitted that he found the practice "revolting" and went on to write of the priests at this time:

> They would have been willing to enter into an alliance with the servants of God, and would have had no hesitation in worshipping Jesus Christ, if they [that is, *the missionaries*] would have worshipped Buddha. According to their ideas, Jesus Christ was a good man, as Buddha was a good man; and if Buddha was only regarded as the best, what should hinder the formation of a compact between the two systems, that would have brought the whole of the Sinhalese people under one religious rule?[4]

The missionaries, of course, did make converts, people who claimed they had become Christians. However, throughout the nineteenth century what leaps out from missionary writings is a struggle to impress upon new converts that their pre-conversion religious practices had to be rejected. Various strategies were adopted, requiring converts and church employees to make statements of faith that rejected Buddhism and Hinduism, for instance, or threatening excommunication. Some converts eventually internalized the message; others did not. To take just one example, Rev. I. Wood from "Cotta," now Kotte, just outside Colombo, in the *Church Missionary Society Report 1858-59*, reports that eleven members were struck off the list because they were present at a heathen ceremony for the recovery of a sick relative. He goes on:

> When this was announced to them they endeavoured to prove that there was nothing in the ceremony derogatory to their profession of Christianity. The fact is, that, like the majority of the people in the immediate neighbourhood of the compound, they thought that some of their heathenish practices might be well grafted upon their Christianity. The prevailing opinion in and around Cotta is, that the being half Christian and half Buddhist is far better than being either decidedly Christian or Buddhist. Between the two they fancy that certain deliverance from future punishment must be obtained.[5]

Dual religious belonging, therefore, would seem to have posed no problem to Sri Lankan Buddhists in the first two-thirds of the nineteenth century. During the Dutch domination of the maritime areas, between 1658 and the 1790s, many had been forced into it. Christian baptism had been a prerequisite for government service. Many, therefore, had gone through this formality and attended Christian worship. But they had not thereby stopped going to their Buddhist or Hindu temples, and the Dutch authorities turned a blind eye, more concerned about trading profits than enforcing exclusivist patterns of religious belonging. The attitude first encountered by the British missionaries, however, cannot be attributed solely to tactics used for survival under the Dutch. Buddhism, as it spread south, north, and east from India, did not invite allegiance through condemning the religiousness it encountered but by demoting it through incorporation. Spence Hardy's reflection that the monastic Sangha would have been quite happy to have made a pact of coexistence with Christianity if the Buddha could have been seen as supreme is written with the sarcasm of horror but, in fact, hits the nail on the head. If the ultimacy of the Buddha's wisdom and compassion is accepted, Buddhism in practice has been willing to draw abundantly from other religious wells in noncompetitive harmony.

Looked at through the prism of contemporary exploration into multiple religious identity, the process was one through which a new identity, Buddhist, entered a particular context, gained dominance, and enabled a reinterpretation, not a rejection, of existing identities or expressions of religiousness. When Christianity entered Sri Lanka, therefore, some Buddhists were willing to incorporate it within their existing framework almost as an additional "religious insurance policy," while retaining the supremacy of the Buddha. Others seemed ready to "pass over" into Christianity, not rejecting their previous religiousness but placing it in subordination to their new choice of identity. Both approaches recognized the need for one system to be dominant but also assumed a certain soteriological compatibility between religions and religious practices.

A NEW PARADIGM ENTERS

Neither approach, of course, was acceptable to the new evangelical missionaries. As a consequence, a new paradigm within the Buddhist world arose, hammered out through the encounter with Christian exclusivism—one of competition rather than coexistence, religious exclusivity rather than a willingness to draw from the "other." The words of the Guardian at the Temple of the Tooth in Kandy quoted at the beginning of the chapter capture this. In retrospect, the process possessed a tragic inevitability. For, no religious community as sophisticated and scholarly as the Sri Lankan Buddhist community could have been expected to remain pliant and unresisting in the face of the missionary attack on its beliefs and practices, especially in the context of a rising, affluent middle class with capital. There had been resistance to Christianity when the Portuguese and Dutch had control of the island, but what happened in the nineteenth century represented a new configuration of forces—religious, economic, political, and international.

The missionary onslaught on Buddhism and religious practices such as exorcism in the first half of the nineteenth century took the form of oral confrontation and the handing out of polemical tracts in the vicinity of Buddhist temples and at religious pilgrimages, and an enforced pattern of biblical studies and Christian worship in missionary schools. In writings sent to the mother society, Buddhism was presented as a false, nihilistic atheism and Sri Lankan Buddhists as benighted, degenerate, indolent, and immoral; in the works of missionaries such as the Pali scholar Rev. Daniel J. Gogerly, reasoned treatises were eventually produced in Sinhala on the superiority of Christianity over the perceived negativity of Buddhism.[6] The sheer weight of the offensive written by missionaries throughout the century was fed partly by home expectations—what better way to raise funds than to appeal to British sympathies for the "benighted"—but its effect on Sri Lankan Buddhists was seismic. Here are just two examples from the 1830s, the second published in Sri Lanka, not the West:

> To say that 'thick darkness covers the people' is not saying too much; for hardly any description can convey to the minds of those who have never witnessed the superstitions of the heathens, their degraded condition.[7]

> The utter extinction of being is the acme of Buddhistical felicity! The utter extinction of the passions is the acme of Buddhistical virtue! According to the Buddha's doctrine, the latter ensures the former. What a degrading and a misleading system! Even with respect to the right regulation of the passions, and the suppression of all that is immoderate and evil, Buddhists 'do greatly err.'[8]

Opposition to the missionaries began early in the nineteenth century. As Kitsiri Malalgoda has ably demonstrated, the first reaction of the monastic *(bhikkhu)* Sangha was to send petitions to the colonial administration appealing for a nonaggression pact between religions in the belief that any right-thinking authority would see that offending the sensibilities of another religious group was wrong.[9] Malalgoda states that these began in the 1820s. The earliest I have found, however, was in 1815, after Methodist missionary Rev. Benjamin Clough had been involved in aggressive preaching against Buddhism near Kelaniya Temple, a place of pilgrimage about seven miles from Colombo. Rarely were these petitions acknowledged by the government. A second approach was for members of the *bhikkhu* Sangha to discourage parents from sending children to Christian schools.

At first this opposition was low key. However, as the *bhikkhu* Sangha became convinced that dialogue based on reason and mutual respect was impossible with the missionaries, resistance became confrontation. This was helped by a number of charismatic monastic leaders, some of whom were not averse to adopting missionary styles of communication, for example, a more aggressive and emotional preaching style in contrast to the normative lowered eyelids and use of protective fans. At first, confrontation through the printing press, preaching, and debates was led by the *bhikkhu* Sangha, lay people either basking in the reflected victory of their leaders, for example, in the famous Panadura Debate of 1873, or helping to cause general disruption at missionary meetings. However, in the last two decades of the century, with Western collaboration from theosophists and freethinkers, lay people from the emerging bourgeoisie took the lead.

In general, the missionaries welcomed these developments. Why? Because the missionaries could now understand the paradigm the Buddhists were working with, since it was, in fact, their own conception that difference between religions meant that they were mutually exclusive systems in competition and rivalry with one another. As early as 1863, one CMS missionary could write rejoicingly from Cotta:

The late controversy, however, has stirred the minds of the people, and, to a very great extent, broken down the old notion, and opened their eyes to the fact, that there is a great distinction between Christianity and Buddhism, and that they cannot profess one without actually denying the other.[10]

And the Methodist District Meeting for South Ceylon could report in 1882 that the "bitter opposition" of the Buddhists is a good sign, "showing that the old period of patronizing Christianity for worldly gain and secular position is passing away."[11]

The Buddhist Revival ushered in what has come to be known as Protestant Buddhism, because it was a protest against Christianity and appropriated from Protestant Christianity several of its forms and practices. One of the features taken over from Protestant Christianity was, not surprisingly, emphasis on difference and non-compatibility between religions. In spirited resistance to the missionary construction of Buddhism, Buddhism was pictured by later revivalists as irretrievably different from Christianity and irrevocably superior to it because of its non-theistic nature, its compatibility with science, its rationality, its optimism, and its sublime ethics, each assertion being a direct challenge to one of the accusations made by the missionaries.[12]

This form of Protestant Buddhism persisted in Sri Lanka, especially among the bourgeoisie, throughout the twentieth century. Although the tendency to demonize Christianity present at the Panadura Debate and in some writings of the Anagarika Dharmapala did not last long into the twentieth century, although mistrust toward Christians periodically flared up, religious identity continued to be asserted through difference. I experienced this personally during the period between 1986 and 1993, when I studied Buddhism in the country. I can remember one lunchtime conversation with a young, committed Buddhist woman toward the end of my stay, after she had learned that I was a Christian. Her reaction went something like this: "After seven years studying Buddhism, how can you possibly remain a Christian? Don't Christians have a lesser goal? They don't have *nibbana*!" Her questions were sincerely asked and her bafflement was genuine, just as the bafflement of the early missionaries had been genuine when they found that curious Sri Lankans were not going to convert when told they were sinners and needed the salvation that only Jesus could offer. Deeply ingrained in her self-identity as a Buddhist was the idea that Christianity was a lower path, that although Jesus might have been a good man, even a bodhisattva, a future Buddha, he pointed people only to a heavenly world, still within the round of birth and rebirth (*samsara*), rather than to the ultimate state of *nibbana*. It was, therefore, almost unbelievable to her that I could have encountered Buddhism at depth and not become a Buddhist. That I could, while remaining Christian, draw deeply from Buddhism in my own religious life was also beyond her comprehension, and I do not believe she was closer to understanding it even after we had talked for several hours. Difference between the two religions precluded for her any form of dual belonging.

TOWARD A NEW RELATIONSHIP

Mistrust toward Christians in twentieth century Sri Lanka took several forms, the most persistent being the accusation that Christians were involved in unethical conversions, namely, using the promise of material benefits to place pressure on vulnerable, poverty-stricken villagers. There was truth in the allegation. The twentieth century witnessed a growth of independent churches in Sri Lanka, led by charismatic leaders who were known to condemn Sri Lanka's other religions, and also a growing conservatism in mainline denominations. However, in the middle years of the century, a remarkable group of Christians sought to pioneer a new relationship with Buddhism—Rev. Yohan Devananda, Anglican; Rev. Lynn A. de Silva, Methodist; and several Roman Catholics, including Tissa Balasuriya, O.M.I., Dr. Michael Rodrigo, O.M.I., and Dr. Aloysius Pieris, S.J. I would like to concentrate on the last two to explore whether they were able to develop new expressions of religious belonging in the context created by the Buddhist Revival. Both were profoundly influenced by Vatican II. Both were painfully aware that the Christian church in Sri Lanka was largely locked in Western structures alien to the predominantly Buddhist culture of the country. As Sinhala people, they were part of Sinhala culture, permeated by Buddhism. As Roman Catholics, who had studied in the West, they were also part of Western Christian culture.

Michael Rodrigo

Michael Rodrigo was born to a Roman Catholic mother and a father of Buddhist background in 1927. At the age of twenty he joined the religious order of the Oblates of Mary Immaculate and studied theology and philosophy at the Gregorian University in Rome, eventually gaining his first doctorate in Buddhist philosophy in 1959. From 1955 to 1971, he taught at the National Roman Catholic Seminary in Sri Lanka but felt increasingly dissatisfied with the kind of theology he was communicating in a country deeply divided socially and economically. In 1971 he set off to Paris to study for a second doctorate, this time on the subject of the moral passover from selfishness to selflessness in Christianity and the other religions in Sri Lanka—Buddhism, Hinduism, and Islam.[13]

On returning to Sri Lanka, he did not go back to the seminary but worked with Fr. Tissa Balasuriya, O.M.I., at the Centre for Society and Religion in Colombo, a pioneering initiative set up to concentrate on issues of human rights, poverty, unemployment, and racial justice. In 1978 he moved again, becoming director of Sevaka Sevana, an institute developing a new contextual training course for priests in the Badulla Diocese of the country. This brought him even more into contact with the unwritten history of the poor in Sri Lanka and led to his next decision, to request to live in an entirely Buddhist village, Alukalavita, on the road between Buttala and Kataragama in Uva Province in the south of the country, one of the poorest parts of Sri Lanka. His intention was not to build a church but to seek to redress a past that had been marred by bitterness toward Christianity. For, in 1818, there had been an insurrection against the British colonial rulers in that area which had been brutally suppressed by the "Christian" power. A slash-and-burn policy had destroyed land and all possible "terrorists" had been killed, that is, all young men over eighteen. The memory of this had not died.

In Alukalavita, Michael set up Suba Seth Gedara, Good Wishes House. Two Roman Catholic sisters were among those who joined him: Sr. Milburga Fernando and

Sr. Benedict Fernandopulle. Suba Seth Gedara, although eventually possessing a class-room and health room as well as living quarters, was built largely of local materials and had no electricity or piped water. Michael was to live there only seven years. On November 10, 1987, he was shot, through the back of the head as he was saying mass at Suba Seth Gedara, not by the villagers themselves, but by forces that did not like his work with the poor.

The movement in Michael Rodrigo's life was both physical and theological. Physi-cally, he began within a comfortable, middle-class, Roman Catholic environment and moved toward an ever-increasing identification with the poor. The theological move-ment can be illustrated by his poems, which I was asked to edit after his death.[14] In 1952, in Rome, Michael collected forty-seven of his poems under the title *Stardust in the Waves.* He was only twenty-five, a young, ardent priest in training. The poems show a sensitive person steeped in traditional Christian theology. An intense yearning to understand the suffering of Christ is present. The symbols of darkness and light, flame and water are used. Christ's sacrifice is a burning, flaming circle of light. Inner turmoil is the darkness of a cave when light is withdrawn. In "Gushwind for My Flame," there is this:

> Were I the oil
> And you, the living flame, Lord
> We'll burn together unto death
> For death is life.[15]

By the 1970s Michael's poems had changed. With a searing directness they spoke of the Sri Lankan social situation in rural villages—cultural domination, poverty, the greed of the few that was exploiting the many. "Buddhi and a Bottle Lamp" gives this autobiographical material:

> How did it begin? I don't know
> I was looking into villages
> And what I found burst in on me
> What a thing it was to see them work much
> Play a little dhang for the New Year
> To see them suffer for ever and a day
> Like their cousins in line-room darkness. . . . [16]

By 1979, just before he created Suba Seth Gedara, his thought had moved on. Speaking of the rural poor, he writes:

> See how He was, hidden, teaching me to find
> His face among his people
> Old hand at Sorrow, He
> Soon I was visiting them, no longer for a
> Survey, bench-mark or data sheet
> Or to be with them as presence, witness,
> what-have-you

> Something else (Someone) pulled me, attracted me
> His joy, his *ananda,* his peace, his *shanthi*
> *Metta, karuna, mudita, upekkha;* say any name's
> The Name.
> Somehow I found out Christ
> I went to the village and was converted
> because He was present.[17]

He went further in the poem "Pieta," which tells the story of a young farmer crushed under the tractor and held in the arms of his wife, the wife becoming Mary, the farmer Christ:

> Lips tight, voiceless, lifeless in your arms
> dispossessed, no lands
> sent away from life-giving tanks
> An urgency in you downcast eyes over His
> closed in death
> In your lap you bear Him once again
> not cold marble but bleeding
> fallen from a tractor.
> . . . .
> There in your lap, we see the human face of
> God, the Son
> Your child.[18]

The theological progression seen in these poems shows an intense awareness of the suffering of Christ; a growing encounter with the social realities of suffering, poverty, and exploitation in Sri Lankan rural life; the realization that it is in this hardship that Christ can be found, not in the structures of the church; the personal imperative to become one with Christ through being one with the poor; and seeing in the poor not only the weakness of Christ but the strength of Christ.

Parallels could be drawn with the conscientization of liberation theologians from South America. But there was one significant difference. The poor among whom Rodrigo discovered the strength of Christ were Buddhist. His own journey into Christ was not only a journey into the reality of poverty but also a journey into Buddhism as lived by the poor. Rodrigo remained a Christian, but his encounter with the heart of his own faith was also an encounter with the heart of another faith. It could be said that it was through the witness of another faith that he encountered what was authentic in his own faith, a process also present in the experience of Aloysius Pieris.

In a paper read in Thailand in 1984 Rodrigo spoke of three "moments" of confessing: confessing Jesus in a Christian context; confessing the Buddha-Dhamma in a Buddhist context; confessing Jesus in a Buddhist context.[19] All were central to his life. His work in the first category was that of liberation theologian. Stretching like a thread throughout the Bible, he would point out to Christians, was the theme of the poor upraised and upheld by a God who had emptied himself to become human. Those who sought God, he insisted, would find God only if they underwent the same self-emptying.[20]

The farmers in Uva, where Michael chose to work, were landless, voiceless, and powerless, providers of rice for the nation yet so indebted that many were not able to eat enough rice themselves. At first, they were suspicious of the Christian group among them. One member of the *bhikkhu* Sangha made it quite clear that he wanted them to go, fearing that they would soon start pouring water and baptizing. But the reverse happened. The villagers found that Michael joined with them to celebrate Vesak, the most important Buddhist festival of the year; in other words, that he was willing to "confess" the Buddha-Dhamma, the teaching of the Buddha, alongside them, although a Christian. At Vesak, in 1981, he got up in the temple and spoke about the five Buddhist moral precepts *(panca sila)*. In 1982, again at Vesak, he worked with a Buddhist lyricist in the village to write devotional songs based on the ten perfections *(paramita)* in Theravada Buddhism. After those songs had been sung, as documented by Michael himself, the Buddhist monk who had asked him to leave announced: "I regret having harassed him at the start, saying he had come to baptize. Now, I know that was not his idea. So, now I tell you, be free to come here or to go there to learn the Dhamma. It is the same. He can guide you."[21] It was through such confessing that trust was built. When I visited Suba Seth Gedara at the beginning of 1987, I felt that I had touched something incredibly precious in Sri Lankan life. Michael and the chief monks from two temples, Ven. Alutwela Sumanasiri and Ven. Alutwela Upananda, were true colleagues and friends, supporting and encouraging one another in a very difficult economic and social context. In Buddhist terms they were, to use a Pali concept, *kalyana mitta*, noble or virtuous friends, united by the Buddha-Dhamma.

Michael Rodrigo was able to confess Buddhism in a Buddhist context because of the well of common emphases he saw stretching across Buddhism and Christianity. Never did Michael stress difference between the two religions when I was with him, only what united them, such as the qualities of loving-kindness, compassion, non-acquisitiveness, and self-emptying. He was able to laud the five precepts *(panca sila)* and promote the ten perfections *(paramita)* because they spoke to him of a common heritage between the two faiths. Similarity, he stressed to me, was present even in the linguistic roots of key words. For example, he pointed out that the Greek word for compassion *(splanchnon)* meant "mercy welling from the bowels," and that the Pali word for loving-kindness *(metta)* was from the verb *mejjati*, "to melt." "Dialogue can intensify when we know that *metta* and compassion are from kindred roots," he wrote.[22] Another example he gave me was the similarity between the Pali word for truth, *sacca*, and the Greek word for righteousness. So, in witnessing to Buddhism among Buddhists, he would stress the Buddha's renunciation as a self-emptying flowing from compassion, the social implications of the *panca sila*, the dangers of greed *(tanha)*, and the benefits of community. "Within Buddhism," he told me, "the individual dies and the Sangha [community] comes up with the idea of a corporate soul." But he would also say that he did not have to teach such concepts. They were there already, and he was the learner:

I have learnt at the feet of the people, the poor masses, and at the feet of the Gurus of the village whom I always revere – the Buddhist monks who slowly but surely try in many places in Sri Lanka to lead the people to the living out of the Dhamma in practice. Everyday I learn from the people, farmers and peasants specially, patience, renunciation, acceptance of their lot, suffering, hope in solidarity and what are generally called the Saradharma, virtues of sharing, brotherhood, rejection of greed.[23]

As for confessing Jesus in a Buddhist context, Michael would say that it was only through the kind of dialogue of life in which he was involved that Jesus could be confessed and known in a Buddhist context. He justified this by pointing to the attitudinal changes that had occurred during his stay in Uva, as shown, for instance, in the words of a youth leader documented for a paper he eventually gave on this experiment in interreligious dialogue:

> I accept Jesus as a founder of a noble religion, one who showed sincere affection for people. He loved all as equals and showed it by his life. . . .
> At the start, some young people watched you carefully; how will you act towards us? Did you come to turn us to your ways somehow? were you an international spy-group or spy-ring to eventually sell out our village? – were questions harassing us youth. But we went beyond observation, worked with you as you worked with the people. There we discovered the true face of what you called 'sabhava' the church.[24]

Rodrigo's communicating of Jesus in a Buddhist context was by making himself an example of the qualities present in the life of Jesus—compassion, empathy, strength.

ALOYSIUS PIERIS, S.J.

Aloysius Pieris is director of Tulana Research Centre, situated in a rural area just outside Colombo, near Kelaniya Temple, where, on the banks of the Kelani River, Benjamin Clough had challenged the *bhikkhu* Sangha in 1815. When I first went to Tulana in 1986, I saw it as an aesthetic jewel. Its roofs and mellow walls reminded me of a temple. There was an appreciation of beauty down to the last detail—leaves and petals drawn into the stone of the pathways, small lotus ponds into which rainwater drained naturally, works of art by Buddhists on Christian themes. Now, the buildings have grown. There is a second library, more accommodation for members of the resident community, and more works of art. The twenty-fifth anniversary was celebrated in 1999.

The word *tulana* comes from Pali and Sanskrit and can be defined as "discernment," "weighing things up," or "discerning action." The metal plaque cast for the twenty-fifth anniversary, hanging in the main room, has a pair of scales at its center. Working toward discernment through research, reflection, and critical deliberation, and engaging in discerning action and encounter in the context of Sri Lanka's religiousness, poverty, war, and economic crisis is what Tulana has been about. The libraries are a treasure trove for indological and theological research. The works of art embody in clay, stone, and paint a message about the way religious traditions can inspire and give to one another. The seminars, talks, and meditations support and nurture many who are working at cutting edges in the country's life, particularly in struggles against economic injustice. Now a media unit is being developed.

Aloysius Pieris is internationally known as indologist and liberation theologian. He has published well over one hundred articles. His theology and work have given subject matter to several doctorates. What I shall concentrate on is his relationship with Buddhism and his message concerning religious identity and belonging. I will not attempt to encompass his writings on Christology, the nature of the cross, cosmic and metacosmic religion, voluntary poverty, or feminism unless they touch directly on the more narrow subject of religious belonging.

Born in 1934, Pieris joined the Jesuit Order when only nineteen. Like Rodrigo, he eventually gained two doctorates, one in Buddhism and one in Christian theology. He was the first Christian, let alone priest, to obtain a doctorate in Buddhism from a Sri Lankan university. One of the first challenges he threw out to the churches, using the example of Jesus' baptism at John's hands, was the need for the Christian church in Asia to be humble enough to "be baptized by its precursors in the Jordan of Asian religion and bold enough to be baptized by oppressive systems on the cross of Asian *poverty.*"[25]

It was a call rooted in experience. For Aloysius Pieris had done what he was encouraging the church to do. Aware that academic knowledge of Buddhism was not enough, in his early thirties, in 1967-68, he had journeyed to the living witnesses to Buddhism themselves. He had prostrated himself at the feet of a learned Buddhist monk and had asked to be taught by him. For a time, his new teacher placed him in a Buddhist monastery anonymously. Looking back on the event, he recalls that the members of the *bhikkhu* Sangha there thought he was an ex-Buddhist monk because his knowledge of Pali was so good! It was an act indicative of a willingness to lose identity as a Christian priest in order to gain a total immersion in Buddhism in a second baptism. It was a true "passing over" in order to come back. The result was that the lived language of Buddhism became part of him.

Much of his thought and indeed action concerning the way religions should relate to one another has flowed from this pivotal experience of putting himself utterly in the pedagogical hands of someone of another faith with absolute trust. What emerged was not a form of Christian-Buddhism but a much deeper appreciation of the nature of religion itself and its role in society. Here are some of the main points he has made in this regard:

- Each religion is stamped by its own unrepeatable identity.
- The different formative experiences of the great religions can be seen as representing mutually corrective instincts of the human spirit.
- Interreligious dialogue is not a luxury but a necessity, especially between those of different religions who are committed to the poor and are open to "the Unspoken Speaker, to the Spirit that is not tied down to any dogma, rite or law";[26] that is, the Word that is larger than any religious institution.
- In this dialogue neither syncretism nor synthesis is appropriate. Symbiosis is.[27]

Three levels, Pieris has suggested, are present in the development of any religion: core experience, collective memory, and interpretation. The first is the liberative experience that gave birth to the religion and continues to condition the language and mood of the religion, for example, the Jesus story in Christianity or the enlightenment of the Buddha. The second is the medium through which this has been mediated—songs, narrative, drama, liturgy, the development of a priestly hierarchy. The last is the way in which the formative, core event has been framed by followers throughout history. The three, in Pieris's view, form an unrepeatable, identity-stamping nexus, a unique offering to the world's spiritual search, and true interreligious encounter must embrace all three. And because each religion is unique, Pieris suggests, those entering into it with empathy and the willingness for a *communicatio in sacris* should expect to discover difference, should expect to be challenged by a new religious language, a new vocabulary. Citing commonalities, however real, is not enough.

In the nineteenth-century world of the evangelical missionaries, to assert difference was, by definition, to imply a distinction between truth and falsity. In Pieris's view, however, difference does not mean that religions are necessarily located along oppositional battle lines. In his earlier writings he became known for juxtaposing gnosis and agape, wisdom and love, when speaking about the formative experiences of Buddhism and Christianity—Buddhism as embodying wisdom or insight into reality through self purification and renunciation, and Christianity as embodying agape or self-giving love. He did not deny that Buddhism emphasized compassion or that Christianity spoke of wisdom but used the two categories to pinpoint a difference in core experience. It was awakening into wisdom, enlightenment, that the Buddha gained. It was self-giving love that Jesus demonstrated on the cross. Pieris's judgment is not that one was superior; both are "salvific." He calls them "both legitimate languages of the *human* spirit" and continues:

> What must be borne in mind is that both gnosis and agape are *necessary* precisely because each in itself is *inadequate* as a medium, not only for experiencing but also for expressing our intimate moments with the Ultimate Source of Liberation. They are, in other words, complementary idioms that need each other to mediate the self-transcending experience called "salvation." Any valid spirituality, Buddhist or Christian, as the history of each religion attests, does retain both poles of experience—namely, the gnostic and the agapeic.[28]

In other words, wisdom is not enough without a language of self-giving love, and self-giving love is not enough without a seeking of insight or discernment through discipline, renunciation, and self-knowledge. Presented in this way, the core experiences of Buddhism and Christianity are seen by Pieris as two essential movements of the spirit that need one another. Christianity, he believes, has crushed to its detriment the gnostic side it once had and now needs to be evangelized by the East into a new emphasis on gnostic detachment and voluntary poverty. Theravada Buddhism, he suggests, needs to have an infusion of agape for it to recover its own emphasis on compassion. Voluntary poverty, or renunciation of acquisitiveness and opposition to Mammon, is where the two movements meet. Difference between religions but not rivalry is therefore affirmed.

In hearing Pieris speak about Buddhism—and it was the same when one listened to Rodrigo—the sense of affinity and appreciation is palpable, combined with scholarly knowledge. In 1995 I interviewed Pieris for a series of programs I was writing and presenting for the BBC World Service on Buddhism. I asked him about the practice of mindfulness in meditation, and this was the answer he gave:

> Mindfulness is a key word in Buddhism, as in most spiritualities outside Buddhism. In Buddhism, the state from which one has to be delivered is a state of sleep, of being drugged, of being doped. Greed or selfishness is a form of drug by which we get ourselves completely mind-less. Therefore, the situation from which the teaching of the Buddha would like to deliver us is precisely this drugged situation. Therefore, mindfulness is the opposite. It is to be completely aware at every moment of what is happening within us. Not to be programmed – that's the ideal. From birth we are programmed and it is so that we can de-programme ourselves and be constantly aware of various forces which make us slaves that mindfulness is important. It is the process by which we awaken ourselves and keep awake constantly. It is a process of constant discernment, constant awareness of what is happening within so that we are not out of control of ourselves. The key word of the Dhammapada, the little manual of spirituality in Buddhism, is *appamado*. It means vigilance, not being doped, getting detoxified, total awareness.
>
> *Moha*, another key word used by the Buddha to describe this situation, is to be completely de-mented. Ninety percent of us are de-mented. And so *amoha*, the opposite, is again a word for *nibbana*. Mindfulness is the process of deliverance that is available to anyone who wants it. It is not something from outside. It is something you can do and it is to be done continuously so that it becomes a permanent state.[29]

This leads on to Pieris's use of the terms *syncretism, synthesis,* and *symbiosis*.[30] Syncretism and synthesis Pieris rejects as invalid paths to worthwhile encounter, since both violate the unique identity of each religion. Those, he claims, who have said Asian Buddhists are syncretistic do an injustice to the rich cosmic religiosity of the poor. Not for him a "pick and mix" postmodern ethic of personal spirituality, a fusing together of practices from different faiths to create a new entity unrecognizable to the adherents of the faiths mined. Symbiosis, in contrast, Pieris defines as a movement through which those who have different religious identities live and work together and in the process are taught by the "other" more about what is significant and unique in their own faith. In other words, Buddhists, through interacting with Christians, learn more about what is uniquely valuable in Buddhism, and Christians learn more about what is uniquely valuable in Christianity. The hidden can be uncovered in encounter; the lost found. There is a drawing from the wells of another tradition— not to create new religious identities but rather to nurture critical self-evaluation and deeper self-knowledge. According to Pieris, for this to be liberative in the truest sense, both to the individual and the community, there has to be common commitment to the poor and sensitivity to "the Unspoken Speaker, to the Spirit that is not tied down to any dogma, rite or law,"[31] the Word that goes beyond any religious hierarchy or structure. Elitist, ivory-tower interfaith encounters he has little time for.

In his writings, Pieris speaks predominantly of two symbiotic fronts—practical action within basic human communities, and art. In the interfaith communities he is in touch with what he sees, a veritable symbiosis of religions. Each religion, challenged by the other religion's unique approach to the liberationist aspiration of the poor, especially to the sevenfold characteristic of their cosmic religiosity mentioned above, discovers and renames itself in its specificity in response to other approaches. . . . It indicates one's conversion to the common heritage of all religions (beatitudes) and also a conversion to the specificity of one's own religion as dictated by other religionists. You may call that interreligious dialogue, if you wish.[32]

As for art, on the wall of Tulana's main room, entered into through an archway straight from the garden, is a mural relief by a Buddhist monk, Ven. Hattigamana Uttarananda; it depicts Christ, in service, washing the feet of his disciples. The setting is Asian. The disciples are wearing the robes of the Buddhist renunciant and carrying alms bowls, although their hair and beards distinguish them from members of the *bhikkhu* Sangha. They enter the house of a lay person for the traditional gift of a meal, a *dana*. The person who comes forward to refresh them after travel, however, is not the servant but the master himself, with a towel wrapped around his waist. One disciple holds up his hand in a gesture that says, "Something strange, unusual, significant is happening here." And to the side, two women, one of high caste and the other of low, observe, side by side, with a traditional gesture of reverence.

Before beginning this work, Uttarananda read the Christian gospels in conversation with Pieris, who asked him to depict something that struck him as unique to Christianity. He chose the revolutionary challenge Christianity holds out to the culture of master and slave. In this mural and the painting alongside it on the woman taken in adultery, he also pointed to Jesus' enlightened attitude toward women. The work is an example of a Buddhist reminding Christians of a pivotal emphasis in their faith, often overlooked.

Another work of art at Tulana is a further large mural relief, this time made of baked clay. The artist is again Buddhist, Kingsley Gunatilleke. Again, it resulted from long hours of dialogue—on Luke's gospel. It shows the young Jesus in the Temple at Jerusalem. His face looks up to his teachers in eager and innocent inquiry. Behind him are his parents, anxiously trying to restrain him. But Jesus refuses to be controlled by them. And the people he is questioning are not the temple rabbis alone. They are the Buddha, Mahavira, Krishna, Laotse, Confucius, and women teachers. The spirituality and the philosophies of the world are there. The message of the mural is that the human search for truth is like a sacred temple "in which the Word is being formed in the exchanges of many holy and learned people who have served humankind with their sacred findings. It is a dialogue in the Spirit."[33] In this search, no one religion should have the arrogance to stand alone. To be truly itself, each religion must engage with others and see itself through the eyes of the "other."

CONCLUDING REMARKS

Has a form of double belonging in religion emerged in Sri Lanka? Or was it present before the British evangelical missionaries? The answer, of course, is dependent on how the phrase is defined. If double belonging implies that a person is 100 percent

Buddhist and 100 percent Christian at one and the same time, such a form of belonging has not been and is not present in Sri Lanka. The curiosity that Sri Lankan Buddhists originally felt toward the message of the missionaries, their willingness to applaud that which was good, was not an affirmation of parity between Buddhism and Christianity. It was rather a willingness to draw that which was good into their own framework. It was a willingness to see Jesus as a person worthy of respect in addition to the Buddha, and devotion to him as a possible "insurance policy," but within a Buddhist worldview. If conversion to Christianity was chosen, through religious conviction or political expediency, a similar dynamic was often present. In other words, religious practices from Buddhism that still seemed good and efficacious were not rejected but were brought into the Christian framework, with the Christian framework becoming dominant. No doubt a few of those who started to go to church in the colonial period simply held Buddhism and Christianity alongside one another. But I would argue that this was rare. At the level of the heart and mind, the framework of one religion was usually dominant.

As for Michael Rodrigo and Aloysius Pieris, neither has ever claimed parity of allegiance to more than one faith. Throughout his life, Rodrigo was utterly rooted in Christianity and used Christian terminology to define his approach to interreligious encounter. The same is true of Pieris. However, both have also used another religious language—that of Buddhism—and have used it with such sensitivity and command that it has been as though a Buddhist were speaking through them.

Can there be a form of double belonging where there is familiarity with and affinity to more than one religious language, even if one language, by choice, remains privileged as the dominant language of the heart and mind? I believe there can. With this definition, Rodrigo and Pieris have both "belonged" to Buddhism as well as Christianity. They have drawn deeply from Buddhist wells as well as from Christian ones, have sat at the feet of Buddhist teachers, and have taken Buddhist vocabulary into their very being. They have been able both to enter the worldview of Buddhism and to articulate the experience in Buddhist terms. But I would want to distinguish strongly between this and a multiple or dual belonging in which a sense of being rooted in one religious language is lost. Pieris's latest books, written as part of a series to mark the twenty-fifth anniversary of Tulana, for instance, are absolutely rooted in Christian discourse.[34] However, and here is the important point, these books could not have been written without a knowledge of other religious languages, without a lifetime of interreligious awareness. They express a spirituality that is at once deeply biblical, although subversive of some approaches that pass as biblical, but also fed by encounter with the poor of the earth who have another religious belonging.

Rooted in one religious language, Rodrigo and Pieris learnt to speak and think in another religious language. Rodrigo in his conversations and writings tended to stress similarity between these languages. Pieris has done this also. The opposition in all religions to Mammon or greed and the stress on voluntary poverty in Buddhist and Christian monasticism has been brought out in his work. But he has also worked with difference and uniqueness in religion, as a resource, when religions meet, for growth, creativity, the rediscovery of that which has been overlooked, and ever deeper discipleship. Peiris in fact holds together the need for rootedness in one religious tradition and the need for plurality of insights into Truth. It is not a case of multiple belonging or dual belonging but a search for the Word that goes beyond structures, mediated through the language of one's own faith in encounter with that of others. It is this, perhaps, that the Sri Lankan experience can offer to this debate.

NOTES

[1] The first missionaries to arrive in Sri Lanka after the formation of the evangelical societies were from the London Missionary Society (LMS) in 1805. The involvement of the LMS, however, did not continue beyond sending this one group. The societies that retained a continual presence throughout the century were the Baptist Missionary Society (1812), the Wesleyan Methodist Missionary Society (1814), the American Mission Board (1816), and the Church Missionary Society (1818). In 1840, the Society for the Propagation of the Gospel entered and, toward the end of the century, the Salvation Army (1885/86) and the Quakers (1896).

[2] Thomas Squance, *The Methodist Magazine* [London] 34 (1816), 197.

[3] Robert Spence Hardy, *The Jubilee Memorials of the Wesleyan Mission, South Ceylon* (Colombo, Sri Lanka: Wesleyan Methodist Bookroom: Colombo, 1865), 36-37.

[4] Ibid., 286.

[5] Rev. I. Wood, *Church Missionary Society Report 1858-59* (London: Church Missionary Society), 156.

[6] In 1849, Rev. Daniel J. Gogerly published *Kristiyani Prajnapti* or "The Evidences and Doctrines of the Christian Religion," a tract that drew on Gogerly's extensive knowledge of the Buddhist texts to present the perceived superiority of Christianity.

[7] James Selkirk, *Recollections of Ceylon after a Residence of Nearly Thirteen Years with an Account of the Church Missionary Society's Operations in the Island and Extracts from a Journal* (London: J. Hatchard & Sons, 1844), 356.

[8] Rev. William Bridgenell, Methodist missionary writing in 1839 in *The Friend*, a magazine published in Sri Lanka by the Methodist Printing Press.

[9] Kitsiri Malalgoda, *Buddhism in Sinhalese Society 1750-1900* (Berkeley and Los Angeles: University of California Press, 1976), 213-14.

[10] *Church Missionary Society Report 1863-64* (London: Church Missionary Society), 176.

[11] *South Ceylon District Minute Book* (Colombo, Sri Lanka: Methodist Church Archives, January 1882).

[12] This can be seen particularly in the writings of the Ven. Anagarika Dharmapala, collected in Ananda W. P. Guruge, *Return to Righteousness: A Collection of Speeches, Essays, and Letters of the Anagarika Dharmapala* (Colombo, Sri Lanka: Ministry of Education and Cultural Affairs, 1965).

[13] An edited version of Michael Rodrigo's thesis was published as *Father Mike and His Thought*, vol. 1, *The Moral Passover from Selfishness to Selflessness in Christianity and the Other Religions in Sri Lanka (Ceylon)*, ed. Sr. Milburga Fernando, *Logos* 27/3 (September 1988). *Logos* is published by the Centre for Society and Religion in Colombo, Sri Lanka.

[14] Michael Rodrigo, *Tissues of Life and Death: Selected Poems of Fr. Michael Rodrigo O.M.I.*, ed. Elisabeth J. Harris, *Quest* 95 (June 1988). *Quest* is published by the Centre for Society and Religion in Colombo, Sri Lanka.

[15] Ibid., 8.

[16] Ibid., 22. Dhang is a board game a little like checkers.

[17] Ibid., 36. *Metta, karuna, mudita,* and *upekkha* are the four "divine abodes" in Theravada Buddhism: loving-kindness, compassion, sympathetic joy, and equanimity.

[18] Ibid., 45. Tanks are manmade irrigation lakes, developed in ancient Sri Lanka.

[19] These "moments" are developed by Rodrigo in the context of the Suba Seth Gedara experience in "The Hope of Liberation Lessening Man's Inhumanity: A Contribution to Dialogue at Village Level," in *Asian Faces of Jesus,* ed. R. S. Sugirtharajah (Maryknoll, N.Y.: Orbis Books, 1993), 189-211.

[20] See Michael Rodrigo, "The Bible and the Liberation of the Poor," in Fernando, *Fr. Mike and His Thought,* vol. 2, *Logos* 27/4 (October 1988), 52-74.

[21] Michael Rodrigo, "Buddhism and Christianity: Toward the Human Future: An Example of Village Dialogue of Life," in Sr. Milburga Fernando, *Harvest Dreams of Fr. Mike: Coming to Fruition* (Colombo, Sri Lanka: Centre for Society and Religion, 1987), 58.

[22] Michael Rodrigo, "Towards a More Intensive Dialogue with Buddhists," in Fernando, *Fr. Mike and His Thoughts,* 2:34.

[23] From "Fr. Michael Rodrigo's Mission in His Own Words," in *Fr. Michael Rodrigo: Prophet, Priest and Martyr* (Colombo, Sri Lanka: Christian Workers' Fellowship, 1989), 14.

[24] Rodrigo, "Buddhism and Christianity," 60-61.

[25] Aloysius Pieris, "Western Christianity and Asian Buddhism: A Theological Reading of Historical Encounters," in *Love Meets Wisdom: A Christian Experience of Buddhism* (Maryknoll, N.Y.: Orbis Books, 1988), 41.

[26] Aloysius Pieris, *Fire and Water: Basic Issues in Asian Buddhism and Christianity* (Maryknoll, N.Y.: Orbis Books, 1996), 133.

[27] The concept is explained in Aloysius Pieris, "Interreligious Dialogue and Theology of Religions: An Asian Paradigm," in Pieris, *Fire and Water,* 154-61.

[28] Aloysius Pieris, "Christianity in a Core-to-Core Dialogue with Buddhism," in Pieris, *Love Meets Wisdom,* 111.

[29] Elisabeth J. Harris, *What Buddhists Believe* (Oxford: Oneworld, 1998), 74-75.

[30] Pieris, "Interreligious Dialogue and Theology of Religion," 154-61.

[31] Pieris, *Fire and Water,* 133.

[32] Pieris, *Fire and Water,* 161.

[33] Ibid., 137.

[34] Aloysius Pieris, *God's Reign for God's Poor: A Return to the Jesus Formula: A Critical Evaluation of Contemporary Reformulations of the Mission Manifesto in Roman Catholic Theology in Recent Jesuit Documents* (Kelaniya: Tulana Research Centre, 1999); idem, *Mysticism of Service: A Short Treatise on Spirituality with a Pauline-Ignatian Focus on the Prayer-Life of Christian Activists* (Kelaniya: Tulana Research Centre, 2000).

8

Double Belonging and the Originality of Christianity as a Religion

CLAUDE GEFFRÉ

The ways are complementary without being contradictory.

—CONFUCIUS

Multiple religious belonging is a symptom of a new sociology of religion informed by the fact of globalization. It is the effect of an increasingly effective network of communication on a worldwide scale, and of a de-institutionalization that furthers the free circulation of beliefs detached from their tradition of origin. But this phenomenon is also an indicator of a profoundly altered theological landscape insofar as Christian theology has come to take seriously the paradigm of religious pluralism, and has come to express a more positive judgment on non-Christian religions. There is a broad consensus in favor of renouncing an absolutization of Christianity as the only religion carrying the key to the salvation of human beings willed by God. We are witnessing much greater optimism about the possibility of salvation from within the other religions of the world, and we have gone beyond a conception of mission oriented in the first place to "conversion," understood as a change of religion.

Multiple belonging or *double belonging:* the difference in vocabulary is not irrelevant. The former expression refers to a typically Western situation. The second evokes more generally the encounter of Christianity with non-Western cultures and religious traditions. Hence, if we would like to exercise a theological discernment of this double belonging within Christianity itself, it seems important to avoid confusing it with the widely present phenomenon of multiple belonging that is characteristic of our Western modernity. To avoid the immediate critique of syncretism with regard to double belonging, I shall begin by facing the typically syncretistic drift of the new religiosities flourishing in our Western societies. We may then distinguish this from double belonging understood as the logical outcome of real inculturation and focus our theological reflection on this latter phenomenon. This will require an interrogation on the originality of Christianity as a religion.[1]

MULTIPLE BELONGING AS A SYMPTOM
OF THE MODERN *HOMO RELIGIOSUS*

The religiosity of the Western person of our times is spontaneously syncretistic. One searches for answers in the wisdom traditions of the Orient with their strong sense of non-duality *(advaita)* between oneself and the Ultimate Reality, between human beings and the universe, and between body and spirit. Or else one resorts to the forgotten wisdom of the Western esoteric tradition (Hermetism, Kabbalism, Alchemy, and so on) which teaches us that mind and body, infinitely small and infinitely large, participate in the same universal cosmic energy, which must be captured.

The success of new syncretistic movements (not to be confused with cults or new religions) is directly linked to the process of globalization. Economic globalization has its parallel in the domain of religion. Following the success of audiovisual communication, there has emerged a religious supermarket that offers the growing number of consumers many products of the living religions as well as various esoteric alternatives in matters of myths and beliefs, practices, secret initiations, and healing techniques for both the body and the mind. Insofar as many of our contemporaries, Christians included, are no longer fixed to a normative tradition with regard to questions of truth and practice, they can accumulate practices derived from very different traditions without contradiction. Beliefs are afloat. This religious mood or mentality may have been captured best by the expression of the British sociologist Grace Davie: "believing without belonging."[2] What is ignored is the credibility of this or that belief, its necessary connection to this or that religious system, and its incompatibility with other beliefs. The only criterion is the enhancement of my being and my most intimate potentialities.

Indeed, one would understand nothing of the syncretistic tendency of modern religiosity if one did not link it with contemporary individualism, the jealous preoccupation with the authenticity of one's personal experience, and a loss of memory of the tradition in which one is born. Christians themselves are not exempt from this temptation to syncretism. Since they are often strangers to the normative tradition of their churches, they may continue to call themselves Christians while at the same time practicing a rather radical selectivity with regard to each different article of the creed, and while engaging in a rather risky synthesis in the areas of both faith and practice. What may well be contradictory in the domain of conceptual logic need not be so in the domain of existential logic. The *immediately believable* is whatever nourishes my well-being.

I thus understand the tendency toward syncretism as a symptom of modern and postmodern religiosity in the context of both globalization and an increasingly jealous individualism. However, it must be understood that the success of this syncretistic orientation (which is often related to neo-paganism) coincides with a loss of credibility, of, if not the Christian tradition itself, then at least the official churches that present an image of the tradition that is too institutional, too dogmatic, and too morally prescriptive. Confronted with the failures of secular society—anonymity and unbridled consumerism—and with the distance between the lived world and an increasingly superficial world, many men and women go in search of a re-enchantment of the world, human beings, and the God they do not find in mainstream Christianity. They are not insensitive to certain forms of Nietzschean neo-paganism that sacralize life in the innocence of its becoming. And they are in search of a God somehow more divine than the all too familiar God of the long Judeo-Christian tradition.[3]

Whatever the ambiguities of these new religious orientations, often given the negative designation of "nebulous esoteric mysticism,"[4] we must listen with respect and attention to this undefined aspiration of much of contemporary spirituality. Who does not feel some nostalgia for a God more divine than the unique God of monotheism, identified as "supreme Being" and "Origin of the world"? Who can embrace a purely profane world governed solely by the demonic tendencies of human nature and without any reference to the divine? Who does not dream of the harmony between body and soul beyond the dichotomies of some of Christian spirituality?

I do not denounce the desire to integrate the riches of the various traditions in a higher syncretism. But we do have the right to ask ourselves whether this syncretism is at the service of a search for an ever greater and more divine God. Or is it no more than a sacralization of our own essential being in a passionate search for any mental or physical technique that can bring about an enhancement of our self?

Before asking if the time may be ripe for new forms of syncretism, I must point out that the ardent search for some essential self strikes me as fundamentally alien to the Christian conception of salvation as a free gift flowing from a complete self-surrender to God. Even if I would stay far from assuming that the monotheistic religions have a monopoly on transcendence, I refuse to believe that the Absolute—whether or not it is conceived of as personal—is nothing but the term of the self-fulfillment of the human being, or the cosmic energy in which we participate in communion with all living beings. It may be true that some forms of Christianity oriented primarily toward political and social change do not respond directly to the spiritual hunger of many of our contemporaries. But one cannot forget that Christianity, as the religion of the gospel, never dissociates the cause of humans, especially suffering human beings, from the cause of God.

DOUBLE BELONGING AS REQUIREMENT FOR INCULTURATION

THE PITFALLS OF INCULTURATION

Faced with the immense theme of inculturation, I will start by exorcising two temptations or pitfalls: that of an incarnationism and that of an abstract dissociation of religion and culture.

In spite of the privilege granted to the term *incarnation,* one tends too quickly to exploit the analogy between the incarnation of the Word of God in the humanity of Jesus and the incarnation of Christianity in a new culture. Contrary to the dream of certain liberal theologians of the nineteenth century, there is no essence of Christianity in its pure state. It is always a matter of a Christianity already inculturated, and this since the beginning of the history of the church. An abstract Christianity does not exist. As soon as one acknowledges the transcultural nature of the Christian faith, one must observe that the Christian message has adopted the dominant culture of its place of origin, including the frame of thinking and the vocabulary of Semitic thought and of Greek culture. This is precisely the historical risk and the theological stake of the incarnation.

It must thus be recognized that the dominant historical image of the church has been shaped throughout the ages by the West, or at least by the Mediterranean basin. We may say that it has emerged within the tension between Jerusalem and Athens, the two emblematic cities of that time. It is only today, at the beginning of the twenty-first century, that the church is starting to take seriously the existence of a *tertium quid*, a different, non-Western person who is neither Greek nor Jew. As Panikkar likes to ask, "Must one be spiritually a Semite and intellectually a Greek to be a Christian?"

But if it is true that there is no *essence* of Christianity floating beyond every culture, it would nonetheless be wrong to conceive of the problem of inculturation in terms of a Christianity that would have to cease to be Western in order to become African or Asian. I believe more in a fruitful and creative encounter between the resources of a Western Christianity and the values of non-Western cultures, which are themselves inseparable from their great religious traditions. This is why I call for a *conversation* between the new theologies born in Africa and Asia and so-called European theology. It is certainly important to relativize those elements that belong to the cultural and historical baggage of the Christian faith of the past centuries. But I believe that it is also illusory to wish to return to an original Christianity beyond all doctrines and later theological developments. In short, the encounter between contemporary Christianity and a non-Western culture is always an encounter between two cultures.[5]

The other pitfall that must be denounced is that of the myth of the inculturation of Christianity into a pagan culture while ignoring the encounter between Christianity and another religious tradition. How could one speak of African or especially Asian culture without taking account of its religious roots? The importance of this question for the problem of double belonging is clear. One may speak of a successful inculturation, in which the Christian identity is combined with complete respect for ethnic, national and cultural belonging. We are familiar enough with the official discourses proclaiming a plural identity simultaneously both fully Christian and wholly Indian, Chinese, or Japanese. But what would the Indian identity consist of outside of Hinduism? What would comprise the Chinese identity without the complex religious mixture of Taoism, Confucianism, and Buddhism? What is the Japanese identity apart from Zen Buddhism and the Shinto tradition?

The relationship between religion and culture is extremely complex, and the Westerners who pride themselves on the autonomy of a culture said to be atheistic often forget that it is still a post-Christian culture. In fact, it is very difficult to distinguish between that which is derived from culture and that which is derived from religion. There is a reciprocal interaction between the two, and it is impossible to assign an absolute origin to one or the other. Every religion worthy of the name has a cultural impact, whether in the area of the symbolic resources or with regard to the enhancement of being and meaning. But, in turn, culture itself has a humanistic and rational function insofar as it represents the victory obtained over the prevalence of human violence in primitive societies. In spite of its rudimentary character and its ethnic particularity, every truly humane culture relates to other cultures insofar as it goes beyond purely utilitarian exchanges and commits itself to the service of the authentically human. Kant would say that it is in the order of value and not only possession or might.

In light of this inseparable link between religion and culture, it is increasingly difficult to imagine the inculturation of the Christian message in a non-Western civilization without evoking the confrontational or dialogical encounter with other great religious traditions. This is particularly the case with regard to South and East Asia. Here, the incarnation of the gospel occurs in a culture permeated by a long religious tradition that has shaped value systems, symbolic resources, and daily life. How, for example, might one distinguish belonging to the Indian culture and belonging to Hinduism? There exists no separate term for philosophy in India, since it is so closely intertwined with the reading of the sacred texts. And if there is such a thing as a black culture in the sense of Senghor, how could one abstract it from the traditional African religions? Even if it is true that Islam is becoming less thoroughly Arabic, how might one distinguish Islam as religion from Islam as the Arab-Muslim civilization?

This understanding of inculturation in the context of interreligious dialogue invites us to revise our purely negative conception of syncretism. There is a *good use of syncretism*, and, in effect, we are already witnessing a "Hindu Christianity" and a "Buddhist Christianity" that are more than mere confusion or patchwork. The fact that in the past the encounter between Christianity and the other religions has been experienced as conflict and exclusion does not mean this situation must be fatally normative for this new millennium. At this juncture the question that deserves our attention is whether there can be a Christian identity understood in terms of a double religious belonging. However, before offering some elements of a theological response to this question, I would like to point to the dynamic of rupture and continuity present in any process of inculturation of Christianity in a new culture.

THE DOUBLE MOVEMENT OF INCULTURATION

The inculturation of the gospel in a culture evokes a complex process of rupture and continuity, or, to use a more classical vocabulary, of purification and assumption. We must say that there is no Christianization of a culture without cultural transmutation of Christianity. To take but a famous example, it is still a point of contention whether the inculturation of Christianity in the Greek culture did not bring with it a process of Hellenization of Christianity. And, closer to home, it was the archbishop of Kinshasa, Cardinal Malula, who liked to say that "so far, we have Christianized Africa, it is now time to Africanize Christianity."

If Christianity is faithful to itself as the religion of the gospel, its encounter with a new culture coincides with a novelty in its thinking, its imagination, and the global culture of the people of a particular era, as was the case with the preaching of the gospel in the pagan world of Antiquity. This encounter can be interpreted in terms of rupture. But it must be asked whether this rupture is related to the newness of the gospel, which is always a sign of contradiction of the status quo and the spontaneous hierarchy of values of a pagan culture left to itself, or is a matter of the strangeness of a Christianity that may be too wedded to an alien culture. In its attempt at inculturation the church is thus challenged to question itself about its spontaneous forms of expression and to practice discernment with regard to the fundamental elements of the Christian message and more contingent structures derived from the dominant culture with which it has been historically associated.

As the word of God, the gospel can find itself in conflict with the self-evident values and the self-sufficiency of the sinful human being. But one must first ascertain whether the church is the mirror of the gospel. Is it the gospel itself that is challenged, or is it the false scandal of a cultural vehicle that is completely alien to the men and women to whom the church is sent? Unless the church practices this attempt at inculturation, there will be no occurrence of the good news. Hence, this would mean that the church of this age can only be faithful to its global mission by itself undergoing a *conversion*, that is to say, by questioning its age-old privileged mode of thinking and expression, namely, that of Western civilization.

This questioning of the historical form of Christianity leads to a process of reinterpretation of its message and practice in contact with a different culture. One may speak of the function of Christianity as "critical catalyst" with regard to all human cultures.[6] This means that the gospel exercises a critical function with regard to the elements threatening, or at least posing an obstacle to, real humanization. But at the same time, every human culture is the vehicle of precious values that help us to understand and articulate what is *authentically human*.[7] Hence, Christianity must succeed in assuming the positive values of a new culture and in using these values to better explain the Christian truth. But as I have said before, especially in Asia, Christianity is confronted with a complex whole in which the cultural and the religious elements are inextricably intertwined. One should thus avoid the illusion that it would be possible to make a clear distinction between the cultural values that might be kept and the specifically religious elements that would need to be discarded. The work of *Aufhebung* (destruction-assumption) must manifest itself with regard to this cultural-religious universe in a way that the leaven of the gospel gives rise to a new historical image and form of Christianity. The church can give evidence to its Catholicity only if it favors the birth of an Arabic, Indian, Chinese, or Japanese Christianity. We may imagine the relevance of this with regard to our problem of double belonging. It would be redundant to affirm the possibility of a double belonging involving Christianity and the different cultures. One can be fully Christian while remaining Indian or Chinese. The question remains open as to whether it is possible to imagine a Christian identity that would also integrate the positive values of another great non-Christian tradition.

Before moving into some elements of a theological response, I would like to specify that the creation of a new Christian identity presupposes a reinterpretation of Christianity, both on the level of the confession of faith and on the level of practice. It is not enough to speak of a simple adaptation.[8] It is not possible merely to translate the Christian message in a different culture without reinterpretation of the content itself of the message. But it would also not be enough to state that this reinterpretation would consist of practicing a critical discernment between the substantial elements of the Christian message and its more secondary or accidental elements. This would imply that Christianity, as the religion of the gospel, coincides with a corpus of truths that would have to be translated in another language. Christianity is first and foremost a matter of being. Truth consists of certain strong ideas that lead to significant practices. Edward Schillebeeckx likes to remind us that, prior to being a teaching to which one must adhere, Christianity is an experience that has become a message.[9] A real inculturation of Christianity must involve the re-actualization of the fundamental Christian experience to which texts of the New Testament testify in a historical context that is both culturally and religiously different from our own. And this leads to a new configuration of Christianity, both on the level of the language of faith and on the level of existence.

It is always the same Christianity. But the historical form to which we have long been accustomed does not exclude the possibility of different historical forms yet to be imagined. When I speak of historical forms, I mean propositions of faith, symbolic resources, institutional structures, and ethical norms. Inculturation involves faithfulness to that which is essential to the Christian experience and which has been transmitted to us since the time of the apostles. "That which is required is that which is sufficient" is the basic principle of ecumenical work which—provided it is not understood in minimalistic terms—may serve as a criterion for the institution of new historical forms of Christianity. One often speaks of the mutual questioning of the gospel and a particular culture, comparing this to a mysterious exchange. A document of the International Theological Commission, for example, offers this very balanced proposal: "On the one hand, the Gospel reveals to and liberates in every culture the ultimate value of the values which it carries within itself. On the other hand, each culture expresses the Gospel in a distinct way and brings out new aspects of it."[10] This is a good expression of the process of inculturation. But in the new context of interreligious dialogue at this dawn of a new millennium, the mysterious exchange operates not only between the gospel and the cultures, but also between the gospel and the other religious traditions of the world.

DOUBLE BELONGING AS A THEOLOGICAL PROBLEM— THE THEOLOGICAL FOUNDATION OF DOUBLE BELONGING

Since Christianity encounters not only cultures but also the religions to which these cultures are directly related, it not only exercises a critical function with regard to cultural and religious totalities but also undergoes a process of assumption and transformation. Hence, to become Christian after belonging to a non-Christian tradition does not necessarily mean alienation from either the previous cultural and ethnic identity or from one's previous religious identity. To be sure, the gospel will exercise a critical function with regard to the idolatrous, immoral, or inhuman elements of a religion. But it is also capable of transforming itself in the act of assuming the positive values of a religion as seeds of truth, goodness, and even holiness. It would be absurd to affirm that one can be both Christian and Hindu or Buddhist from the perspective of these traditions as religious systems. But if religion is understood as an interior experience and as the total surrender of oneself to a transcendent and Absolute reality, it would be possible to affirm a continuity between my Christian experience and my previous spiritual experience. It would be the same experience of the Absolute that is mediated by different symbolic conceptual and ritual ways of objectifying the experience. But this is not the whole truth. The structuring elements of Christianity may undergo a metamorphosis in the contact with those of the tradition to which I belonged. One may then speak of the emergence of a new form of being Christian. This is what I mean by the good use of syncretism. To be sure, this risky syncretism, which is more than a confusion, will take different forms depending on the diverse capacities of the *homo religiosus*. For example, it will be more difficult on the level of the mind than on the level of the spirit or the heart.

This generous view of things is not without theological foundation. It can only be accepted by those who regard religious pluralism as a providential destiny given by God in the service of a better manifestation of the fullness of truth coinciding with the mystery of God and of God's providence of salvation fulfilled in Jesus Christ. This pluralism must be more than a compensation for the guilty blindness of humanity throughout history and more than a consequence of the failure of the mission of the church during the past twenty centuries. In speaking of the principle of religious pluralism corresponding to the mysterious will of God, we are in accord with the clear teaching regarding the universal salvific will of God. We rejoin the most original intuitions of the Second Vatican Council and we continue the bold teaching of the church fathers on the seeds of the word which had been distributed throughout the history of humankind long before the coming of Christ.[11]

In other words, the economy of the Word incarnate is the sacrament of a larger economy that coincides with the spiritual history of humankind, which has never been left solely to itself. This history is under the dominion of the Word of God and of the Spirit of God, which has become the Spirit of the risen Christ. As such, God draws near every human being through grace, and the religions of the world can be the agents of salvation outside of the history of salvation that begins with the calling of Abraham and finds its fulfillment in Jesus Christ. In spite of their shortcomings and their errors, the religions may in their own ways be signs of the universal love of God. The singularity of the Christian experience of God is not compromised by the recognition that God is also at work in other religions.

Like cultures, religions are under the sign of ambiguity insofar as good and evil are inextricably mixed. But in being manifestations of the stammering search for this Ultimate Reality we call God, they fulfill an irreducible function that finds its mysterious fulfillment in Jesus Christ as the full manifestation of the love of God. Hence, when we take the risk of speaking of double belonging as a new synthesis of the positive values of Christianity and those of another religion, it is with the conviction that the positive values of another religion may have been brought about by the Spirit of God itself. They may be transformed and even transfigured. But they may also reveal certain potentialities that have not been expressed in historical Christianity. Each religious tradition is unique and irreducible in its way of mediating the Absolute. This may express itself on the level of meditation, on the level of the understanding of oneself and the world, or on the level of the symbols and the forms of the sacred. As a consequence, it would be no doubt illusory to dream of a synthesis or even of a complementarity of the great religious traditions in this world. That is precisely the error of all syncretisms. But on a more existential level, our new Christian identity, which has Jesus Christ as absolute center of reference, could very well assume spiritual attitudes, mental schemes, symbolic resources, and ascetic rituals and practices belonging to other religions while transfiguring them in continuity with our own ethnically and culturally lived world. It is in that sense that, it seems to me, we would be authorized to speak of double belonging without falling into contradiction or confusion. These experimental searches for integration are the seed and the promise of new forms of Christian life that testify to the worldwide vocation of Christianity in the midst of the diversity of cultures and religions.

Yet when I refer to the integrative role and the worldwide vocation of Christianity, one must not confuse this with the true universality of Christianity. Only the Christ is universal. When we proclaim him as the Son of God, he coincides, paradoxically in his historical particularity with every moment of history. But Christianity itself as a historical religion is relative and cannot claim to comprise totally that part of religious truth that finds itself disseminated in the infinite diversity of the religions of the world. This is why it is probably too much to speak of implicitly Christian values with regard to the positive values in other religions, as if these would find their perfect fulfillment in Christianity. They are simply different, and it is in this very difference that they will find their mysterious fulfillment in the plenitude of the mystery of Christ. One may speak with Panikkar of "Christianness" or of the "Christic seed."[12] I would speak of the *Christic values* that will never be fully expressed in the different forms of Christianity in the world, even if they retain a revelatory potential with regard to the richness of the Christian singularity.[13] In reaction to every false absolutization of Christianity as historical religion, we are invited to understand that Christian truth is neither exclusive nor inclusive of all other truth. It is singular and relative to the irreducible truth of every religion. Our Western theology is just beginning to understand that religious truth is not necessarily under the sign of the principle of noncontradiction. If Christianity is the true religion, this does not mean that every other religion is false. It only witnesses to a different truth. And in interreligious dialogue, I discover that the confrontation between different truths can help me to discover a deeper truth than the one that I once believed to possess a monopoly. It is the attitude of dialogue itself, which is adopted in the heart of the religious subject who turns to the person of Jesus Christ without necessarily rejecting the different religion of his or her birth.

THE SINGULARITY OF CHRISTIANITY AS A RELIGION

Can one be simultaneously Christian and Hindu or Buddhist, Christian and Muslim? If it is possible to ask this question without falling into absurdity, a more radical question is immediately raised. What is most important in Christianity? Is it a whole of mental or symbolic objectifications, rites, and practices or the unpredictable power of the gospel? In short, the problem of double belonging leads us to the question of the originality of Christianity as the religion of the gospel.[14]

In order to answer this question, we are invited to reflect on the historical origins of Christianity in its relationship to Judaism. The new covenant introduced by Christ did not immediately lead to a new ritual, a new temple, and a new priesthood. And from an ethical point of view, the new commandments of Jesus Christ are in fact a radicalization of that which had been written in germ in the Torah as the law of the love of God and love of neighbor.

It is the urgency of the mission to the Gentiles that has led to a distinction between the contingent elements of the religion of Israel and the gospel message itself. At first, the Jews who had become disciples of the path of Jesus found it completely normal to continue to visit the synagogue, to circumcise themselves, and not to eat certain forms of impure meats. They thus believed in the possibility of remaining Jewish while becoming Christian. It is a matter of balancing the two sayings of Jesus: "I have not come to destroy, but to fulfill," and on the other hand, "One does not put new wine in old skins." If there is rupture and newness, this manifests itself in the event of Jesus Christ, which coincides with the coming of the kingdom of God and the new relationship to God and to the other. This newness expresses itself especially in terms of a *new spirit* with which one approaches a universe of thinking, a vision of humankind and of the world, and a style of living that itself may remain traditional.

We are never done with reflecting on the origin of the split between Christianity and Judaism. It is not a matter of substituting one religion for another, but—to use an expression of Michel de Certeau—the coming of Jesus that coincides with an *instituting rupture* of something new in an ancient world.[15] And even if it is a matter of a simple analogy, the relationship of Christianity to Judaism has a paradigmatic value with regard to the relationship of Christianity to the other religions. Just as the church does not integrate or replace Israel, in the same way it can not be said to integrate or replace the religious truth that may be present in another religion.

In any case, the coexistence of the Jewish religion and Christian practice following Jesus invites us to reflect on the originality of Christianity as a religion. Strictly speaking, Jesus did not found a new religion, if by religion we mean a system of doctrinal propositions, symbolic representations, a whole of rituals, a catalogue of prescriptions, and a program of determined behavior. Christian life is not determined a priori. It exists wherever the Spirit of Jesus gives birth to a new being in the individual and collective person. The question of the specificity of Christianity is often irritating. There is no Christian "species." There is only a Christian genre, which is often difficult to ascertain. On the level of action, one cannot speak of Christian practices that would stand over against simple humane practices. One will more properly speak of Christian actions as *significant* actions when certain humane actions, whether profane or religious, witness to the *evangelical difference*.

There is a Christian way of being a man or a woman, a Christian way of loving, of working, of suffering, or of rejoicing. There is a Christian way of being European, African, or Asian. Must one go so far as to say paradoxically that there is a Christian way of being Hindu or Buddhist or Confucian? In any event, if Christianity is the religion of the gospel, that is to say, if it defines itself more by the *spirit* than by the *letter*, then it should not be compared or contrasted to other religions.

This interrogation on the originality of Christianity as a religion brings us to the debate on the opposition between faith and religion, which in the modern era was exploited most greatly with the apologetic purpose of announcing Jesus Christ to irreligious people. Christianity is better than a religion; it is a faith. Hence, it is not necessary to rely upon specific religious preconditions in order to receive the Good

News of the gospel. However, we are aware of the fact that the historical form of Christianity as we know it is comparable to other religions insofar as the lived faith is always translated in a number of institutional, doctrinal, and ritual expressions. We cannot follow Karl Barth all the way when he claims to oppose Christianity, as the religion of grace, to all other religions, which would be religions of works. The distinction between works and grace may be found in every religion. Christianity itself (and Barth is the first to admit this) may become idolatrous and lead to the self-sufficiency of the person, whereas religions that are supposedly of the law may be the mediators of grace for the sinful human being.

One must thus avoid attributing to Christianity a *unicity of excellence* in contrast to all other religions. But at the same time, it is important not to sacrifice the *Christian difference*, regardless of what the historical expression of Christianity may have been. In this sense, following Karl Barth, we have not yet made the most of the Pauline tension between law and grace, between the letter and the spirit. Insofar as it remains faithful to its own genius, Christianity is religiously singular, even if it possesses all the classical traits of a great religion in the eyes of the historian of religions or the sociologist. This singularity defines itself essentially with reference to the gospel, that is to say, to the good news of a liberation, not only with regard to the law of Moses, but with regard to every religious code and all prescriptive and ritual systems that would pretend to be pleasing to God.

Paul Beauchamp writes: "In its double rapport with the Jewish law, accomplishment and rupture, the Gospel marks from the outset its relation with every possible culture."[16] I would like to add that the gospel marks from the outset its relation with every possible religion. Like Judaism, the different religious traditions may be "pedagogues" with regard to the discovery of the real face of God and with regard to the truth of the religious relationship to God who has become manifest in Jesus Christ. But it must also be said that, like Judaism, the religions are bypassed, or at least displaced by the newness of the gospel. The religious history of humankind may attest to the fact that religions are unique insofar as they are rooted in particular ethnic and cultural traditions. But the gospel may become the good news of every man and woman beyond his or her race, language, culture, and even religious belonging. Indeed, it does not offer the grace of salvation to one race, to one land, to one law, or to one religious or cultural tradition.

The gospel has a worldwide mission insofar as it rejoins in every human being the aspiration to become liberated from a religious code that still contains "elements of the world," in the sense of Saint Paul. But, of course, Christianity as a historical religion cannot pretend to carry a judgment on the "dilapidated" character of the other religions unless it submits itself to the judgement of the gospel.

CONCLUSION

To conclude these overly theoretical reflections on the possibility of double religious belonging, I would just like to recall that concretely in the life of the individual the question of the coexistence of two religious universes in one person points to the burning question of belonging to the church and indeed points to the very threshold of belonging. What would be the criteria of Christian identity for all those who remain at the doorstep of the church and who already live in the Spirit of Christ? And what about those who have taken the step of baptism, but who continue to observe the practices and the rituals of their original religion? There is no general answer to these questions. But it is good to remind ourselves that *ubi Christus ibi ecclesia* (Where Christ is, there is the church). This implies that many people who do not belong officially to the church are already members of the kingdom of God and are working toward the edification of the kingdom each time they perform evangelical deeds.[17] In other words, the visible belonging to the church guaranteed by the confession of the same creed and the communion in the eucharistic body of Christ can be a sacrament of an invisible belonging to Christ, who transcends the borders of the visible church and who may coincide with belonging to the other great non-Christian traditions.

Christian identity is always a matter of becoming, and it is important to privilege the notion of the threshold, not only with regard to the degrees of belonging to the church, but also with regard to the adult age of Christian existence, which may go through a number of partial realizations with regard to the confession of faith and the practice of the gospel.

I cannot conclude this daring reflection on these unusual cases of double belonging without calling upon the parable of the sower and the seeds. Who can claim to know the good soil in which the seed of the gospel will take root? For centuries it was thought necessary to bring about a tabula rasa of all cultures and religions that were foreign to Christianity. Today, one would be rather tempted to believe that they can be the opportunity for the emergence of new expressions of the gospel of Jesus Christ.

NOTES

[1] I am fully aware of the fact that double belonging is often conceived of from the point of view of Christians who wish to nurture themselves through the wisdom traditions of the East. Here, I focus rather on the reverse approach: How can one become Christian without denying the positive values of one's religion of origin? This, I believe, is an increasingly pressing question for the inculturation of Christianity, one that presents the theological problem of double belonging in its most radical form.

[2] Davie's expression is cited by Massimo Introvigne in his well-documented study "L'explosion des 'nouvelles religions,'" in *La Documentation Catholique* 2209 (August 1-5, 1999): 732-44.

[3] This is, at least, the hypothesis I have tried to develop in a short article, "La quête de Dieu dans les courants esoteriques contemporains," *La Vie Spirituelle* 718 (March 1996): 732-44.

[4] See especially, F. Champion, "Les sociologues de la postmodernité et la nébuleuse mystique ésotérique," *Archives de Sciences Sociales des Religions* (1989), n. 67-1: 155-69.

[5] I have explained myself more elaborately on this subject in "Pour un christianisme mondial," *Recherches de sciences religieuses* 86 (1998): 53-75.

[6] This is the expression readily used by Hans Küng in "Towards an Ecumenical Theology of Religions," *Concilium* 203 (1986): 139-48.

[7] For the meaning that I give to this term, see my study "L'humain authentique," in *Une parole pour la vie: Homage à Xavier Thevenot*, ed. G. Medevielle and J. Doré (Paris: Cerf/Salvator, 1998), 61-73.

[8] See my "La Révélation comme histoire: Enjeux théologiques pour la catéchèse," *Catéchèse* 100-101 (July-October 1986): 59-76.

[9] "Christianity is not so much a teaching which must be endorsed as an experience of faith which becomes a proclamation" (Edward Schillebeeckx, *Expérience humaine et foi en Jésus-Christ* [Paris: Cerf, 1981], 50).

[10] Commission théologique internationale, "*L'Unique Église du Christ*" (Paris: Le Centurion, 1989), 29.

[11] I have already discussed this issue in various publications. I refer specifically to my study "La place des religions dans le plan de salut," *Spiritus* 134 (February 1995): 78-79.

[12] See, for example, Raimon Panikkar, "The Jordan, the Tiber and the Ganges," in *The Myth of Christian Uniqueness*, ed. J. Hick and P. Knitter (Maryknoll, N.Y.: Orbis Books, 1987), 89-116.

[13] But I also refer various times to the idea of *Christianness* in my latest book *Profession théologien: Quelle pensée chrétienne pour le XXIe siècle?* Dialogues with Gwendoline Jarczyk (Paris: Albin Michel, 1999).

[14] I have already discussed the issue of double belonging in "Pour une théologie à l'heure chinoise. Évangelisation et culture," *Concilium* 146 (1979): 93-106. See also my book *The Risk of Interpretation. On Being Faithful to the Christian Tradition in a non Christian Age* (New York: Paulist Press, 1987).

[15] See Michel De Certeau, *La faiblesse de croire* (Paris: Seuil, 1987), 183-226.

[16] Paul Beauchamp, *Le Récit, la lettre et le corps* (Paris: Cerf, 1982), 244.

[17] Jacques Dupuis, "L'Église, le Regne de Dieu et les autres," in *Penser la Foi: Mélanges offerts à Joseph Moingt*, ed. J. Doré and C. Théobald (Paris: Cerf, 1993), 327-49.

9

Belonging or Identity?

Christian Faith in a Multi-Religious World

WERNER G. JEANROND

Christians belong to God and to each other in Christ. However, this basic orientation of Christian faith (cf. Jn 8:47; Rom 12:5; 1 Pt 2:9; Rv 7:10) has led to various forms of discipleship within the local frameworks of this world. Not only a large number of particular traditions of ecclesial formation, but also various strands of linguistic, geographical, social, philosophical, cultural, political, and economical existence contribute to the shape of every Christian's personal experience of belonging to *the* Christian tradition in this world. Yet any experience of Christian belonging is always already in need of being assessed in the light of this basic Christian vocation of belonging to God and to one another in Christ.

Thus, every Christian life takes place and is shaped in response to this vocation and the need to follow this vocation within the different traditions and communities that support it. Moreover, although Christian faith without the church is unthinkable, authentic discipleship can never be identified totally with one or the other church tradition. Rather, all ecclesial communities belonging to the Christian church need to be assessed in terms of how much they each belong to God and to one another in Christ. Hence, the ultimate criterion for evaluating all forms of Christian belonging is and remains *belonging to God and one another in Christ.*

However, even this ultimate criterion needs to be interpreted afresh in any given situation. What it means to belong to God and one another in Christ needs to be discerned within the churches. Moreover, this process of ecclesial discernment occurs within the larger horizon of the world in which all Christian faith praxis takes place, that is, finds its space, time, and expression. In that sense, Christians always already "belong" to a number of traditions and communities, however, this belonging is not understood in terms of ultimate belonging. Rather, Christian faith understands any form of belonging within this world as temporary and transient; however, this does not mean that it is insignificant or unimportant. Without belonging to the world, no form of Christian belonging can materialize in the first place. Therefore, we have to distinguish between *necessary belonging* and *ultimate belonging,* that is, between necessarily belonging to a context marked by space, time, sociality, and language, on the one hand, and ultimately belonging to God and one another in Christ within any such context, on the other hand. The tension that characterizes this multiple belonging of a Christian is eschatological: Christians live in this world, though orientated by their desire to participate in the eternal life that only God can give and that God has offered to humanity in Christ. Thus, Christian existence that can be said to be radically theocentric and christomorphic by nature requires forms of multiple belonging which, however, all stand under the judgment of this primary eschatological orientation. Therefore, multiple belonging is a necessary predicament of Christian existence, though all particular forms of belonging need to be assessed against the vocation of ultimate belonging.

It is thus evident that any consideration of the various forms of belonging as well as of ultimate belonging require hermeneutical decisions, that is, strategies of interpreting authentic forms of Christian life and of developing criteria of authenticity for Christian life. No form of human belonging can escape this hermeneutical predicament. That means no reference to the Bible, to tradition, to human reason, to divine revelation, or to any form of ecclesial teaching authority can ever remove the need to develop strategies of interpretation within the Christian church. The Christian hermeneutical task concerns not only the interpretation of texts and traditions, but also the interpretation of any attempt to define Christian identity in this world. Moreover, the world becomes itself an object in any act of interpretation that wishes to be conscious of its contextual complexities.

In the light of these initial observations I would like to discuss Christian belonging in three steps: (1) the ambiguity of the Christian tradition; (2) the impact of the present multi-religious context on the search for Christian identity; and, finally, (3) the problematic nature of any search for identity and the eschatological orientation of any form of authentic Christian belonging.

THE AMBIGUITY OF CHRISTIAN TRADITION

In a theological context, *tradition* has at least two different though related meanings: it may refer to the extra-biblical apostolic heritage in the church, or it may refer to the entire development of the Christian church until the present time.[1] Here I am more interested in the second meaning, though I shall pay less attention to the actual development of the different branches of the Christian church or to their doctrinal relations. Instead I wish to pursue a systematic analysis of the criteria that might help us to assess this development, its achievements and failures, and the need for reform and change.

Such a critical assessment of the larger Christian tradition is necessary today especially in response to the calls for church reform arising both from within the ecumenical movement and from interreligious encounter and dialogue, but also in order to meet expressions of suspicion both from outside and inside the Christian movement with regard to the theological legitimacy of our present ecclesial traditions. These and other questions concerning the identity of the Christian church have directed the attention of many theologians and church leaders toward reinterpreting the Christian tradition. Once again the Christian tradition has become an object of interpretation, at the same time when interpretation theory itself has become anew the focus of theological attention.

Since no interpretation is ever free of interests, it is important to discuss the spectrum of interests operative in a reinterpretation of tradition, a spectrum reaching from those approaches that aim at supporting any given ecclesial status quo to those that aim at critically examining the present situation of the Christian church. In many of the current debates in the churches (for example, the participation of lay people in the church, the role of women in church and ministry, the hierarchical constitution of ministry, attitudes toward gays and lesbians, interreligious encounter, and more) *tradition* is used either to protect the status quo or to challenge it.

Given this confusion about tradition as a resource for Christian praxis and theory, it must be the task of the theologian to serve the Christian community through attempting both to clarify the issues as far as possible and to develop adequate methods that will allow the churches to develop criteria for a critical and constructive examination of their common Christian heritage. The Christian faith must be critically and self-critically appropriated, and not just repeated, by every generation of Christians. The handing on of the gospel and the acts of appropriating it never make for a smooth process but always entail the emergence of new tensions. Therefore, the legitimacy of any given liturgical, personal, doctrinal, and communal manifestation of the Christian tradition has to be examined again and again. This process adds new life to the Christian movement and at the same time protects it against all forms of traditionalist incrustation.

The Christian church has repeatedly faced the need to develop a set of criteria of Christian authenticity. Whether in response to the Gnostic crisis, medieval legal thinking, the Protestant reformers' critique of the church in the sixteenth century, Enlightenment thinking, modernity and postmodernity, or the growing awareness of religious pluralism in our world, the resources of the Christian tradition, including the Bible, apostolic succession, doctrinal development, liturgical and contemplative praxis, and the conciliar movement, have been searched afresh in order to identify strands of authenticity and stability in the ongoing process of Christian ecclesial existence.[2]

These and other struggles for the official preservation of the Christian faith and the formal continuity of the church have always been in danger of becoming matters of ultimate concern in the church at the expense of the continuing and fearless experience of Christian faith in different times and cultural circumstances. Moreover, the concern for the intact preservation of Christian identity has often led to a kind of "colonial" attitude toward differing models of Christian praxis, especially toward those that differed from the models advocated by the European centers of the church. This Eurocentricity of Christian identity is rejected today by many non-Western and Western Christians alike. Moreover, occasional outbursts of neurotic anxiety of losing Christian identity and the authoritarian measures adopted by church authorities to prevent this from happening have ironically accelerated this very loss.

In our contemporary intellectual context and radically pluralistic cultural environ-ment no religious movement can be saved from decline or death through simplistic references to its old age (antiquity), or its formal continuity with the original apostolic witnesses to the originating event (succession), or episcopal or synodal agreements on its values (consensus).[3] In the eyes of contemporary men and women these criteria alone do not at all guarantee that a tradition merits further continuity. The possible and actual distortions and ideological features in Christian claims to tradition have only further burdened the ongoing search for Christian identity.

However, the most challenging critique comes from within the Christian tradition itself. It asks whether the strong concern for ecclesiastical continuity is not in itself a betrayal of the eschatological faith that God's reign is at hand. In other words, is the existence of a formally and institutionally organized church not only not a valid crite-rion but in itself a possible obstacle to authentic Christian praxis? The continuing examination of the attitudes toward the Holocaust that were adopted by the churches in Germany as well as by the Vatican puts new emphasis on that question.[4]

These observations of theological and ecclesiological challenges to the Christian tradition have drawn our attention once more to the necessity of a proper theological methodology to help us to understand the Christian vocation and message, but also to interpret the multidimensional context in which we are trying to grasp the heart of this Christian project today.

The context in which the current search for Christian authenticity takes place is marked by an increasing awareness and experience of religious pluralism. Christianity is not the only religious tradition claiming people's attention today, and previously homogenous Christian spaces are quickly developing into areas of a lively religious pluralism as a result of such factors as mass migration, easy international communica-tion, and globalization.[5]

Religious plurality and the increasing fragmentation of traditionally Christian societies, not only in the Northern and Western hemisphere of the world, have made it imperative for all adequate Christian theology to confront the task both of theologi-cally coming to terms with the fact that there exist other religious movements and of discussing their particular forms of worship of the divine, their view of human life, and their understanding of salvation. Parallel with this inner-Christian attention to other religions, we can witness an increasing actual encounter (not always peaceful) between different religions on a number of levels as well as an increasing number of interreligious dialogues on theological, parish, and hierarchical levels. Moreover, in the aftermath of the Holocaust, a new Christian awareness of the particular nature of Christian-Jewish relations has moved to the forefront of Christian conscience the question of to what extent Christian identity since the beginnings of the Christian church has been constructed at the expense of Judaism.

In the meantime, a number of official Roman Catholic and Protestant documents have significantly contributed to the Christian reassessment of other religions and opened the door widely for many forms of more comprehensive interreligious en-counters and dialogues.

It goes without saying that this new interreligious context has had an important effect on all current projects of redefining Christian identity. But before attending more closely to some examples of Christian responses to this new multi-religious and interreligious experience, I wish to emphasize once more the necessity for proper hermeneutical strategies when discussing the theological nature and the transformation of tradition in Christianity.

When we understand the Christian church not as a museum that displays once meaningful deposits, but as a living organism, then the practical tasks of all Christians will have to change accordingly. In such a living organism theologians function as interpreters of the always ambiguous tradition, of its experiences, insights, contributions, and failures. Moreover, theologians assess the context in which the Christian tradition articulates itself. And they must be critical of their own possible distortions, biases, and failures. Theologians will have to be careful not to become "intellectual tyrants."[6]

The best precaution against such a temptation may be the willingness to respect otherness and even radical otherness. That is to say, theologians must not understand appropriation of the multiform tradition as an act in which every text, every liturgy, every praxis, every phenomenon is interpreted in such a way that it fits their preunderstanding. Rather, by adopting critical and self-critical methods of interpretation, theologians ought to be prepared to challenge and transform their own preunderstandings and interpretative horizons.

The originating event of Christian faith, and thus of the Christian tradition as a whole, is accessible to us only thanks to and in spite of the Christian tradition itself. The Christian disciple of today encounters Jesus Christ and his particular theological initiatives through the various biblical witnesses and through the pluriform witness within the ongoing Christian movement. Hence, both of these encounters are pluralistic and ambiguous by nature. The pluralistic witness of the Christian tradition is, however, not without critical focus. And it is precisely the task of adequate theology to strive to articulate this focus again and again. It is then the task of the entire community of disciples to validate or challenge the always limited interpretations of this focus.

Any interpreter of the Christian tradition ought to realize that already the earliest witnesses had warned the Christian disciple of the possibility of ideological appropriations—that is, distortions—of the significance of Jesus Christ. The portrayal of Christ's disciples in Mark's gospel, for example, is full of dramatic corrections of false interpretations and anticipations of Christ's identity. The reader of the gospel is explicitly alerted to the temptation of reducing the gospel to his or her biased and limited perspective. Mark demands a new seeing, a new perspective from his readers. Analogically, the Christian disciple of today must be willing to interpret the apostolic tradition through always fresh and critical perspectives. As Mark's gospel emphasizes, the apostolic tradition itself is burdened by inauthentic acts of discipleship. The self-critical dimension of Markan and other New Testament texts has added to their "classic" character. That is to say, they have successfully resisted efforts of automatization, domestication, and manipulation by their hearers and readers.[7]

More reflections upon the need for critical and self-critical hermeneutical strategies are needed. But the above considerations of the pluralistic and ambiguous nature of the Christian tradition may have convinced the reader of the fact that the Christian community—the church—requires a continuous assessment of all its manifestations, including its doctrinal and other symbolic expressions. This assessment may well lead to a thorough rethinking of all the present criteria of ecclesial authenticity and to an always renewed search for more adequate understandings of and responses to Jesus Christ's call on Christians to participate in God's creative and redemptive project at work in the Christian church and—in spite of the manifestations of its own fallibility—through the church in the world.[8]

Any discussion of Christian belonging takes place within the framework of this pluriform and ambiguous Christian tradition. This tradition itself cannot offer ultimate belonging, but it can narrate and encourage concrete expressions of responses to God's offer of ultimate belonging in Christ. Moreover, this tradition's own search for identity takes place in a world where many religious forms of belonging are experienced and critically assessed.[9]

THE IMPACT OF THE GLOBAL MULTI-RELIGIOUS CONTEXT ON CHRISTIAN BELONGING

During the twentieth century we saw a shift in some of the Christian approaches to other religions. New and increasingly easier means of travel facilitated meetings among people from different religious backgrounds. Mass migration as a result of both the two World Wars and the sharp inequality in the distribution of labor and wealth in the world led to a much greater level of encounter between followers of different religions and of different traditions within one and the same religious movement. Formerly homogenous Christian countries or regions in the richer West underwent a transformation into increasingly multi-religious spaces.

Since the second part of the twentieth century individual Christians as well as entire churches have been willing to reassess their view of other religious traditions as well as of other Christian traditions. This opening toward the Christian "other" and the religious "other" has transformed traditional missionary paradigms and provided new challenges to the inner-Christian identity project. Christian identity can no longer be formulated without due attention to a new and more enlightened Christian ecumenism *ad intra* and a new and more enlightened Christian theology of religions *ad extra*.

One prominent example for an individual life's career at the interface between traditional missionary identity and a genuinely Christian openness toward an other religious tradition is the German-Japanese Jesuit Hugo M. Enomiya-Lassalle (1898-1990). In the words of his biographer Ursula Baatz, "Hugo Lassalle's journey is a bridge between the Christian spirituality of the past centuries and a new way of being a Christian."[10]

Long before the interreligious initiatives within the Roman Catholic Church since the Second Vatican Council opened the way for an officially encouraged encounter and dialogue between Catholic Christianity and other religious traditions, Lassalle began to explore Zen-Buddhist spirituality in Japan. He did not reflect first upon the theoretical viability of a meeting between Christian mysticism and Zen contemplation; rather, he entered into the meeting in a more direct and personal way (21).

After the normal Jesuit education Lassalle left Germany in 1929 in order to work as a missionary in Japan. His clear goal was to win Japanese men and women for

Christ (120). He quickly developed a great sensitivity for the subtlety of Japanese religiosity, language, and culture, and identified a number of in-depth connections between Christian faith and expressions of Japanese religiosity. His particular attention, however, was directed toward Zen. After 1943 Lassalle participated regularly in Zen meditation sessions under the guidance of prominent Japanese Zen masters. He saw no difficulty in interpreting his Zen experiences in the light of Christian praxis (124). As his diaries document, Zen was for him one means of purification on the inner journey toward spiritual perfection and sanctification (134).

Asceticism, according to the Christian monastic tradition, was a necessary way of preparing for total union with God; it was necessary for the purification of the soul from all worldly trappings. Both Buddhist masters of asceticism and Christian saints served Lassalle as examples for his own spiritual journey and for his teaching in Japan. Thus, the traditional mystical images of the ascent to the mountain, the image of the spiritual marriage from the Song of Songs, as well as the image of *kenosis* (self-emptying) inspired Lassalle's mystical-spiritual journey.

After the end of the Second World War Lassalle became a Japanese citizen. His Japanese name, Makibi Enomiya, connected him with Hiroshima, where he had survived the nuclear bomb's devastating destructiveness, and also with some of the roots of Japanese culture. Enomiya is the name of the Shinto-Shrine in Hiroshima, and Kibi no Makibi is the name of a Japanese reformer who lived in the eighth century. This reformer had been sent to study in China from where he returned with books, weapons, musical instruments, and Buddhist pictures and writings in order to promote further cultural development in Japan (175). In Hirsohima, Lassalle worked for the planning and construction of the Peace Memorial Church, which was built and finally inaugurated on August 6, 1954, the ninth anniversary of the nuclear bomb's explosion over that city.

In this article I cannot assess the implications of Lassalle's many religious, social, musical, and wider cultural and pedagogical initiatives in Japan and on behalf of the inter-cultural meeting between that country and the West. Rather, I wish to concentrate on his increasingly double religious belonging. Lassalle shared the curiosity of a number of Western religious persons, such as Thomas Merton and Henri Le Saux, for Eastern religious experiences and resources that could promote the renewal of the Christian mystical tradition. Moreover, in his longing to experience God as God, Lassalle was guided by the writings of the Jesuit founder Ignatius of Loyola, the Spanish mystics John of the Cross and Teresa of Avila, and the fourteenth-century mystic Jan van Ruysbroek, but increasingly also by his own Zen masters, among them Harada Roshi, Watanabe Genshu, Yamada Roshi, and others. However, he did not share the Buddhist interpretation of the experiences gained during the Zen sessions. Rather, he attempted to interpret these spiritual experiences in a Christian way. What he explored was thus the connection between the practice of Zen and Christian spirituality (244). Lassalle was fascinated by the possibilities Zen offered for the coordination of an active and a contemplative life and also by the in-depth dimensions of prayer that were revealed to him through the practice of Zen (249).

The neo-Scholastic Roman Catholic theological distinction between "natural religions," that is, the non-Christian religions, and "supernatural religion," that is,

Christianity, made it easier for Lassalle to integrate Zen into his own Christian spiri-tuality. Because the practice of Zen could be interpreted in terms of a natural way toward the supernatural goal (253), Lassalle became increasingly convinced that a liaison between Zen and Catholicism might be able to counteract the decay of values in Japan—and in the West (256).

Lassalle never advocated a mixture of Buddhism and Christian faith. Rather, he considered Zen to be a natural method not linked with a particular religious confes-sion and therefore explored its use within Christian faith (270). Lassalle tried to use Zen in order to deepen his own contemplation on Christ (273f.). In Zen he saw a path that leads away from the world and into the innermost of the human soul, a way that leads to a deeper experience of God.[11]

In spite of the clear expression of his belonging to Christ as the basis of his interest in Zen, Lassalle's enthusiasm was not shared by all of his Jesuit confrères in Japan or by some of the church authorities in Rome, although his fellow Jesuit in Japan, Pedro Arrupe, later general of the Jesuit order, never ceased to encourage Lassalle's attempts to develop a Japanese expression of Catholicism (283). Early in 1961 Rome forbade Lassalle to teach the "Zen method" either to Jesuits or to lay people. In addition, his book, *Zen—Weg zur Erleuchtung*, published in Vienna in the previous year, was blocked from further publication.[12]

In the 1960s, however, in spite of the Jesuit and Vatican efforts to squash Lassalle's attempts to integrate Zen into Japanese Christianity, his views spread in Europe and beyond. The new openness in the Roman Catholic Church following the Second Vatican Council provided further fertile ground for Lassalle's vision of interreligious encounter and spiritual symbiosis. His works appeared again in print and reached a wide readership.

Lassalle's personal longing to experience *kensho* (the experience of awakening) was not to be fulfilled until in 1974, when Yamada Roshi finally examined and confirmed Lassalle's *kensho* (358f.). As a result of this confirmation Lassalle could embark further on the path of Zen, now attending to koan-praxis. Once again, Lassalle emphasized that the practice of Zen has nothing to do with Buddhist philosophy. A glance at the collection of koans he recommended in his preface to a book by Yamada Roshi will easily confirm this. However, to follow the path of Koan certainly involved another option than to embrace the worldview of Scholastic philosophy. The question that was to trouble Lassalle during his last years, therefore, very much concerned the shape of Christian theology: What remains of Christian religion if one sheds two thousand years of theological tradition built upon and around the Christian gospels? We can ask, Who is the Christ to whom Lassalle wished to belong, and what does it mean to be a Christian? (365f.).

In the 1970s the practice of Zen became very successful in the West, yet at the same time questions regarding the compatibility between Zen and Christian faith were raised anew. Is Zen dangerous for Christians? Hans Urs von Balthasar warned against the practice of Asian meditation and called it a betrayal of Christian faith. He asked how the Asian unity mysticism and its world-denying attitude could ever be reconciled with the Christian affirmation of the creation made possible by Christ's incarnation.[13]

Ursula Baatz, however, notes that von Balthasar did not realize that neither Buddhism nor Hinduism teaches that the world would need to be negated in order for human beings to experience the absolute (381).

Lassalle never questioned the potential of Zen meditation for Christians, although he was aware that theological problems needed to be addressed. He remained faithful to his original intuition that Zen paved the way for a deeper experience of God, an experience so necessary in a rationalistic age (390). Christian theology had neglected the dimension of both mysticism and a spiritual anthropology. Like his fellow Jesuit Karl Rahner, Lassalle therefore stressed the importance of a deeper spiritual experience for every Christian.[14]

Moreover, Lassalle was keen to free our word *God* from all those images and conceptions that hide the experience of that which cannot be signified by name, the absolute, the unending, the incomprehensible, the all-encompassing. Through zazen, Lassalle had been able concretely to experience the very mystery of God of which Christian dogmatics speaks (398).

The question whether or not Zen is compatible with Christian faith has remained important for many Christians—even after Lassalle's death in 1990. At the end of his life Lassalle had no doubt whatsoever that Zen was one way toward a better understanding of God and Christ. Union with God was Lassalle's aim, and he did not accept the boundaries that traditional Western Christian thinking tried to impose on his own search for that mystical union in Japan. He paid a high price for his Zen mysticism, yet he grew firmer in his experience of the objectless reality of God. Hence, Christian identity was no longer a concern for the mature Lassalle. Of course, until the end of his life he tried to find Christian expressions, mostly from the mystical tradition, for his own experiences of God, yet it was the union with God and Christ that ultimately concerned and moved him and not any kind of Christian-identity project.

The priest who once set out to win souls for Christ in Japan had been able to grow in Japan toward a new experience of God's presence thanks to a particularly Japanese movement of contemplation. He appreciated "that the oriental religions had been able to use the natural energies of the human person better than Christianity had done."[15]

Lassalle returned to Europe in order to share the meditative practice and spiritual wisdom that he had personally gained in Japan with a great number of people through his lectures, his Zen sessions, his publications, and his wide-ranging correspondence. There was no doubt in Lassalle's mind as to the primary nature of religious experience. Theology always came in the second place and was not to be allowed to destroy or endanger the personal exploration of God's presence through prayer and meditation.

Lassalle's journey is far from unique as far as the Western Christian search for wisdom in Japan or other parts of Asia is concerned. A significant number of Western Christians have since moved to Japan in order to explore the possibilities of a Japanese-inspired renewal of Christian mysticism and theology.[16]

Moreover, many European and American Christians have moved to India, Sri Lanka, Taiwan, and other Asian countries in order to experience God in new depth.[17]

Thomas Merton's recovery of the contemplative tradition for ordinary Christians and his explorations of Asian religiosity would need to be assessed more fully in this context than is possible here. Hence a few hints must suffice. "As Merton looked at

Zen, he understood it as helpful to Christians precisely because it was a way to release the dominating hold, so prevalent in the West, of the exterior or illusory self, the individual or the empirical ego, on the whole person. Zen offers a way of releasing the inner, metaphysical, natural self that is the substratum for what Christianity describes as the action of grace or the 'birth of Christ' in the person."[18]

As with Lassalle, Merton's interest in the spiritual practices of the East concerned their particular approach to consciousness. Merton did not set out for Asia in order to transform Christian theology. Of course, this transformation will unavoidably follow as a result of any deeper exploration of Eastern views of the human self.[19]

Merton was interested in uncovering the spiritual wisdom of the religions. Yet "Merton's search, however open to the thought worlds and the categories of other traditions, was that of a monk who remained convinced that the monastic experience had something important to offer the ordinary readers in the West for whom he wrote."[20]

Neither Merton nor Lassalle ever questioned their belonging to God in Christ and to the community of Christian disciples. However, though in often quite different ways, they very much questioned some of the philosophical trappings and ecclesial expressions which that belonging had received in Christian history. Both fought against false consciousness in church and society and attempted to offer ways of penetrating toward a deeper, non-clinging attention to God, self and world. Thus, they problematized the very notion of a Christian identity.

IDENTITY AND BELONGING IN CHRISTIAN FAITH

Why do Christians search for their identity? What is identity? In order to answer these questions it might be useful to distinguish among various identity projects. First of all, identity can refer to continuity. A person or even a movement may seek to identify aspects of continuity that allow that person or movement to be recognized over a period of time. One might also speak here of the character of a person or of a movement, for example, the Christian church.[21]

Second, identity can be sought by persons or movements themselves, or it could be established by others. For instance, we have no direct access to the character of Jesus. Instead we are dependent on the gospels' narrative strategies in order to ascribe Jesus a character or to establish his identity. Moreover, we are dependent on certain strategies and acts of reading, in order to receive the narratives offered to us as hearers or readers, as believers, or as academics.[22]

Although we have no direct access to the identity of Jesus, the biblical and post-biblical texts formulate aspects of Christian identity. This is done both in terms of descriptions of Christian vocation and in terms of confronting Christian ways of responding to God and to other ways of religious behavior, for instance, the Jewish way. More and more it had been emphasized that Christians were not Jews and that the New Testament was not the same as the Old, although it has always been recognized that Christians stand in a unique relationship with Jews and that both Testaments need to be read together. Moreover, the church fathers stressed the differences between Christian and Gnostic *gnosis*, between orthodox and heretical faith. Identity thus may be constructed in order to highlight difference and to erect boundaries against other traditions. However, it might also be appreciated as a task, a public task linked to the search for truth over against a mere private esoteric inner discovery.

Third, the search for identity could involve a genuine reflection upon one's own personal vocation and religious authenticity or upon the corporate search to retrieve and renew the vocation and faithfulness of the entire Christian movement or of its various branches. Any search for Christian identity is contextual and therefore necessarily limited in scope. Different linguistic, religious, geographical, social, gender-related, theological, philosophical, cultural, political, emancipatory, and other aspects are operative in such a search for Christian identity at any given time and place. Against those theoreticians that claim that human beings are determined or bound by their tradition or language it needs to be stressed, first, that men, women, and children are well able to cross borders, to move into new languages and traditions, and to overcome boundaries, and second, that traditions may be transformed from within. Hugo Enomiya-Lassalle is one example of such a personal cross-border transformation. The Christian church itself can be seen as an example of such a corporate cross-cultural movement. It entered the Hellenistic world and was transformed in the process. Today it is being transformed in the process of entering the Asian, the African, and the Pacific worlds.

Fourth, it is always necessary to reflect upon the interests that motivate any search for identity. Does one look for a renewed personal or corporate identity in order to organize a defense against challenges from outside or inside? Does one look for identity in order to retrieve basic characteristics that have been lost over time? Does one look for identity in order to find orientation in new and different contexts in which one has not lived or functioned before? Does one search for a renewal of identity in order to promote personal and communal development? Does one wish to define identities in order to draw clear boundaries against "others"? Does one believe to be able to distill pure identities not affected by body, context, time, and the other factors mentioned above? And finally, who in any family, community, or church has the power to define identity for the whole group or tradition? Who restores repressed identities?[23]

It has become evident that any identity search is a second-order operation loaded with questions and problems. Moreover, searching for Christian identity in any cultural context of our world (past, present, and future) is a complex, multidimensional exercise. The Christian encounter of and dialogue with other religions have challenged the traditional Christian self-understanding, but at the same time promoted new demands for the secure establishment of markers of Christian identity in today's world. Since the middle of the last century, efforts to retrieve the essentials of Christian revelation have characterized the theological search for Christian identity. Since the middle of the 1980s the Trinity has been treated by some theologians as the ultimate sign of Christian identity.[24]

It has even been suggested that the Trinity "is the transcendental condition of interfaith dialogue with the Other."[25]

There can be no doubt that both themes—revelation and the Trinity—are of great significance for Christian self-understanding: How to treat of God's self-communication and of its reception in history, and how to understand the particular Christian approach to God are both important tasks for Christian thinking. Yet, the challenge of Zen to Christian theology undercuts both theological efforts. For Zen asks whether human consciousness and identity formation are adequate approaches to God in the first place. To be sure, Zen does not deny the importance of theological thinking, but it adds a question mark to its Western foundations and thus reopens the discussion of how essential one particular cultural tradition is for the dynamics of Christian belonging to God and to each other in Christ.

The discovery of Zen by Christians and the retrieval of Christianity's own apophatic traditions as a result of the meeting between Western Christianity and Japanese Zen show how creative the interreligious encounter can be. They shed new light on the complex search for Christian identity. Moreover, even on the theoretical level of the Western encounter with Buddhism, new insights into the understanding of the self are opened up for Christian thinking. David Tracy offers the following summaries: "Perhaps the greatest affinity between much French deconstructive and Kyoto Buddhist thought is the common insistence on the illusionary character of the self and thereby of any modern Western attempt to use that self to ground or provide a foundation for 'reality.' . . . The anti-dialectics of the deconstructionists celebrate difference and the anti-dialectical dialectics of the Kyoto school signal non-duality."[26]

Tracy appreciates that "the Buddhist way forces modern Westerners to confront our cultural and psychological notions of ego, self, and subject beyond the usual alternatives."[27]

Tracy is fully aware that the Christian-Buddhist dialogue has a number of difficult differences to confront and discuss. Nevertheless, he welcomes the opportunities not only to get to know the other in the other tradition and that tradition as other, but also to learn how to retrieve repressed or forgotten strands in our own Christian tradition.[28]

In the context of his famous discussion of "anonymous Christianity" Karl Rahner stated that even Christians must consider themselves as anonymous Christians. That means that even they are not in full possession of their Christian identity but on the way toward an always deeper participation in and more explicit expression of the salvific nature of the divine mystery.[29]

Belonging to God and to one another in Christ is the basic Christian orientation, according to the New Testament. We have seen that this orientation has been interpreted very differently throughout the Christian tradition, a tradition whose ambiguities but also whose abilities to stimulate a new awareness of God's self-disclosure in Christ have become evident. We have also seen that the christomorphic nature of Christian faith in God describes a way of ultimate belonging. However, this ultimate belonging must not only be proclaimed but lived, celebrated, and shared in the different and shifting contexts of this world. As the example of Enomiya-Lassalle has demonstrated, every form of ultimate belonging must be embodied and at the same time tested and transformed in the different ways of explorative belonging. And in this regard the dynamic meeting between Christian faith in God and other religious approaches to God and/or Ultimate Reality seems to be very promising indeed for all participants.

In order to be transformed by God, human beings as well as religious communities need to expose themselves critically and self-critically to the other in the other and to the other in their own selves and traditions. The Christian traditions not only provide many examples of failed meetings with human otherness and with the radical otherness of God, but they also offer important orientation and encouragement for this lifelong spiritual journey. When the resurrected crucified Lord meets his former disciples after his violent death, to be sure a meeting that dramatically transformed all known religious knowledge and tradition, he asked them not to be afraid. He pointed to his identity (in the sense of continuity and identifiability) with his former self, though an identity now utterly transformed by God's surprising action. Moreover, he invited a deeper and lasting form of belonging, a belonging that does not bind the individual disciple to any image of the past, but a belonging that inspires the disciple to follow Christ to the radical transformation God has been preparing for anyone who wishes to belong to God.

Belonging to God, however, does not mean to assume Christ's own identity. Rather, it means, as the Markan Jesus tells the crowd after he—in no uncertain terms—had rebuked Peter's misinterpretation of discipleship: "If any want to become my followers, let them deny themselves and take up their cross and follow me" (Mk 8: 34).

Christian belonging is always dynamic; it is open to God's transformative action. This eschatological nature of Christian faith frees Christians from all forms of narrow definitions of identity and forms of cozy or neurotic belonging to their tradition. They do not need to be afraid to meet their own otherness or the otherness of others, for their ultimate project is not to stabilize their own selves but to belong to God and one another in Christ and prepare themselves for God's transformative actions in all of their life as well as in the entire universe.[30]

CONCLUSION

The search for a better and deeper praxis of Christian belonging to God and to one another in Christ must continue. The praxis of Christian belonging requires both concrete steps and thorough efforts of critical reflection as well as constructive religious imagination. One inspiring example for the ongoing exploration of multiple belonging on the way toward ultimate belonging to God and each other in Christ is SEIMEIZAN, a Christian-Buddhist place for prayer and interreligious dialogue on the Southern Japanese island of Kyushu.[31]

This monastic settlement has the form of a branch temple *(Seimeizan Betsuin)* of the Buddhist Albert Schweitzer Temple nearby. Thus, this Christian monastery as a branch of the Buddhist Temple witnesses to the network of prayer and meditation inspired by multiple belonging. Among the different levels of contemporary interreligious dialogue, that is, dialogue of life, of works, of theological exchanges, and of religious experiences, at SEMEIZAN one has opted for the latter form, a dialogue of "religious experience," "where the partners, in mutual respect and sincere friendship, but also in total faithfulness to each one's tradition, express to one another their religious experience, especially in the form of prayer or those symbolic-ritual forms which alone can make visible, through material signs, the invisible, inner, religious life and its mystery. It is here, at this level, that each religious tradition reaches its purest identity and expresses it in the most adequate way."[32]

The founder of SEMEIZAN, Franco Sottocornola, thus expresses the intimate link between the *gift* of pure identity and the prayerful transformation of either tradition. Organizing the different prayer sessions by incorporating the subtle Japanese attention to nature and by combining a special emphasis on silence, both Christian and Buddhist prayers may become richer and open the heart of the praying person. "The practice and the attitude of 'prayer' makes all those who are involved in it aware that they are not dealing with something that 'belongs to them' or that *they* are going to decide about: we are called to be faithful servants of the Truth, and humble disciples of Love. Prayer will open our hearts to the grace needed for this marvelous mission."[33]

NOTES

[1] In this section I draw on some reflections in my book *Theological Hermeneutics: Development and Significance* (London: SCM, 1994), 165-82.

[2] See ibid., chaps. 2, 3, 6, 7.

[3] Antiquity, universality, and consensus were the criteria recommended by Vincent of Lérins (see his *Commonitory*, in *A Select Library of Nicene and Post-Nicene Fathers of the Christian Church*, 2d series, vol. 9 (Oxford: James Parker; New York: The Christian Literature Company, 1894), 127-59. References to the uninterrupted succession of ministerial authority in the church have been made by, among others, Irenaeus of Lyons (see his *Adversus Haereses*, 5 vols., Sources Chrétiennes (Paris: Cerf, 1965-82). Cf. Jeanrond, *Theological Hermeneutics*, 18-26.

[4] See Michael Phayer, *The Catholic Church and the Holocaust, 1930-1965* (Bloomington and Indianapolis, Ind.: Indiana University Press, 2000).

[5] See Robert J. Schreiter's analysis in his book *The New Catholicity: Theology between the Global and the Local* (Maryknoll, N.Y.: Orbis Books, 1997), 1-27.

[6] See Stephen Sykes, *The Identity of Christianity: Theologians and the Essence of Christianity from Schleiermacher to Barth* (London: SPCK, 1984), 7.

[7] For a discussion of the notion of a classic, see David Tracy, *The Analogical Imagination: Christian Theology and the Culture of Pluralism* (New York: Crossroad, 1981), chap. 3; and Werner G. Jeanrond, *Text and Interpretation as Categories of Theological Thinking*, trans. Thomas J. Wilson (New York: Crossroad, 1988), 133-42.

[8] For a closer examination of the different dimensions of the Christian church see Werner G. Jeanrond, *Call and Response: The Challenge of Christian Life* (New York: Continuum, 1995).

[9] See also Robert Schreiter's reflection upon theological criteria for Christian identity in *The New Catholicity*, 81-83.

[10] Ursula Baatz, *Hugo M. Enomiya-Lassalle: Ein Leben zwischen den Welten* (Zurich and Düsseldorf: Benziger Verlag, 1998), 8. All translations from this work are my own. Numbers within the text refer to pages in this work.

[11] In his most famous book, *Zen—Weg zur Erleuchtung: Einführung und Anleitung* (Freiburg im Breisgau: Herder Taschenbuch, 1992 [1960]), Hugo M. Enomiya-Lassalle clearly stated his Christian intentions. See, for example, page 73.

[12] It was republished, however, as soon as the Second Vatican Council changed the official orientation of the church in these matters, and it has since appeared in many editions and translations.

[13] Cf. Baatz, *Hugo M. Enomiya-Lassalle*, 381. Ursula Baatz refers to Hans Urs von Balthasar's article "Meditation als Verrat," *Geist und Leben* 50 (1977), 260-68.

[14] See Karl Rahner, *Schriften zur Theologie*, vol. 7 (Einsiedeln, Zurich, Cologne: Benziger, 1966), 22.

[15] Enomiya-Lassalle, *Zen—Weg zur Erleuchtung,* 86 (my translation).

[16] See ibid., 89-100.

[17] See the account of this movement in Michael von Brück and Whalen Lai, *Buddhismus und Christentum: Geschichte, Konfrontation, Dialog* (Munich: Beck, 1997). For an example of a Western woman meeting Zen in Taiwan, see Meister Hsin Tao, *Weisheit und Barmherzigkeit,* ed. Maria Reis Habito [German edition] (Adyar, 2001), esp. the introduction by Maria Reis Habito, 7-49.

[18] Anne E. Carr, *A Search for Wisdom and Spirit: Thomas Merton's Theology of the Self* (Notre Dame, Ind.: University of Notre Dame Press, 1988), 88.

[19] Cf. ibid., 89.

[20] Ibid., 94f.

[21] In this section I draw on some of the thoughts presented in Hermann Häring, Maureen Junker-Kenny, and Dietmar Mieth, eds., *Creating Identity, Concilium* 36 (2000/2), esp. Hille Haker, "Narrative and Moral Identity in Paul Ricoeur," 59-68.

[22] For a theological discussion of reading theories, see Werner G. Jeanrond, *Text and Interpretation as Categories of Theological Thinking,* chap. 2; and Jeanrond, *Theological Hermeneutics,* chap. 5.

[23] See Felix Wilfred, "Identity: Suppressed, Alienated, Lost," in Häring et al., *Creating Identity,* 31-38.

[24] Cf. Gavin D'Costa, *The Meeting of Religions and the Trinity* (Maryknoll, N.Y.: Orbis Books, 2000). See Werner G. Jeanrond, "Revelation and the Trinitarian Concept of God: Are They Key Concepts for Theological Thought?" in *God: Experience and Mystery,* ed. Werner G. Jeanrond and Christoph Theobald, *Concilium* 2001/1 (London: SCM, 2001), 120-30.

[25] Kevin J. Vanhoozer, "Does the Trinity Belong in a Theology of Religions?" in *The Trinity in a Pluralistic Age: Theological Essays on Culture and Religion,* ed. Kevin J. Vanhoozer (Grand Rapids, Mich.: Eerdmans, 1997), 41-71, esp. 68.

[26] David Tracy, *Dialogue with the Other: The Inter-Religious Dialogue* (Louvain: Peeters, 1990), 70f.

[27] Ibid., 75.

[28] Cf. ibid., 94. See also David Tracy, "Kenosis, Sunyata, and the Trinity: A Dialogue with Masao Abe," in *The Emptying God: A Buddhist-Jewish-Christian Conversation,* ed. John B. Cobb, Jr., and Christopher Ives (Maryknoll, N.Y.: Orbis Books, 1990), 135-54.

[29] Cf. Karl Rahner, *Schriften zur Theologie,* vol. 5 (Einsiedeln, Zurich, Cologne: Benziger, 1962), 136-58; *Schriften zur Theologie,* vol. 9, 2d ed. (Einsiedeln, Zurich, Cologne: Benziger, 1972), 498-515; and *Schriften zur Theologie,* vol. 10 (Einsiedeln, Zurich, Cologne: Benziger, 1972), 531-46.

[30] For a broader discussion of the eschatological nature of Christian faith, see Werner G. Jeanrond, *Gudstro: Teologiska reflexioner* (Lund: Arcus, 2001), 13-31.

[31] Franco Sottocornola, "SEMEIZAN: A Place for Prayer and Interreligious Dialogue in Japan," *Svensk Teologisk Kvartalskrift* 75 (1999), 118-25.

[32] Ibid., 120. In SEMEIZAN the visitor discovers quickly that from prayer flows a deep commitment both to the service of hospitality and to a number of social projects that are undertaken in communion with the Buddhist Schweitzer Temple (see ibid., 122-24).

[33] Ibid., p. 125.

10

On Christian Identity
Who Is a Christian?

RAIMON PANIKKAR

For whoever wishes to save one's own life will lose it;
yet whoever loses one's own life for my sake, will find it.

—MATT. 16:25[1]

This entire study is a meditation on this text.[2] A free translation of it would be: "Whoever cares to preserve one's own identity is lost; whoever gives it up for my sake, will attain the true identity"—which for the christians is called the christian identity.

IDENTITY IN PLURALISM

The question is double: *Who* is a christian? and *what* is a christian? A purely 'subjective' or a merely 'objective' answer will not do justice to the problem. We shall have to blend the two together and take a standpoint which overcomes the modern philosophical split between subject and object. Who and what is a christian is answered neither by a personal subjective feeling nor by an impersonal objective doctrine.[3]

Furthermore, the answers are manifold. There is no single answer as to who a christian is or what the christian identity may be.[4] The answer to the question of christian identity is in fact pluralistic. What does it mean? A strictly univocal answer condemns all the other answers as inadequate or even false, while an equivocal answer

---

To accommodate the author's desire to bring into his writing experience and insights derived in usage and linguistic structures he has encountered in Sanskrit, German, Greek, Latin, English, Italian, Spanish, and Catalonian—to name just a few of the languages Professor Panikkar speaks and works in—this chapter has not been forced to conform to American or British English language conventions.

would not be an answer at all. But the answer is not even analogous. If we were to succeed in finding a deeper or a common core underlying all the plural answers, then this *primum analogatum* would become the basis for a super-system, which would in turn reduce the plural answers to mere psychological or sociological variations on one and the abstract core. Christianity cannot be reduced to an abstraction. We would then have a mere perspectivism and not take seriously the different opinions. The problem is then simply transferred, for we may equally ask why one perspective is better or broader than another. If the question has many answers involving thinkers, people saint and plain, who for two millennia have given different interpretations, we have a case of true pluralism. Indeed, if the answer were only objective there would be no contradiction in defending a single true answer, say the roman catholic answer. But even then the most strict roman catholic answer has changed substantially along the ages—up to the most recent times: we may adduce the excommunications of non-catholics as a single example. And this very "strict catholic orthodoxy" forbids to abide by the last official document of the hierarchy which contradicts previous official statements.

In short, the answer has to be a pluralistic answer, but this is not an easy task. It implies embarking on a way of thinking which overcomes the above-mentioned split between objectivity and subjectivity.

I would like to venture a pluralistic approach. Pluralism, by definition, does not admit of *a* pluralistic system. Pluralism belongs to the order of the *mythos* and not of the *logos*. We speak of pluralism not when we discover a plurality of possible answers to a problem but when, while recognizing that these answers may be mutually incompatible, we find we cannot deny their legitimacy given a certain standpoint, albeit one which we cannot accept intellectually.[5] Pluralism is a fact which challenges rational analysis. It allows us to discover our own personal and collective contingency.

In the Eucharistic Congress of Bombay, 1964, after affirming that christians have no monopoly on goodness, truth, or salvation, I proceeded to describe a christian as "a conscious collaborator with Christ in the threefold function of creating, redeeming and glorifying the world." On that occasion I was trying to speak from within the broadly acceptable christian myth.

We may agree that a christian is somebody who acknowledges a special relation to Jesus Christ, but the understanding of this relation is not interpreted in any univocal way and the analogy cannot go beyond the formal or structural contents of the word "relation".

Karl Rahner's efforts to find a general basis for his "transcendental Christology" depend not only on the postkantian and evolutionary mentality of modern western Man, but also on a maximalist position that many christians would not accept and would even refuse to acknowledge as being implicit in their "christian belief".[6] Many would declare themselves christians without necessarily admitting that Christ is the "absolute Saviour" and even without giving to Christ a metaphysically central place.[7] A certain type of christian humanist would consider Christ a great human master of the western civilization along with others and would not accept the metaphysical claims of the major orthodox traditions of the past. It is a well-known fact, especially in modern times, that many people, in particular intellectuals, acknowledge Jesus Christ and reject explicitly christianity.[8]

At the very outset I should prevent a misunderstanding. I do not minimize in any way the importance of the doctrinal contents of the christian identity, but history shows and "sociology of knowledge" highlights that at any given point in time (and I would add in space as well) there are prevalent myths which make plausible and even evident doctrines which are contested or forgotten in other times and places. Nor am I denying the role of authority to declare what is orthodox and what is heterodox. This is not our question. I am approaching the fundamental theological and philosophical problem stated in the title.

A THESIS BY *WAY OF HYPOTHESIS*

The problem of human identity is a thorny and thoroughly debated philosophical problem.[9] The question of identity in self-conscious beings entails self-identity. Human identity cannot be satisfied with external marks. It is not just "objective". It has to be *self*-identity. But it cannot be merely "subjective".[10] It consists of the conscious and somewhat never-ending search for 'something': a self or a non-self, which will guarantee the unity or at least the continuity of the person. I say never-ending because the question of human identity inevitably leads to the impossible enterprise of individual self-awareness: It is the I asking for its own 'I'.[11] But this assumes already an I asking for a 'me'—supposedly identical to the I. Identity is, in the final analysis, not the result of one's particular reflection upon it (self-identity depends on my underlying notion of self), but the radical fact of that reflection (the myth underlying my 'self-consciousness'). Ultimately our thesis addresses a particular instance of a more general problematic concerning the peculiar nature of the human being *(Dasein)* as distinct from any other entities. I shall not, however, pursue this line of inquiry but concentrate rather on our concrete question.

The thesis runs like this: *the criterion for christian identity lies ultimately in the sincere confession of a person, validated by a corresponding recognition of a community.*

In other words, the question of christian identity cannot be resolved if it is formulated in the form of "*what* is a christian?", or in the form: "*Who* is a christian?". *A christian is one who both confesses oneself to be such and as such is accepted by a community* (usually christian). More pointedly: I am a christian if I sincerely confess to being one (subjective factor) and am accepted as such by a community (objective element). The point I am making is that christian identity is an existential fact and not just an essential feature. Thus, it does not need a perennially fixed *context*, nor always the same minimum of *text* (doctrine). Christian identity expresses itself differently in different times and places, according precisely to the peculiar self-understanding of both individual and community.

The problem is painfully acute for catholic identity which was based for a long time on merely objective grounds, probably in order to counterbalance the predominantly subjective protestant answer. Many a disorientation after Vatican II may have its cause in this fact. What or who is a catholic? We shall approach the question in its christian generality. The catholic answer will be just a corollary.

Our thesis affirms that what constitutes christian identity is the sincere personal confession, *martyría*, which finds a positive resonance in a community. It is neither the *mere* whim of an individual or group claiming to be "christian" (if no other individual or group accepts it) nor is it a matter of *merely* doctrinal statements—*necessary as these statements are in any given situation*. Nor is there any christian identity without knowing it. It has to be human self-identity—and therefore conscious.[12]

If I am right in this thesis, the consequences are far-reaching indeed. But I shall restrict myself to clarifying this theologumenon. Before doing so, we shall have to reflect a little on the pluralistic situation at the root of our present-day crisis in christian identity. After analyzing the thesis I shall conclude with some philosophical reflections followed by other, more theological, considerations.

THE PLURALISTIC GENESIS

When a single myth hovers almost palpably over a culture, forming as it were a horizon in terms of which truth and reality can be defined, there is little doubt as to who is a christian and what christian identity means. Either the question does not arise, so thoroughly the answer is taken for granted, or *orthodoxy* proclaims itself the undisputed criterion, with all the refinements that theologians may consequently append to the central fact of a universally recognized orthodoxy accepted as christian identity. Orthodoxy is considered the true mirror of *orthopraxis*, which constitutes the practical and existential aspect of religion. In times of a unified myth, orthodoxy becomes the crucial criterion, not necessarily due to a cartesian identification of the true nature of Man with reason, but rather to the lack of differentiation between the *doxa* and the integral human being. In such a time *orthodoxy* is so much taken for granted in its fundamental tenets, that a denial of these tenets is seen as tantamount to a denial of plain humanness. The heretic was and still is condemned not because he holds false ideas, but because of the contumacy of existentially persevering in an allegedly de-humanizing, i.e. in itself damning attitude.

This is not the modern problem because christians recognize different models of and loci for orthodoxy. Ways of thinking have been disentangled from ways of being. This, of course, has to be defended by all those who hold that "christianity claims to transcend cultures and find expression in a variety of cultures".[13] This feature has been common since (at least) the schisms of the XI and especially the XVI centuries. Heresy and apostasy are well-studied phenomena.[14] But today the problem arises mainly because the very conception of orthodoxy does not seem to be sufficient for christian identity; so polyvalent has it become, and to some so irrelevant, that it offers no common foothold and certainly no criterion of identity.[15] If the *ortho-doxa* of a particular church has become problematic, that of the sum of the different christian groups is patently nonexistent. If by an artificial "tour de force" one could extract some rather vague common denominator of all christian beliefs at a given time, by the next decade there might well appear another "christian" church which would belie the hypothesis.[16] What then makes a christian christian?

The question applies with special pungency to roman catholicism because the apparently monolithic block of one single doctrine held by 800 million catholics has collapsed.[17] How can a single person, the Supreme Pontiff, have *immediate* jurisdiction over almost a billion individuals?

Orthodoxy refers to belief, while faith transcends the doctrinal realm. We distinguish *faith* as a constitutive human dimension, namely that dimension which keeps us constantly open to a 'plus', an 'other', or simply to 'transcendence', from *belief* as the articulation of our ultimate convictions.[18] If faith, then, is no privilege of the christian, what kind of belief makes a christian a christian? It all depends on where we draw the line at any given point in time and space. The thesis I am proposing affirms that *from a doctrinal standpoint* there is no absolute and everlasting criterion as to where to put the christian 'boundaries'. Life is constant change.

We all know many people today—but we could as well cite a C.G. Jung, B. Russell, B. Croce, A. Gide or J. Ortega y Gasset and also Simone Weil and M. Heidegger (to draw from the european generation immediately preceding our own)—who have declared themselves non-christians because they were unable to accept what they considered essential to the christian tradition.[19] And yet, we could easily adduce followers of all the thinkers just mentioned who declare themselves christians because they see no contradiction between their own beliefs (often even those of their masters) and the christian tradition. How to explain such a change?

In point of fact, there are today christians who believe in the nicean creed, others who reinterpret it in such a way which amounts to not accepting it, and some who straight-forwardly reject it as obsolete. People declare themselves christian marxists, christian atheists, hindu-christians, and so on, a development unheard of only a few decades ago. Just where is the line to be drawn?

Our thesis is that there is no everlasting doctrinal line to draw. We need only to look at history in order to witness the retrieval of the boundaries of orthodoxy. We are beginning to witness in christianity something which is almost a commonplace in some other traditions, notably the hindu one. A hindu is not constituted by her views or beliefs ("orthodoxy"), but rather by that person's more or less explicit or implicit 'confession', by her practice of being a hindu, and her acceptance by a hindu community. It is well known that a theist, a deist, a polytheist, an atheist, etc., all can be hindus without finding any conflict or contradiction therein. But then, it will be objected, christianity is not a religion like hinduism. Nevertheless, there hardly remains a baptist, a presbyterian, an 'orthodox' or a 'catholic' who will today contest the propriety of calling christian those who do not happen to belong to their particular persuasion. Religions are existential facts, not merely doctrinal systems. This does not deny, I repeat, that at any given time christian existence 'incarnates' itself in particular doctrines, intellectual statements, dogmas, rituals and the like. Let us not forget that the first christian creeds were called *symbols* (of the Apostles) and not conceptual doctrines.

Who then is a christian, if the name cannot be given any *particular doctrinal* content? To go back to a purely ontic, karmic or metaphysical reality totally independent of our consciousness will not do either. To say, for instance, that every baptized person is a christian—like anyone born of a hindu father is a hindu, or any person born of a jewish mother is a jew—i.e., to reduce christian identity to a biological or material act, even if the fact is deemed to be sacramental, is hardly convincing nowadays. To say this does not imply necessarily disputing the efficacy of a sacramental act, the power of a metabiological karma, or the reality of blood relations. All these are valid issues, although perhaps debatable on other grounds. The reason such an opinion is unacceptable is, first of all, the bare fact that many undisputed christians today—who will even quote Scripture in their favour—do not accept this opinion. Some may not go so far as affirming that the "baptism of desire" is not (obviously) the desire for baptism, but rather the baptism of any authentic desire. Yet many christians after Peter and Paul would not stifle the work of the Spirit by imposing some sort of christian circumcision. Baptism is certainly not christian circumcision (Acts 15:1ff.).

Secondly—and most important from our point of view—once we have become aware of the problem, i.e. once we raise the very question of christian identity, a merely material fact will not suffice. If we are to say, continuing our example, that a christian is a baptized person, then in order to accept this answer we are obliged to interpret it. But in this very interpretation, the ontic fact becomes ontological and thus subject to a variety of interpretations. In other words, once we ask about christian identity, this identity can no longer remain a mere fact of which the subject is unaware. Even if this were 'the' answer, consciousness of it has already crept into the supposedly bare fact for those who support this thesis and superimpose it on others.

Stretching—even straining—the meaning of words, we may speak of the identity of a stone, meaning by this its singularity, which may be determined irrespective of however the stone might (per impossible) identify itself. "Per impossible", because if there were the slightest possibility that the stone could identify itself, then it would be illegitimate to ignore that self-identification. We cannot reduce human identity to such a merely objectifiable characteristic; the stone has singularity but not individuality, specificity but not identity. Identity here implies the individuality of that particular being which recognizes itself for what it believes to be.[20]

ANALYSIS OF *THE THESIS*

The two parts of our thesis mutually condition each other and are, properly speaking, not separable. I could hardly declare myself a christian if there were no community to make sense of my declaration. And vice versa, no sociological group could have any meaningful idea of what a christian might be if there were nobody declaring oneself to be such. For the sake of analysis, however, we shall have to treat one aspect at a time.

The Christian Confession

Christian identity is a personal category. It is not primarily a tag applied to an idea, to a culture, or to anything else; it is the confession of a person. If the designation is applied to other things, this is done analogously and subsequently to the christian identity of a person. I may hold that christian politics is incompatible with war and I may quote christian scriptures and examples in my favour, but other christians may be of a different opinion and also adduce holy texts and christian examples on their side. The hotly debated issue of some decades ago about "christian philosophy" betrayed the underlying crisis of christian personal identity.

We may leave aside the issue of an anonymous christianity, because this depends utterly upon whether we understand by christianity an ontological, metahistorical fact or a historico-religious fact. I submit that the category of anonymous christians cannot properly be applied to the problem of christian identity.[21] Christian identity is a personal category, and thus it is also a conscious one. Even in the case of little children, it is the vow of the godparents that is supposed to stand for the community's guarantee of the infant's implied intention. It is my free confession of being a christian, in whatever sense we may interpret it, that is necessary for me to be a christian. The entire history of christianity would fall apart if the christian confession were not necessary to christian identity. Not only would martyrs and confessors, heretics and schismatics, persecutors and persecuted become meaningless, but the entire christian fact would be reduced to an amorphous and confused turmoil caused by certain historical groups over the past twenty centuries.

I have inserted the word 'sincere' into the thesis for obvious reasons. I assume that there is no conscious fraud, no intention to lie, but rather the expression of one's deepest and most intimate conviction. I assume that if I confess myself to be a christian I *believe* myself to be one; I assume further that we have to do here with a normal human being, so that I exclude the extreme possibility that I might sincerely declare myself the king of El Dorado and be hailed as such by some group of mad fellows.

I am well aware of the ontological understanding of the christian fact, according to which sacramental power works even on the unconscious level. From St. Augustine's dispute with the donatists up to Graham Greene's more recent descriptions of the inner workings of an ontologically present and psychologically unconscious grace, an entire tradition stands for the relative independence of the "opus operantis Christi" (which is the proper theological understanding of the "opus operatum"—otherwise it would be magic). I personally believe that the christian fact, like any authentic religious belief, is grafted onto the metahistorical core of the person, but all this in no way contradicts the affirmation that christian identity implies a free consciousness of it. We may have christian character, christian culture, christian grace, etc., but personal identity presupposes the consciousness that affirms and recognizes itself for what it claims to be. Can we identify human beings only from the exterior as we identify geological strata?

"Christian identity," if it is to have any meaning *qua identity*, means that in our self-consciousness the name "christian" denotes an appropriate view of our self-understanding. In other words: the affirmation of christian identity cannot be separated from the consciousness which affirms it. Can I meaningfully and legitimately be called a christian if I deny myself to be one?

It could be retorted that one does not need to know that one is a christian in order to be one: an adult, for instance, who was baptised as a child and does not know it. I have theological difficulties for accepting such a hypothesis; yet, even accepting the 'story', that adult might be a christian (for those who have such a magic idea of the sacramental "opus operatum"), but this naked fact is not christian identity.

I may be wrong in affirming that "I am a christian", but without confessing it, without being aware of it, I can certainly not speak of my christian identity. If I am wrong, I should be proven wrong according to criteria accepted in common by myself and those who argue the contrary. If we do not agree on the criteria we may then have two different understandings of the word christian and, unless otherwise mutually recognized, there is no higher criterion of further instance to which we may appeal.

Here the judgment of dialectics may prove final; that is, we may both cling to our respective criteria until one of us finds the other guilty of self-contradiction or incoherence.

The christian confession is also of capital importance in recognizing and accepting the reciprocal character of human communication; so that the declarations and opinions of the other must be treated on a par with our own (or our group's) opinion. The dialectical approach is inapplicable here. The dialectical method is too impersonal and assumes from the start a contradictory position. It recognizes only the principle of non-contradiction as its final court of appeal; it assumes that Being follows the laws of thinking and that thinking is exclusively dialectical. Here the dialogical method becomes imperative.[22] Dialogue is based on confidence in the other *qua alter*, and not only insofar as I can understand or co-opt the other. We trust each other in the dialogue and not only the *tertium quid* of our impersonal rationality. We are now entering the second part of the thesis.

The Community's Acceptance

I can scarcely be identified as a christian if I do not recognize myself as one. This first part of the thesis is a *necessary* condition but it is not *sufficient*. My confession must find a positive echo in a human group. The word "christian" as I use it must have meaning for others besides me. A purely private interpretation, like any private language, not only defeats its purpose, which is to communicate, but destroys its very nature, which is relational. If I were to insist on calling myself christian in a way which nobody finds acceptable, I should strive to prove convincingly (to others) that the adjective "christian" applies also to me. In other words, if I were to claim the name "christian" in a way that seems strange to others (cf. the case of Paul) then I will have to convince them that my understanding is not wrong and it is at least compatible with if not implied in theirs. In order to do this, I shall have to base my arguments on certain criteria acceptable at large by my fellow-beings. Pure equivocation would serve no purpose, for in such a case my "christian identity" would have a meaning totally different from any other use of the word, which amounts to declaring that I am not a christian in the sense in which the word is understood by all the others.

We ought to recall the classical discussions on the nature of christianity which seem to be normative for the question of christian identity. Here would be the place to discuss the different criteria which have existed down the ages, still exist today, and which make it possible for one to be considered a christian.

Let us recall that excommunication is an exclusion from the community, i.e. an annulment of the second condition (recognition by a community) only from a legal point of view stipulated by the hierarchy of a community or by an entire community, as a punishment of the culprit and for the welfare of the particular community. In no way does the excommunication imply that the excommunicated is not a christian. It says only that the excommunicated is a bad christian, and for this is censured by exclusion from the communion of the faithful.[23]

Ever since Romano Guardini's epoch-making study of *The Essence of Christianity*,[24] which could be considered as a certain climax in the problematic set in motion since

Adolf von Harnack,[25] the perennial search for christian self-understanding has been situated not on the doctrinal level, but on the existential. The 'person' of Jesus Christ (and not his teaching or any idea) is the essence of christianity[26]. Or, avoiding the concept 'person', we find the *symbol* Christ at the very centre of christian identity.[27] Hans Küng's book is a study of modern Man's criteria for "being christian", i.e. for christian identity, and the very success of the book underscores the vitality of the issue.[28]

What we find, following this line of research, is the effort of thinkers and theologians to reformulate what they consider to be a christian, employing all the hermeneutical tools at their disposal at a given moment and in a given cultural setting. Today's answers must be clearly discerned and evaluated on their own merits. I shall give later on my understanding of my own catholic identity; but our problem is not how I may give a convincing answer *hic et nunc*, but the attempt at a genuine "fundamental-theological" consideration.

We are not going to discuss the contemporary opinions on the essence of christianity. Valid and convincing as these may be, they are answers and—legitimately—christian answers within the cultural and religious field of the modern plurality of views. Our question is the general one about the principles on which christian identity is based. There are christians who belong to diverse cultural and religious matrices, and a complete answer to the question will have to be rethought over against this wider context of religious and cultural pluralism.

By way of example, let us recall one case: Keshub Chunder [Sundar] Sen, the great leader of the Brahmo Samaj as an exponent of the bengali renaissance of the last century had written movingly about Christ, and a man like Max Müller could assure him that there was nothing non-christian in the Samaj, so that he even encouraged Sen's successor Protap Chunder Mozoomdar [Pratab Sunder Mazumdar] to declare the entire Samaj as christian without caring for affiliation with any established christian church.[29] Yet: "Why is it that, though I do not take the name of Christian, I still persevere in offering my hearty thanksgiving to Jesus Christ?", asked Sen in 1875. "A wholesale acceptance of the Christian name by the Brahmo Samaj"—wrote Mozoomdar to Müller—"is neither possible nor desirable, within measurable time."

They 'were' christians for Max Müller. Yet the spirit of the times some hundred years ago made impossible both the confession of being a christian and the acceptance of it by any group. None of the parties were ready for it. It would have been a mere lie and not a genuine name, a real word. Neither the confession nor the acceptance is left to the whims of somebody. They would not have been accepted; they could not make such a claim (of being christians). This is the power of the *myth*.

Another example is that of Mahatma Gandhi. The christian influence on Gandhi was great.[30] He was confronted by christians and deeply moved by the figure of Jesus Christ. Yet he did not join christianity: "If then I had to face only the *Sermon on the Mount* and my own interpretations of it, I should not hesitate to say: «Oh yes, I am a Christian»." Our first condition is fulfilled. But he then goes on to say: "But I know that, at the present moment, if I said any such thing, I would lay myself open to the gravest misinterpretation."[31]

It is just this problematic which leads me to add the two following sections.

PHILOSOPHICAL REFLECTIONS

Let us imagine that a certain christian group or individual has the criterion m for judging who is a christian, and another group or individual has the criterion n, and similarly o and p are other such criteria held by different groups. A criterion of criteria is not ascertainable if there are mutual contradictions among the particular criteria. In other words, if m, n, o and p are mutually incompatible, there can be no common criterion. We could still think of a purely formal common denominator z, and say, for instance, that the criterion underlying all criteria is the bare reference to Christ without ever specifying what that word means or how its centrality is envisaged. But that z would satisfy nobody, and such a criterion for being a christian would be no criterion at all. In so many words, z is not a criterion for being a christian because unlike m, n, etc. it is not recognized as a sufficient criterion by anybody. We do not even know where the limits of such a criterion would lie. In fact, z could be common not only to m, n, etc., but also to other groups which do not even claim to be christian. Hence it is not a criterion.

It may clarify the issue if instead of casting about for criteria, we try to understand what identity might possibly mean.

Two Ways of Thinking about Identity

The identity of a thing can be determined in two different ways, according to the bent of one's thinking. If we apply a kind of thinking based on the primacy of the *principle of non-contradiction*, we shall reach the notion of the identity of a thing by defining the differences between that particular thing and the rest of the world. Entity a is all the more what it is the more it is not *non-a*. This is the active mode of defining identity. Here identity leads to, and is reached through, differentiation. Christian identity will accordingly be seen in terms of its specific difference over against a generalized "non-christian" identity—meaning all the rest of mortals. Every attempt at defining christian identity will be geared to discovering those features which are different, separate, and allegedly "unique" in the christian tradition or in the christian self-understanding. Christian mysticism will thus be labeled "supernatural" in contradistinction to "natural" mysticisms, "christian grace is unique", "only christians will possess the fullness of revelation", and so forth. Nowadays, when the "supernatural" is in crisis and the *humanum* (as a more qualified successor to the waning "humanisms") takes precedence, christian identity will strive to distinguish itself from any other way to understand the human and attain full humanity.[32] And since we are today also under the sway of the democratic-egalitarian myth, the point will be to find something specifically christian which need not necessarily offend others by calling itself better or superior. It will only be "distinctive". Typical of this enterprise are the present-day theological reflections which try to sort out christian identity in the field of world religions. If an "Absolutheitsanspruch" cannot be defended, where does christian identity lie? What kind of uniqueness?[33]

If the difference is not one of exclusivity or superiority, it has to be a historical difference. The western christian myth of history provides the horizon for almost all the answers focused along this line of thought. The christian belongs to a particular historical period, with all that this implies: historical mission, historical consciousness, historical identity. Jesus Christ becomes then fundamentally a *historical* symbol. There is only one (historical) Jesus of Nazareth. History is the matrix of reality. And in that history Jesus has performed a unique role which is different from all the other "manifestations" of the "Divine". Christian identity implies belonging to a particular historical people. In a very uncritical although well-meaning way Vatican II calls christians "the people of God". What about the others?

Basically different is the way of thinking which relies on the *principle of identity* to identify an entity. In this case *a* is all the more *a* (the identity is more perfect) the more it is *a*. Linguistic analysis will take exception to speaking of "more" identical, but linguistic analysis is also familiar with the logical paradox that if we do not recognize degrees of identity, any analysis is either contradictory or banal. If the analysandum is identical to the analysans there is no new information conveyed, no gain in knowledge, and thus the analysis is banal. But if they are *not* identical, the analysis is false, for then the analysans would not express the analysandum. All this has led me to speak elsewhere of ontological principles as *qualified tautologies.*

In any event, identity in this view is not based on difference but on unity. Thus christian identity does not need to be seen in contrast with non-christian identity, though it is almost meaningless to speak of a "non-christian" identity—since it all depends on the notion of "christian identity". The identity of the "non-christian" should lie in something that the non-christian *is*, and not in what it *is not.* A christian can be christian without having to distinguish oneself in a contradictory way from a non-christian simply because the core of one's own identity does not lie in any external distinctive criterion. To the contrary, it lies in the internal consciousness of one's own being, which is not threatened by communion or even 'fusion' with 'others'.[34]

This is related to what I have called, in a polemic mood, the "classificatory mania" of the West, schematised by Aristoteles, hallowed by Porphyrios and consecrated by modern sciences. The principle of non-contradiction is here paramount. But as I have argued elsewhere the classificator cannot enter into the classification. Christian identity is not a label in a classification. It is personal identity, and personal identity belongs to the classificator. It is unclassifiable.

This being the case, the question of christian identity cannot be appropriately approached on the merely doctrinal level, which would imprison it within one particular mode of thinking or one particular culture. We have to look for something more basic than doctrinal differences—important and inescapable as these are, given a particular field of intelligibility.

THE NON-OBJECTIFIABLE NATURE OF *SELF-IDENTITY*

Christian identity cannot be segregated from the self-identity of christians. To do otherwise it would imply that our group takes upon itself the prerogative of defining and deciding for everyone who is a christian. Even this fact of appointing ourselves as judges of the christian identity would not obviate the difficulty. In fact, in order that our 'magisterial' decision of deciding who is and who is not a christian be intelligible to others, it would have to pass through the others' understanding, interpretation and acceptance of it. This is but one special case of a more general problematic affecting all human self-affirmations, and bound up precisely with pluralism.

We are so imbued with modern scientific thought that we are prone to judge scientifically and "objectively" facts and events which belong to another order. Not even the worst inquisitorial times would dare to judge *who* a catholic is. The condemnation of the heretic was a political and juridical act, not a decision on catholic identity: *de internis non judicat ecclesia*. But I shall restrict myself to our case by going back to our example of the pebble.

If I affirm "this is a stone", we can easily agree by appealing to the (qualified and critically checked) testimony of our senses. One thing, however, is clear: in our prevalent scientific cosmology at no point has the stone anything to say for itself. The affirmation: "This is a christian", by contrast, does not allow the same ultimate recourse to such independent and critical perception, because the self-understanding of the one "who is a christian" belongs also to the problem itself. The judgement about who is a christian does not depend only on our examination of some objectifiable "thing", as is the case with the stone, it depends as well on the one who is being examined. And the examination of a conscious being entails also asking what and how it examines itself.

We may agree that the word—"christian" in our case—has a meaning and that it has for all the same referent; yet this is patently not enough. Let us assume that according to my understanding a south-african white citizen is not a christian because that person does not believe in the basic trinitarian structure of the nicean creed and accepts (or accepted) apartheid, while according to that citizen this belief is not at all necessary in order to be a christian. We may go on *ad nauseam* debating where to draw the dividing line, but there is no superior reason—if we do not accept it—that could decide the question for us. In short, when a human identity is in question, the self-understanding of the subject of inquiry belongs to the very nature of the object to be understood. I have to treat you as a source of self-understanding, and with the same respect I accord to myself, even if I can neither agree with you nor understand why you take the stand you take. This is pluralism: the acceptance of the other's opinion (as issuing from another source of understanding) which is incompatible with my own.

In philosophical parlance: your self-understanding belongs to you as *you* and not only as *yours*—so that in order to understand *you*, I have somehow to grasp how *you* understand *your* self. In order to say in truth who you are (your identity) I have to integrate also in my saying who you think and believe you are.

We cannot bypass this first step of respecting and accepting what we may neither understand nor agree upon. To do it reasonably we have to make the assumption that the others are sources of intelligence, as much as we are, and thus that the others are equally entitled to their opinion, although we may find it wrong and try to convince them of their 'error'—or even fight them as 'evil'. But meanwhile, i.e. until we do not reach agreement, we shall have to trust in something other and greater than our personal insights—greater even than the faint 'hope' that we may one day convince them, for such an expectation may easily prove to be in vain. True pluralistic tolerance is more than the strategic expectation of a future victory. My point here is that to rely only on our own criteria for deciding such an issue implies an abuse of power unwarranted by the nature of the problem itself. For centuries christian identity has been a political problem. Tolerance is not just a lesser evil, but a mystical virtue. The problems loom large. Why is the modern West more inclined to tolerate 'error' than 'evil'? Heretics are not imprisoned; law-breakers are.

Whatever this may be, we should pursue our search as far as possible. Although we may reach some conclusion for "the time being", as long as "being is in time", the problem cannot be considered closed—a third opinion might well shatter all our past agreements.

It is also this reflection which leads me to formulate the question of identity in terms of function and not of content.

THEOLOGICAL CONSIDERATIONS

THE CATEGORICAL AND THE TRANSCENDENTAL CHRISTIAN IDENTITY

Christian thought has since its inception approached christian affirmations or, traditionally speaking, christian revelation, in two divergent moods: the one focuses on the cognitive meaning or the intellectual content of the affirmation, and the other concentrates on its referent, its intentionality or intentional function. The first is a theoretical or doctrinal approach; the second a pastoral or practical approach. The former is proper to councils and schools, the latter to the parish and ordinary life. The first is sensitive to the essence of truth, the second to its existence.

To say that the word "christian" has many meanings (according to different groups) but only one referent does not resolve the question but only shifts it. Who then is this *referent* to which people refer with different meanings? If *what* a christian is seems polysemous, *who* a christian is must remain an unanswered question as long as we take a solely doctrinal approach to it.

I may call the two approaches the *categorical* and the *transcendental.* The categorical approach focuses on the doctrinal statements: *it means what it says.* The transcendental approach concentrates on the intentional symbol: *it says what it means.* In the last analysis both are required: we say what we mean, because we mean what we say. The category is a translation of a transcendental situation; the transcendental needs a particular category for its expression. I shall describe them briefly.

Categorical Identity

We may introduce the issue by a sociological rather than a theological consideration. There are today many catholics who have decided to cease calling themselves catholic because they do not agree with either the doctrine or the praxis of the official catholic church. They consider their own identity incompatible with such teachings or practices and make it "a question of conscience" to clear out from such company. They believed that christian tenets were supposed to embody the truth. Once they discovered that they could no longer accept those tenets, they felt duty-bound, out of loyalty, honesty and truthfulness to themselves and others, to take their leave from the catholic community. The gamut of reasons is immense, from ceasing to believe in the

Trinity to disagreement over the economics or politics of the Vatican, from marxist leanings to disgust over the birth-control interdict, disagreement with the present Pope, etc. If these people do not consider themselves catholic, or christian for that matter, we may well say that it is due to a fundamentalist interpretation of what it means to be a catholic, or a christian. We may still believe they are christians, but we have no right to call them christian in spite of and against their will. You may burn your north-american passport and refuse to go to the Gulf to wage war, but the U.S Government will imprison and punish so-called army-deserters. Whatever abuse of power it may entail to subject yourself to the laws of a State for having been born within certain geographical boundaries, the fact of being reborn a christian is neither a biological act nor a merely juridical action which you can delete by burning your baptismal certificate. The entire theology of the sacraments hinges on that point. The fact is that there are a good number of catholics who have denied their catholic identity because of the above motives.

In this first case catholic identity is detectable sociologically and historically. A catholic is someone appertaining to a particular and univocally recognizable group of people. The problem of identity, seen from the outside, would then lie in their membership, which is an empirically recognizable fact. And they will willingly consider themselves outside the Church. Voluntary apostasy is a well-studied phenomenon.

Without going back to the Middle Ages or the modernist crisis, one hears in our present times the comments of people who say they would not have broken with the Church if they would have known of the coming Vatican II. What an attitude does it entail to want to remain in the fold while expecting that things will move on and change? This is linked with the much-vexed question concerning the evolution of christian doctrine.

Now, within the categorical framework the problem is not solved by reverting to the evolution of christian self-understanding. One cannot console the impatient by telling them to wait since a heresy today may become an accepted doctrine tomorrow, because this evolution is detectable only *a posteriori*. This "evolution" is the gift of the Spirit and not the conclusion of a syllogism. Besides, this attitude would betray a mere opportunistic membership of the Church: a comfortable community as long as we find advantages in it.

I am speaking all the time about the profound problem of the search for one's own identity. If I reject my catholic identity it is not because while abhorring the Inquisition or the lack of feminine rights in the Church I expect things will change. It is because I consider that such doctrines or practices are radically incompatible with my experience of Truth or the mystery of reality. We cannot console ourselves with vain expectations. At any given time we cannot foresee, much less predict, what evolutionary path christian self-consciousness is going to take. We may certainly pay attention to the signs of the times and (perhaps sociologically) predict a few trends of thought, because the seeds of these future tendencies are already stirring in our present situation. We may envision what north-american christians are going to say, or what stand they are going to take in the coming decade, but we cannot possibly yet know what impact african christians may one day have on the entire christian self-understanding or whether hindu-christians are going to succeed in breaking the semitic and Old Testament paradigm within the christian community itself. The point I am making is that no laplacean spirit or theoretically perfect computer can ever predict the dynamism of the human spirit in its quest forward. By the same token, no one can have an exhaustive understanding of christian identity. Identity has much deeper roots. We do not know the happiness of a person until we know the entire life of that person—said already Aristoteles.[35]

We are dealing here with the christian fact as a case in point of an issue that concerns the very nature of reality itself: the problem of what 'in fact' a fact is. Facts are not merely actualizations of possible potentialities. They are, first of all, real events. They present a radical novelty not necessarily foreseeable or even thinkable (as real possibilities) for human consciousness at a given point in time and space. To stay with recognized christian 'facts': What a Paul, a Constantine, a Palamas, a Francis of Assisi, Thomas d'Aquino, Luther or John XXIII have made possible in christian consciousness does not result from *mere* conclusions of syllogisms or deductions of previous facts. Rather those 'facts' presented themselves as utopias in their time. They were events breaking into the framework of reasonably foreseeable facts. Only *a posteriori* can it be seen that they maintained a certain continuity with previous christian self-interpretations. This continuity, as our thesis coherently affirms, is only a historical continuity, an existential succession, and not a necessarily rational one. The Spirit blows where, when and how she wills; her ways are not our ways.

There is no possibility of having "deduced" that from the Sermon on the Mount and the Gospels in general could not have derived Crusades, Inquisitions and Capitalisms. I am saying that a sociology of the christian community may be a necessary but it is not a sufficient condition for describing christian identity. I am saying even more. I maintain that this degree of freedom (even from logical constraints) is constitutive of reality.

In other words, if even the most elementary movements of matter itself show a radical indeterminacy, I assume that the movement of the Spirit will never be quite reducible to rational laws. The "expansion" of the real universe is more than just an unfolding from a given point—material, logical, or spiritual; the radical novelty of creation does not belong only to the past. It is a *creatio continua*, as the scholastics maintained. Christian identity can be no more fixed or guaranteed immutability once and for all than anything else in our relative universe.

Categorical identity goes as far as it goes; and it serves a purpose as long as nobody challenges the given and accepted notion: A christian is one who believes in the nicean creed, in the augsburgian confession, in the divinity of Christ, or the like. But the christian identity crisis arises the moment that the particular myth is for one reason or another no longer accepted—or found acceptable. Within a homogeneous myth, christian identity has an accepted content, like what a christian attitude represents. I do not think present-day christian conscience would condone slavery as an institution; but I wonder if future christians will not ask themselves how twenty-first century christians could condone capitalism as an institution.

Transcendental Identity

In the second case, we have the awareness of a transcendental identity, that is, the awareness that any categorical formulation is nothing but a crystallization of an ever elusive and never exhaustive manifestation of a reality which transcends every human attempt to pinpoint it.

This other approach reacts to conflict in exactly the opposite manner. It clings to christian identity because what matters is not some theoretical content or any contingent practical attitude, but rather the trust that the truth is expressed in christian tenets and not that christian tenets are the truth, so that if truth proves to be elsewhere—then, by definition, the christian tenets will go there. The oldest formulation of this attitude—after a similar buddhist one—may be that of St. Justin in the second century affirming that "whatever sublime things have been said by anyone belong to christians",[36] probably echoing the words of Paul: "everything is yours" (1 Cor. 3:22). We find the same mood in St. Ambrose of Milano, quoted and endorsed by Thomas Aquinas when he affirms that whatever truth is ever uttered comes from the Holy Spirit.[37]

Modern theologians will sympathize, of course, with the apparently broader idea standing for truth, wherever it may be.[38] But the problem is not so easily solved, for two reasons: first, no truth is totally independent of our understanding of it, and thus of our formulation, so that we cannot completely disentangle the one from the other. Secondly, if every truth is a christian truth, i.e. if the adjective "christian" really is no adjective because it does not add anything, then, christian identity means merely genuine human identity: I confess myself a christian because I acknowledge myself as truly human.

In this case christian identity is either devoid of any specific meaning, for it coalesces with humanness, or it can have any meaning whatsoever, without restriction, for anybody could say that the individual understanding of the transcendental christian identity is best expressed by his or her own particular formulation. If there is truth in buddhism, the buddhists are thus bound to be anonymous christians.

In either case, the remedy seems worse than the malady, since it creates more problems than it solves. Our thesis, on the contrary, says that christian identity is a concrete identity, although neither fixed once and for all, nor left to the private interpretation of the individual. *Christian identity consists rather in the dialogical interaction between a sincere confession and a collective recognition, according to criteria considered valid at each particular juncture.* It then falls to the history of theology to seek an underlying intelligibility in the series of statements affirming christian identity, and my suspicion is that there is no other one than the existential continuity which I would like to call apostolic or historical succession. I am affirming that history in general and christian historical continuity in particular is neither dialectical materialism, nor dialectical historicism, spiritual as this latter may be conceived to be.

An important point should be made here. We should not minimalize the value of history, but we should not absolutize history either. Christianity is undoubtedly a historical religion, but the transcendental christian identity is not reduced to a merely historical fact. If we destroy the mystical core of human religiousness we reduce religion to a historical fact and 'theology' to an ideology. This leads me to a final consideration.

THE NATURE OF CHRISTIAN IDENTITY

With all the provisos deriving from the foregoing, we should be able to formulate a relatively satisfactory answer to this question for our time and place. This is what I may attempt, by reformulating the categorical statements which translate the transcendental interpretation of christian identity for our times. Christian identity is a categorical identity which translates into a particular historical framework that I have called transcendental identity.

Unless we are to fall prey to mere semantics, a christian, according to an understanding which would encompass every self-declared christian *today*, is a person who meaningfully (for herself and her community) confesses herself to be such. This confession and recognition may *hic et nunc* take approximately the following form:

A christian is someone for whom the Christ symbol discloses or illumines or in one way or another touches the central mystery of one's own existence. A christian believes that the Christ symbol—with all the polysemy and polymorphy proper to a symbol, as distinct from a concept—reveals, expresses or manifests something appertaining to the very core of the real in general, and of one's existence in particular. Of this belief the christian finds an echo and confirmation in a community. Individual christians and christian community imply each other. The individual's confession presupposes an understanding of what a christian is. The individual perceives "what is christian" in a community. What we perceive is not a doctrine but a life, a practice, a liturgy in its broadest but also deepest sense of the word *leit-ourgia* [an *ergon*, a work of the *laos*, people]. The community is the keeper of the symbols and gestures which give meaning to the name christian. It is not just doctrinal accuracy but the individual's adhesion to the life and symbols of the community which constitutes christian identity. Today, when there are not only many communities but their number keeps increasing not only in churches or groups, but also in communities of theologians or active movements; today, when the very idea of a universally valid and necessary doctrinal content is becoming more and more problematic, this traditional truth, that the christian's identity depends on one's own *witness, martyria*, acquires greater clarity and relevance. A martyr is always a witness for somebody.

The assumption I am making is that the nature of being a christian is not detectable as a physical reality, but only knowable as a human fact. In other terms, as Indian logicians have known since ancient times, fool's gold is an illusion precisely because it is not gold; it only appears to be gold. But there are objective means to assay the worth of true gold. Just so, in assaying christian identity we cannot bypass the testimony of both the alleged christian and the community.

History past and present shows us that some christian groups will not recognize as christian other individuals or communities. The issue here is whether the fact that different communities hold to different criteria contradicts our thesis or, on the contrary, illumines it from an unsuspected angle.

If we have different groups proclaiming certain minimal conditions for being a christian, and thus if we find some communities considered "christian" according to one criterion and "non-christian" according to another, this means that unless we share the opinion of one of the parties, our thesis uses the word christian to denote different understandings of what or who is christian. From a phenomenological point of view we may be in a quandary if we try to ascertain the *noêma* proper to being a christian, but we may solve the difficulty if we introduce the notion of *pisteuma*: the belief of the believer as belonging to the phenomenon itself. The *pisteuma* is neither merely subjective (it has to be recognized as such) nor purely objective (I have to believe in it). A byproduct of christian ecumenism is the aperture in christian identity. If catholics today consider also christian those who until now were considered apostates and perhaps even non-christian, they can no longer brand-mark as non-catholics those who do not hold the same idea of catholicity. Küng, Boff, Curran, Bermejo, to put forth living examples from four continents, may be 'punished', but they cannot be called non-catholics: their catholic identity is not at stake.

But there is still more to this apparent proliferation of meanings for one and the same symbol. It shows the continuing vitality of the symbol and reveals something about its very nature, namely that it is an important symbol which cannot easily be discarded, because so many different groups claim to have the correct understanding of it, instead of just giving it up and using altogether another name if need be. This makes obvious the power of the symbol itself and suggests that christian identity is not the same as belonging to some arbitrary social group, like membership in a club. Why such a coveted symbol? Why do people with such divergent opinions insist on their right to use this name?[39]

Is a merely cultural answer enough? Why are christians the anti-liberals of one era, and the liberals of the next? Why do some marxists nowadays want to be christian or, for that matter, some christians (who do not wish to cease being christian) want to be marxists or atheists or the like? What kind of dynamism is detectable here? Christian identity in a time of pluralism seems to reveal another, hidden, facet of the problem. It seems to illumine a peculiar aspect of reality (call it a need of the human being, or a feature of human history, or a moment in the divine economy): the need of continuity, of rootedness for Man, which is not merely cultural or biological or ethnic, but also religious.

CONCLUSION

Modern western culture by and large, christian philosophers and theologians being no exception, almost panics at losing one's own distinctive singularity. The fear of pantheism, 'oriental' confusion, intellectual chaos and ultimately of individual death are very heterogeneous names for a rather homogeneous attitude. The will to preserve separate identity is also tied with the will to power and the preoccupation (not to say almost obsession) both for certainty on the intellectual level and security in the political sphere.

No wonder that the words of Christ about losing one's own life have most often been interpreted *cum grano salis*: "an oriental exaggeration",—obviously.

This would be my gloss: to take more seriously and more literally that our life is not private property, that our main task is not to be concerned with ourselves (Matt. 6:19-34), and, on the contrary, to be carefree 1 Cor. 7:32) and without worries (Matt. 6:25), not only regarding how we shall eat and clothe ourselves, but also concerning our own identity (Matt. 6:3, 25:37). I would, paradoxically, submit, that the mature christian identity is the discovery of the existential christian contradiction of such an identity. "Lord, when did we see you hungry . . . thirsty . . . a stranger or naked . . . " (Matt. 25:38). Neither those of the right nor those of the left had identified (recognized) Christ. Why do we worry about christian identity? Only by letting it go may it be bestowed upon us.

This seems to be a great intuition—should I say revelation?—of the Rig Veda (I, 164, 37):

> What I am, I don't know;
> I wander secluded burdened by the mind.
> When the Firstborn of truth comes
> I partake in the same Logos.

The christian identity is that trust that we are known and loved and do not care unduly about ourselves—because our identity is to be identified with the Firstborn of the Cosmos.

Not much later than the quoted text of the Rig Veda the Sibyl at Delphos uttered another oracle complementary to the vedic mantra and which has shaped western mentality: "Know thyself".

Indeed, according to Plato and repeated by the christian tradition and the Qur'an to know oneself is to know God. But when the sacred injunction becomes a profane statement the human being is at a loss. Here begins the "crisis of identity" about which modern philosophers speak.[40] Having severed the "Thou" from the "Self" modern Man clings to the *ego* and under this influence the christian is worried about the own identity and forgets not only Christ's words, but also Plotinus' wisdom: Let it all be, eliminate everything, cut away all.

This was our motto; now in the strong words of John: "The Man who loves himself is lost (He who loves his life will lose it)." The worry about identity may turn pathological . . .

When all this is said and done, as I am myself not outside my own horizon, I may be allowed to express what it does all mean for me:

To be a catholic, for me, means the conviction, the belief that the Divine Spirit, similar as in the case of Jesus (although *minutis minuendis* obviously) has descended upon me and has become incarnated in me, making of me not another Christ (*alius Christus*), but the same Christ (*ipse Christus*)[41] of which Jesus is the head (to follow Paul) and I a member in the process of becoming it more and more fully. It means to be a person in whom the divine Spirit dwells not as a host, but as its 'soul' (in the sense of the *intimior intimo meo* of St. Augustin). This is what baptism means for me. A christian is a person baptised (in this sense) by the Holy Spirit. A christian is then for me the person in whom the divine spirit has become flesh. I may make a series of distinctions:

a. The ontic christian, in whom the divine spirit is the living principle. In this sense any human being, and even any being is a christophany—in as much as any being is more than a material entity and Man more than a merely developed ape.

b. The ontological christian, in whom there is a certain consciousness of the immanent-transcendent mystery that enlivens one's life. That person does not need to use a christian vocabulary, not even a theistic one. Anybody conscious of and believing in the indwelling mystery (again another word to be relativized) in one's own life, i.e. believing in the fact that one does not have absolute possession of one's own being, whatever name one may use to express it, is what I believe a christian is.

c. The historical christian, for whom the christian language makes sense and has appropriated it while retaining the freedom of finding a more and more acceptable interpretation. Christ becomes then the name for that Symbol.

d. The sociological christian, which could be also called the ecclesial one, who owes allegiance to one of the existing christian groups or churches.

e. The catholic christian, who embodies in a very particular way that mysterious consciousness. I would like to retain the scandal and concreteness of the geohistorical symbol of Rome at least for those first two millennia and in spite of the possible arrogance of the word "catholic" if interpreted as universal and not as the call to concrete wholeness—of every one. A roman catholic would in fact mean, for me at least, not the fan of the last Pope (whoever he may be) or the spiritual citizen of the Vatican (without criticizing this loyalty), but the person whose spiritual pedigree passes through those two millennia of roman history, not to get entangled in it or to glorify it, but as the historical springboard from which the catholic tradition may still jump into the transhistorical Unknown.

What makes then a christian christian? My answer is simple: Christ's Spirit living in Man. This Christ Spirit is the Holy Spirit. This Holy Spirit is the Divine Life. This Divine Life is just the Mystery of Life. The interpretation of this fact is its interpretation, and there are traditional christian interpretations, and other versions which the christian tradition has rejected. But I am not speaking about what is an orthodox christian (then we should previously agree on the criteria of orthodoxy—and not necessarily by a democratic procedure), I am trying to express what I understand by christian identity.

I have implicitly distinguished between conscious and non-conscious identity. If the *idem* of the identity needs to be a self-recognized identity, then it becomes an *ipse* and my general thesis stands. Christian identity is the sincere self-confession as such. The confession entails a receiver, i.e. a community. And this was my thesis. If the *idem* has an ontic value independently of its ontological consciousness then my larger personal thesis, as it has been just described, would be the case.

To the objection: "Then everybody is a christian", I have little to object, for to me my christian consciousness is nothing that severs me from my fellow-beings, but just the contrary, that which establishes the deepest bond of communion, namely that we all are pervaded by the divine Spirit, as the Isha Upanishad so beautifully puts it. When I confess myself a catholic I do not have the feeling nor the will nor the understanding that I belong to a religious sect (in the best and traditional sense of the word) that has existed on earth for only two millennia. It is the transcendental identity cast into the mold of my categorical identity. I confess to belonging to the human race, and even more to the entire reality which for eons has taken the shape that has taken in me. *Ecclesia ab Abel*, said the Fathers of the Church[42]

To the retort: "What is then the use of being a christian?" I have equally nothing to reply. I am not moving on the area of usefulness and am far from any utilitarian consideration. I would even retort that this is a wrong way of being a christian, a bourgeois ideology. But this is not the point now. The point is that being a christian belongs to another sphere altogether, and as I believe, to the ultimate one.

To the further objection: "It is however a particular language" I would again say yes. But add immediately that the particularity is not so much that of the answer as that of the question. I did not ask the question. There is no need to put it. But once it is put the answer has to play within the limits set by the question itself.

And this is what I have tried to do.

NOTES

[1] It is interesting to quote traditional and modern translations: "For whosoever will (would) save his life shall lose it; and whosoever will (shall) lose his life for my sake shall find it" A.V. (R.V.). And practically the same is said by the "New Revised Standard Version", the "Revised English Bible", the "New American Bible", the "New Jerusalem Bible", and many others. Only the "New English Bible" translates: "Whoever cares for his own safety is lost; but if man will let himself be lost for my sake, he will find his true self." Cf. also Matth. X, 38 39; Luk. XVII, 33; Joh. XII, 25; etc.—besides the scriptural texts on the cosmic Christ.

[2] This topic was discussed in Strasbourg, June 30-July 9, 1976 in the "X International Ecumenical Seminar" sponsored by the Institute for Ecumenical Research under the theme: *Christian Identity—Confessional Identity—Christian Unity.* Cf. a review in *Journal of Ecumenical Studies*, XIV, 1 (Winter, 1977): 195-196. It was also the topic of the Fall Meeting (November 19-20, 1976) of "The Pacific Coast Theological Society", under the title of *Christian Identity in a Time of Pluralism.* I held there one of the position papers. An abridged version of the present article was delivered as the No. 17 of the *Warren Lecture Series* at the University of Tulsa (USA) on October 4, 1991. I refer also to the contributions of other publications: Michael Amaladass et al. (eds.), *Theologizing in India*, Bangalore (T.P.I.) 1981; Paul Putnanangady (ed.), *Sharing Worship*, Bangalore (N.B.C.L.C.) 1988; Paul F. Knitter (ed.), *Pluralism and Oppression*, Lanham, N.T. (University Press of America for College Theology Society) 1991. The international review *Concilium* did also dedicate its issue nr. 216 (March 1988) to the question of christian identity. Lately the same review *Concilium* insists on the theme of the "biographic, moral and religious perspective of identity" in the issue 285 of April 2000. Charles Duquoc, one of the editors, introduces the issue affirming that "christians are not sure of their own identity." Cf. also *Vivre de plusieurs religions*, Jacques Scheuer et Denis Gira (eds.), Paris (Ed. l'Atelier; Ed. Ouvrières), 2000.

[3] Although I go a step further, cf. the enlightening article by Pierre Bühler: "Christian Identity between Objectivity and Subjectivity" in *Concilium*, nr. 216 (1988).

[4] Cf. a standard modern definition: "A christian is ordinarily defined as 'one who believes in Jesus Christ.' He might more adequately be described as one who counts himself as belonging to that community of men for whom Jesus Christ—his life, words, deeds and destiny—is of supreme importance" . . . H. Richard Niebuhr, *Christ and Culture*, New York: Harper Colophon Books, 1975, p. 11.

[5] Cf. Bernard Lonergan, *Doctrinal Pluralism*, Milwaukee: Marquet University Press, 1971, defending a pluralism of communications and distinguishing a number of necessary differentiations of consciousness; Hans Urs von Balthasar, *Die Wahrheit ist symphonisch—Aspekte des christlichen Pluralismus*, Einsiedeln: Johannes, 1972; David Tracy, *Blessed Rage for Order*, New York: Seabury, 1976, with the subtitle *The New Pluralism in Theology*, and which assumes that there is a "basic meaning of the Christian Faith Itself" capable of many articulations and symbolic representations. The problem then becomes 'the pluralism of faith'.

⁶ "This absolute Relationship to Jesus Christ in History may have been sufficiently or not sufficiently interpreted in the theological reflection, [but] its factuality in every single [person] may disappear in the unreflectivity of the last existential decision of the singular Christian: Where it is, is Christianity… where this Relationship is not accomplished and interpreted, ceases to be actually (explicit) Christianity" *Grundkurs des Glaubens.* Freiburg: Herder, 1976, p. 205.

⁷ Cf. Karl Rahner, op. cit., p. 204.

⁸ Cf. the two volumes of Xavier Tilliette, *Le Christ et la philosophie,* Paris: Cerf, 1990 and *Le Christ des philosophes,* Namur: Culture et Vérité, 1993.

⁹ Cf. Godfrey Vesey, *Personal Identity,* London: MacMillan, 1974, and the 122 bibliographical entries of the appendix; and also Paul Ricoeur's Gifford Lectures, 1986: *On Selfhood, the Question of Personal Identity,* published afterwards as *Soi-même comme un autre,* Paris: Seuil, 1990.

¹⁰ Cf. Amelie Oksenburg Rorty, ed., *The Identity of Persons,* Berkeley: Univ. of California Press, 1976. See also the useful bibliography, pp. 325-333.

¹¹ Cf. my "Das unwissende Bewusstsein" in *Bewusstsein und Person,* Gunter Rager / Adrian Holderegger (eds.), Freiburg: Herder, 2000, pp. 124-144.

¹² Paul Ricoeur makes the fundamental distinction between "identité-*ipse*" and "identité *idem*". "Our constant thesis will be that identity in the sense of *ipse* does not imply any assertion concerning an assumed unchanging core or the person" *op. cit.,* p. 13. We shall deal, of course, with the *ipse* (I myself) and not with the *idem* (same).

¹³ Michael Amaladoss, op. cit., p. 52.

¹⁴ Cf. the efforts of Charles Journet in a pre-Vatican II roman catholic climate to save the concept of 'heresy' from existential connotations of bad will, sin, evil, etc. *Théologie de l'Eglise,* Paris: Desclée de Brouwer, 1957.

¹⁵ Cf. my "Sécularisation de l'herméneutique et l'herméneutique de la sécularisation" in Enrico Castelli (ed.), *Herméneutique de la sécularisation,* Paris: Aubier, 1976, pp. 213-248.

¹⁶ The case of Africa and North America, with new and basically different 'christian' groups every year could offer us ample evidence of the futility of research along these lines. We have to look at the problem differently.

¹⁷ Bishops Lefebre and Casaldaliga, theologians Balthasar and Sobrino, politicians like Pinochet and Aristide, and priests like the communist jesuit Llanos and the ex-president of Notre Dame Hesburgh, women like Dorothy Day and the Duchess of Alba all belong to the catholic fold in spite of the most divergent doctrines, attitudes and ideas. Cf. the intelligent and pathetic defense of Crusades, Inquisition and political power of the Church in Charles Journet, *The Church of the Word Incarnate,* London: Sheed & Ward,1955 [english translation], and the public "mea culpa" asking forgiveness for the sins of the Church by the Pope John Paul II on occasion of the Jubilee of the Year 2000.

¹⁸ Cf. my chapter on Faith in *Myth, Faith and Hermeneutics,* New York: Paulist, 1979, pp. 185-229.

¹⁹ Just a single example: "Why I am not a Christian" was Bertrand Russell's lecture in 1927 (reprinted in a collection of his essays—under the same title—in New York: Simon and Schuster, 1957.) Russell said there that the word christian is used "in a very loose sense these days". It has not that "full-blooded meaning . . . as it had in the times of St. Augustine and St. Thomas Aquinas". Yet today it can be reduced to a minimum: "you must believe in God and immortality", and secondly "you must have at the very lowest the belief that Christ was, if not divine, at least the best and wisest of men". Russell, then, goes on to prove that he does not believe in God, criticizing the traditional arguments. Regarding Christ he candidly confesses that he agrees "with Christ a great deal more than the professing Christians do" and that he "could go with

Him (sic) much further than most professing Christians can". Yet he finds "defects in Christ's teaching" and is outraged "that He believed in hell," while he does not feel "that any person who is really profoundly human can believe in everlasting punishment." It is astonishing today and significant of the contemporary change, that a Man of the moral and intellectual stature of Russell could have held such a simplistic idea of christianity only a few decades ago.

[20] Cf. Raimundo Panikkar, "Singularity and Individuality. The Double Principle of Individuation", *Revue Internationale de Philosophie*, 111/112 (1975), pp. 141-166.

[21] Cf. Karl Rahner, "Die anonymen Christen" in *Schriften zur Theologie*, Einsiedeln (Benzinger) 1965, vol. VI, pp. 545-554. The first time, to my knowledge, that Rahner spoke about it was in a Conference in 1961 (Cf. *Schriften zur Theologie*, 1962, vol. V, pp. 136-158, especially 155 sq.). At that time I made him publicly the same basic remarks I am making here. Cf. also Rahner, "Atheismus und implizites Christentum", *Schriften zur Theologie*, 1967, vol. VIII, pp. 187-212.

[22] Cf. my reflections in Joseph Prabhu, *The Intercultural Challenge of Raimon Panikkar*, Maryknoll, N.Y.: Orbis, 1996, pp. 247-262.

[23] The classical definition of excommunication runs: "censura qua quis privatur ecclesiastica communione fidelium" and practically all commentaries agree that "non repugnat ut excommunicatus sit in statu gratiae sanctificantis et post mortem in regno coeli", Dominicus M. Prümmer, *Manuale Theologiae moralis*, Friburgi Br.: Herder, 1940, vol. 3, p. 359.

[24] Romano Guardini, *Wesen des Christentums*, Burg Rothenfels/Main, 1938.

[25] Adolf von Harnack, *Das Wesen des Christentums*, Leipzig 1900. (*What is Christianity?* New York: Harper and Row, 1957).

[26] Christus ist nicht Zentrum, sondern Mittler; Gesendeter und Heimholender; "Weg, Wahrheit und Leben . . . ", Guardini, *Das Wesen des Christentums*. Würzburg: Werkbund Verlag, 1939, p. 85.

[27] Cf. my essay "The Meaning of Christ's Name in the Universal Economy of Salvation" in *Evangelization: Dialogue and Development*. Documenta Missionalia, 5 (1972) (Roma), pp. 195-218.

[28] Hans Küng, *Christ Sein*. München/Zurich: Piper, 1974, *passim* and especially pp. 531 sq.

[29] Cf. for a brief summary of the correspondence and the problem, Nirad C. Chaudury, *Scholar Extraordinary*, Delhi: Orient Paperbacks, 1974, pp. 330 sq.

[30] Cf. Mohandas Gandhi, *What Jesus means to me*, compiled by Ramadas K. Prabhu, Ahmedabad: Navajivan, 1959.

[31] Mohandas K. Gandhi, *The Message of Jesus Christ*, edited and published by Anand T. Hingorani, Bombay: Bharatiya Vidya Bhavan, 1964, p. 24. The text is from 1927 (*Young India*, Dec. 8).

[32] Cf. Hans Küng, op. cit., pp. 520 sq. for a careful dialectic between "Menschsein" and "Christsein".

[33] Cf. the success of the very title of John Hick and Paul F. Knitter (eds.), *The Myth of Christian Uniqueness*, Maryknoll, N.Y.: Orbis, 1987.

[34] I could personally feel the difficulty of taking such an approach when, four decades ago, I began to express my identity as both christian and hindu without eclectic or syncretistic confusion. "If you *are* a christian", I was constantly told, "you *are not* a hindu." "If I am a christian", I retorted "I am certainly not a non-christian." Between a hindu and a christian there may be opposition, but not necessarily contradiction. Even aristotelian logic is on my side.

[35] *Eth. Nic.*, I, 10 [1100 a 10—1100 b 10].

[36] "Quaecumque igitur apud omnes praeclare dicta sunt, nostra christianorum sunt", *Apologia* II, 13 (P.G. 6 465). This dictum has been also exploited in the opposite direction by an imperialistic mentality: the whole truth is 'ours'—instead of we stand wherever truth is.

[37] St. Thomas quotes this text with certain predilection and knows its source, relating it also to St. Paul: cf. etiam Ambrosiaster I Cor. XII, 3 (P.L. 17, 245 B): "Omne verum, a quocumque dicatur, a Spiritu Sancto est." *Sum. Theol.*, II-II, q. 109, a 1, in 1. In *ad* 1 adds an important thought: " . . . omne verum, a quocumque dicatur, est a Spiritu Sancto sicut ab infundente naturale lumen, et movente ad intelligendum et loquendum veritatem."

[38] Cf. David Tracy's statement concerning "the truth that Christianity taught", namely, "that one's fundamental Christian and human commitment is to the value of truth wherever it may lead and to that limit-transformation of all values signalized by the Christian demand for agapic love", *Blessed Rage for Order*, op. cit., p. 135. We may remember the christian criticism of Gandhi's inversion: not God is the Truth, but "Truth is God." *Satyagraha. Non-Violent Resistance*, Ahmedabad: Navajivan 1951, p. 38.

[39] A pungent example: a well-known spanish lay theologian was recently called by his bishop, who, after congratulating him for his theological contributions, asked him not to say that he was a catholic theologian, since his opinions differed so widely from the statements of the hierarchy.

[40] Cf. Pierre Bühler and Charles Duquoc in *Concilium*, nr. 216 (1988). "If the Church in India lived for centuries on a borrowed identity…" begins A. Karokaran, the chief Editor of the indian journal *Third Millenium* (III, [2000] 1, p. 29) an article on "Mission: An alternative Model". The catholic bishop emeritus of San Bartolomé de las Casas, Mexico, Samuel Ruiz García, speaks of the loss of identity of the indigenous christian population of Chiapas (cf. *National Catholic Reporter*, Feb. 18, 2000).

[41] The expression is of Pius XII referring to Christ in the liturgy (and not only in the Eucharist). Cf. Denzinger, § 3855.

[42] Cf. Henri de Lubac, *Méditation sur l'Eglise*, Paris: Aubier, 1954; Yves Congar, *Esquisses du mystère de l'Eglise*, Paris: Cerf, 1941; Hugo Rahner, *Symbole der Kirche*, Salzburg: Müller, 1964, for references.

Contributors

Francis X. Clooney, S.J., is Professor of Comparative Theology at Boston College. He received the Ph.D. from the University of Chicago in 1984 and has become one of the leading Christian theologians engaged in the dialogue with Hinduism. His interest in Hinduism focuses predominantly on the Tamil Srivaisnava tradition of South India. His publications include *Theology after Vedanta: An Exercise in Comparative Theology* (1993), *Seeing through Texts: Doing Theology among the Srivaisnavas of South India* (1996), and most recently, *Hindu God, Christian God: How Reason Helps Break Down the Boundaries between Religions* (2001).

John B. Cobb Jr., born in Japan in 1925, is Emeritus Professor, Claremont School of Theology and Claremont Graduate School. He is Co-director of the center for Process Studies and one of the leading thinkers in the area of the Buddhist-Christian dialogue. He has authored more than thirty books that focus not only on philosophical and theological questions, but also on issues relating to social and ecological justice. His writings include *Christ in a Pluralistic Age* (1975); *God and the World* (1969); *Beyond Dialogue: Toward a Mutual Transformation of Christianity and Buddhism* (1982). He is co-author (with Herman Daly) of *For the Common Good* (1989), which won the Growemeyer Award for Ideas Improving World Order.

Catherine Cornille, born in Belgium in 1961, studied theology and history of religions (Asian religions) at the Catholic University of Leuven and at the University of Hawaii. Having taught at the Catholic University of Leuven from 1990 to 2000, she currently teaches theology of religions and interreligious dialogue at Boston College and at the College of the Holy Cross. Her publications focus on the question of inculturation, on new religious movements in Asia, and on the theory of dialogue. She is currently working on a book on the conditions for the possibility of interreligious dialogue.

Jacques Dupuis, S.J., born in Belgium in 1923, lived in India from 1948 to 1984. Having obtained the doctorate in theology from the Gregorian University in Rome, he taught systematic theology at the theological faculty of Kurseong (India), at the Vidyajyoti Institute of Religious Studies (India) and at the Gregorian University in Rome, where he retired in 1998. He was Director of the theological review at Vidyajyoti and is at present Director of the philosophical and theological review of the Gregorian University, *Gregorianum*. From 1985 to 1995 he was consultor of the Pontifical Council for Interreligious Dialogue. His main recent publications in English include *Jesus Christ and the Encounter of Religions* (1991); *Who Do You Say I*

Am? Introduction to Christology (1994), and *Towards a Christian Theology of Religious Pluralism* (1997).

Claude Geffré is a member of the Dominican Order. He is Honorary Professor of Theology at the Institut Catholique in Paris and former Director of the prestigious "Ecole biblique et archéologique" of Jerusalem. He is also director of theological series *Cogitatio Fidei,* and a prominent member of the journal *Concilium.* His publications focus mainly on the problem of Christian hermeneutics and on the challenges of religious and cultural pluralism for Christian theology. His English publications include *A New Age for Theology* and *The Risk of Interpretation: On Being Faithful to the Christian Tradition in a non-Christian Age* (1987).

Elisabeth J. Harris is Secretary for Inter Faith Relations for the Methodist Church in Britain and an Honorary Lecturer at the University of Birmingham. She lived in Sri Lanka from 1986 to 1993. During this time, she worked as a Research Assistant at Tulana Research Centre and gained a doctorate in Buddhist Studies from the Postgraduate Institute of Pali and Buddhist Studies of the University of Kelaniya. Before taking her present position, she was a Research Fellow at Westminster College, Oxford. Her publications include "What Buddhists Believe" (1998) and "Ananda Metteyya: The First British Emissary of Buddhism" (1998).

Werner G. Jeanrond, born in Germany in 1955, received the Ph.D. in theology from the University of Chicago in 1984. From 1981 to 1994 he taught at Trinity College at the University of Dublin. Since 1994 he has been Professor of Systematic Theology at the University of Lund in Sweden. He was a member of the board of directors of *Concilium* from 1991 to 2001 and was appointed a member of the Swedish Research Council in 2002. His main publications, which also have been translated into several other languages, include *Text and Interpretation as Categories of Theological Thinking* (1988), *Theological Hermeneutics: Development and Significance* (1994), and *Call and Response: The Challenge of Christian Life* (1995).

Joseph S. O'Leary, born in Cork, Ireland in 1949, studied literature, philosophy, and theology at Maynooth College, the Gregorian University, Rome, and the Ecole Pratique des Hautes Etudes, Paris. Resident in Japan since 1983, he teaches literature at Sophia University and collaborates with the Nanzan Institute for Religion and Culture. Drawing on the thought of Heidegger and Derrida he has interrogated the place of Greek metaphysics in classical Christian texts, especially those of Origen and Augustine. His interest in Buddhism centers on the Madhyamika philosophy of emptiness. His book *Religious Pluralism and Christian Truth* (1996) won the Frederick J. Streng Award in 1998.

Raimon Panikkar may be regarded as one of the seminal figures of the Hindu-Christian dialogue and of the dialogue between religions in general. Born of a Hindu father and a Christian mother, he has come to embody the challenges of multiple religious belonging not only physically but also spiritually and philosophically. His book *The*

Unknown Christ of Hinduism (1964) has been a landmark in the Hindu-Christian dialogue and the title of the book *The Intrareligious Dialogue* (1978) has become a concept in the discipline. Other important publications in English include *The Silence of God: The Answer of the Buddha* (1989) and *The Cosmotheandric Experience* (1993).

Jan Van Bragt, born in Belgium in 1929, has been a Catholic missionary in Japan since 1961. He received the Ph.D. in philosophy from the Catholic University of Leuven. From 1976 until 1991, he was Director of the Nanzan Institute for Religion and Culture at Nanzan University. His main publications include the standard English translation (with introduction) of Keiji Nishitani's *Religion and Nothingness* (1982) and (with Paul Mommaers) *Mysticism, Buddhist and Christian* (1995).

Index

Other Titles in the Faith Meets Faith Series